The Collection of Quotes Credited to prophet jesus

By Gregory Heary

Prophet Jesus the Messiah is a character who needs nearly no introduction as his fame has spread far and wide throughout the world amongst religious and non-religious people. However while being one of the most beloved of people he is also simultaneously the most controversial, misunderstood and misrepresented despite his global popularity. Why is this? Primarily because people use modern contemporaries who have never met Jesus face to face in the flesh on earth to learn about him. Rather than learn about Jesus from Jesus they learn about him from their family, friends, preachers and books that have more data from the author's perspective of who Jesus was than the actual information which Jesus taught people. The problem is primarily in having non-prophetic sources of information about Jesus leading humanity to collectively misconstrue his doctrines, deeds, development and mission. Many extremes exist regarding the figure of Jesus with those who hate him to the point of combat and those who love him to the point of worship and many various levels in between. Originally to get to the core message of Jesus I intended to collect in this book almost every textual quote I could find attributed to him from every published source. I was only planning to omit some of the quotes textually attributed to Jesus from well-known fabricated sources such as the Book of Mormon and the "secret gnostic sources" because such quotes which are claimed to have been secret non-public teachings of Jesus or via a far-fetched trip to pre-colonial America as Mormons claim are not worthy of quoting. This is because they are clearly corruptions that cannot be scholastically or academically discussed let alone religiously treated as being mentionable among the rest of the Jesus texts. If you quote every fool that says Jesus said something then you are likely to confuse the message and lend credibility to the corrupted. This previous sentence justifying my omission of Mormon and gnostic material haunted me as I compiled the data for this anthology of Jesus quotes because the more I researched what was textually attributed to Jesus, the more I learned that much of what has been attributed to Jesus was never truly said by him. I came across an immense problem. Shall I collect everything every scrap of paper that says "Jesus said:" into a book or do I stick to what is authentic and abandon the rest despite the inauthentic being vastly more popular and numerous? Then I considered the personal spiritual consequences again and again and again. To attribute a lie to a prophet is a sin too grievous to commit, even if it is done indirectly, unknowingly or unintentionally. Therefore I decided that I did not want to spoil a meeting with Jesus in Paradise and have him ask me why I quoted so many false quotes and false scriptures about him, knowing full well they were false and contradictory to his true prophetic pearls. I considered the question, "What will I say if Jesus asks me why I quoted a heretical invention about him, even if I labeled it as heretical?" Finally I concluded that as exhaustive and educational as it may be to compile everything anyone has ever said Jesus said, it goes against the very essence of Jesus and the prophetic faith to do so. This is because the heretics already know their heretical false quotes and are unlikely to abandon them even if given the evidence of their error. Whereas those who don't know the lies in Jesus' name would have learned such lies from me and thereby possibly misremembered even if I labeled lies as lies. So many times one can read a book and forget the citation as to the authenticity or source of information, but they remember the quote. Finally I realized that I did not want the burdensome responsibility of having passed along a lie in the name of Jesus even if in a condemnatory manner of forbiddance and exoneration of Jesus.

For that reason I have not quoted everything ever historically textually attributed to Jesus in totality but I have quoted more than just the biblical quotations because Jesus said much more than what is biblically attributed to him. So to limit oneself to the biblical teachings alone is to limit one's knowledge of Jesus and his teachings which in turn will mean limiting one's religion and spirituality. Also the bibles scholastically to date have not preserved 100% of Jesus' quotes nor are all the Jesus' quotes within the bibles true or authentic. The Christian Scholastic world knows this very well and declares it loudly but the majority of Christians don't communicate with their scholars but typically are only exposed to their local preacher, family or friends. Most believe orthopraxy (correct practice) is more important than orthodoxy (correct dogma) and that as long as that tiny group of family and friends thinks you are good morally then you are destined for paradise. Yet if one doesn't have the correct doctrines or correct information from which to derive doctrines, nor the correct doctrine deriving methodology then you can be a pious saint following the path of the devil setting a great example for people on how to think they are good while going to the deep parts of the hellfire for eternity. Many alleged saints throughout history have done this to others by choosing the path of pious ignorance and end up going to hell while they think they are doing good striving hard in innovations and errors none the wiser. Whereas the wise repenting sinner is much better than the sinless fool. Yet by and large people idolize the sinless and debase the knowledge as unvaluable preferring to follow the pious over the wise though the wise are in reality more pious than the foolish saintly figure because ignorance is a sin in itself. Don't misunderstand thinking practicing religion is unimportant as the other extreme leads to, rather knowledge and action go hand in hand. You cannot have correct actions without correct knowledge and it all starts with having the correct true information.

 Surprisingly Christendom today has not a single Christian scholar amongst them that says the biblical portrayal of Jesus is accurate. The problem is their masses don't even read the various bibles versions to begin with and those few who do rely on their own interpretation of denominationally biased translations without even thinking of the necessity of unprejudiced scholastic commentary, research, verification or inquiry. The majority remain ignorant of the Christian scholastic world's scientific grading of textual reliability levels done by Christian scholars. Line by line of the Greek New Testament has been analyzed and graded by Christian Scholars who have rated the percentage of authenticity each line of the biblical texts today has according to Christian research. For example, the Jesus Seminar in the 1980s CE concluded that about 82% of Jesus quotes in the New Testament were not and could not have been actually said by Prophet Jesus. The Jesus Seminar was a study group of 50+ Christian Scholars of every denomination and sect, highly credentialed, all literate in ancient Greek who came together and graded each statement attributed to Jesus in the most popular gospels. This too is another thing most Christians don't know, is that the oldest surviving copies of the gospels dated to over 175 years after the departure of Jesus. All of them are in Greek but Jesus spoke Aramaic and it is uncertain if he spoke Hebrew. However Jesus didn't need to speak Hebrew to be a Jewish religious authority figure at that time because Hebrew did not have the sacrosanct-status it has today in Jesus' time.

Yet it is known with 100% certainty that Jesus did not speak Greek. Thus there is a scholastic problem in that all of the gospels available are hearsay evidence. The gospel writers were not eye-witnesses despite the mythology that the local storytellers in Churches preach. Whereas the original authors of the gospels are all anonymous, meaning their names are unknown. So anything in a gospel that says "Jesus said:" has been translated multiple times and since no ancient gospels exist in Aramaic there is only one fact that can be concluded. Another problem is that historically 97-98.5% of Jews at that time were illiterate, the rate for gentile illiteracy was even higher. Historically very few Jews in 1st century Palestine spoke Greek, the Jewish historian Josephus even wrote in 37 CE that he only knew of 1 or 2 Jews who were fluent in Greek. Jews viewed Greek as the language of their Gentile enemy occupiers and even the Greek texts themselves confirm that they are translations. Jews tended to treat those who learned Greek as traitors collaborating with their Hellenistic oppressors and some rabbis even forbade Jews from learning Greek. Many Jews believed it was sinful to even learn Greek. For the followers of Jesus to allegedly come out with Greek books is one of the most unrealistic notions because it would mean those whom Jesus preached to would not be the target audience but the pagans would be. The texts in Greek were written in Greek to be read by Greeks and not the Jews to whom Jesus preached. What better way to corrupt the religion of Jesus than by teaching a religion in the name of Jesus to the enemies of Jesus in a language which the followers of Jesus didn't know and couldn't speak or write? Factually the original direct testimony regarding what Jesus said in the language he said it has been lost to mankind. Prophet Jesus did not leave any authentic handwritten record himself of what his teachings were that has survived until today nor did any of his students or companions. In fact a few hundred years after Jesus left earth we likely had no more direct testimony or even secondhand indirect testimony available at all.

The philosopher Celsus is quoted to have written from 170 to 180 CE about Christian tampering with scriptures that "as if in a drunken brawl with one another, (they) alter and remodel the gospel from its original written form—three times, four times, many times—so that they might be able to give a rebuttal in the face of critical accusations." Now Celsus wrote that about 200 years before

Constantine published anything or decreed the synoptic gospels sacrosanct. Christians today readily admit that heretical bible publishers exist who tamper with texts to publish bibles that say what they want them to say. Yet it is documented this happened to the gospels long before any bible ever existed. So the source documents of the first bible which Constantine ordered to eventually exist where corrupted beyond use and so even in the 300s CE we were completely disconnected from Jesus because there was nobody to stop nobody from changing gospels or information about Jesus. The official Roman and Jewish government policies in place said to systematically kill Christians and destroy their documents for hundreds of years.

Originally there were many different gospels written by many different people and each early church had their own collection of scripture. Every church practiced Christianity differently because they didn't all have access to the same scriptures. Before the version of Christianity practiced in Rome became the state religion of the Roman Empire by Theodosian decree in 380 CE many Christian denominations existed, there were the Adoptionists, Agnoites, Alogians, Apellaeans, Apocarites, Apollinarianists, Aquarians, Archonticks,

Artemonites, Artotytrites, Asclepidoteans, Ascodrogites, Ascodrutes, Bardesanistes, Basilidians, Beryllians, Bonosians, Cainians, Carpocratians, Cerdonians, Cerinthians, Chiliasts, Colluthians, Collylyridians, Docetists, Donatists, Ebionites, Elcesaites, Encratites, Eudoxians, Eusebians, Eustathians, Eutuchites, Eutychians, Florinians, Gacianitae, Gnostics, Helsaites, Heracleonites, Hermogenians, Heterousians, Hieracites, Lucianists, Luciferians, Macedonians, Manicheans, Marcellians, Marcosians, Maronites, Massalians, Melecians, Melchizedichians, Menanderians, Monarchianists, Monophysites, Montanists, Nazareans, Neonomians, Nestorians, Nicolaitians, Noetians, Novations, Ophites, Originists, Ossenians, Patricians, Paulianists, Pelagianists, Photinians, Priscillianists, Proclianites, Psaytrians, Ptolemattes, Proto-Coptics, Quartodecimani, Quintillians, Sabellians, Sachophori, Satanians, Saturnians, Secundians, Seleucians, Semi-Arians, Semi-Pelagians, Serverians, Sethians, Simonians, Soldins, Stilites, Subordinationists, Tatianites, Theopaschites, Trisormiani, Tritheists, Valentinians, Universalists, Zacheans, and that's just to name a few. I'm not being sarcastic either, that is only a few of the many which existed. All the diverse early Christian groups each had their own gospels supporting their views. Not all of these gospels were actually written by the one whom the texts claimed, often they were written pseudonymously. Some were forgeries and others were changed after being written by the copiers, intentionally and unintentionally. Essentially every church had a different understanding of Jesus based on different scriptures and there was little uniformity among early Christians. This continued for some time with different denominations denouncing the others as heretics while Romans and Jews persecuted every denomination. Everyone was claiming to be followers of Jesus, frequently their arguments would turn violent and blood would be shed. This continued until Constantine became the Emperor of Rome and wanted the chaos to stop in order to rule over a unified empire. Constantine called for the Council of Nicaea in 325 CE inviting the leaders of different denominations to end the bickering and agree, hoping that one day Christianity could potentially unify the expansive Roman empire and be used as a political tool for control. Many bishops from all over the world with different theologies attended this council. The various bishops all brought their own scriptures with them in order to support their religious beliefs. Some bishops had all their expenses paid for by Constantine before they were "convinced" they should attend. A pagan at the time, Constantine was no theologian, he was a politician who had no patience for further arguing. The bishops adjourned for the day and were ordered to leave all their gospels behind them in a big pile in the center of the room. The doors were locked and the bishops were told to pray that God would sort it all out. It is documented that there were between 270 to 4,000 different gospels in there such as the Gospel of Phillip, the Gospel of Peter, the Gospel of Thomas, the Gospel of Judas, the Gospel of Truth, the Gospel of Mary, the Gospel of Mary Magdalene, the Gospel of the Nazarites and many others we don't know the titles of. When they opened the doors the next day, under the impression that no one had been inside since the day before, it was discovered that all but 4 books were thrown about and scattered across the room making it completely disorganized while the 4 gospels attributed to Matthew, Mark, Luke and John were neatly placed on the long meeting table. The bishops were told it was a sign from God that no one could doubt, except there were no witnesses and it is unknown who had the keys to the doors on that night. Irenaeus says there had to be exactly 4 gospels no more and no less, because there are 4 winds of the earth and 4 corners of the earth.(because people thought the world was flat due to Hebrew Scriptures) In 367 CE the Bishop of Alexandria, Athanasius, created a 27 book compilation in his 39th Festal letter, this would become what we know today as the "New Testament". However not every Christian agreed with Athanasius' compilation and it was heavily disputed and continues to be disputed until today. At the Council of Carthage in 397 CE the Catholic Church decreed what the books of the bible would be, certain books were declared scripture by a vote of 568 in favor with 563 against. Meaning that the bible was created via democratic elections and not direct divine revelation or prophetic endorsement. 49.7% of those priests present voted against the bible being considered Sacred Scripture. If merely 3 more priests had voted no then the bible would not be labeled Sacred Scripture or divine revelation. Yet even after this "decisive vote" the apocalyptic "*Book of Revelation*" wasn't included at the end of the bible until 419 CE at another Council of Carthage. Meaning for 24 years after democracy barely declared the bible to be completed and authoritative, the famous *"Book of Revelation"* was not part of the bible. Thus we have to keep in mind that different parts of the bible were added to it at different times. For all we know a new book might be added to the bible tomorrow. So know the bible is an anthology, which is a collection of literary works of various authors chosen by a certain compiler. Without a doubt it was humans who compiled the bible and humans also wrote the bible, but did God inspire all the authors, compilers and translators? I addressed that question in my book *"Which edition of the Bible is from God?"* so we will not delve into that topic as this book is an attempt to collect the credible teachings of Jesus rather than analyze the bibles which incorrectly are commonly thought of as having a monopoly on the teachings textually attributed to Jesus. Yet it is crucial to know that the first official bible composition as we know it came into being well over 360 years after Jesus left earth.

Instead of the originals, translations were used when creating what we today know of as the New Testament. One can only hope they were translated honestly with integrity having as few mistakes as possible without the translator intentionally changing the texts, as ancient translators had a tendency to do. It's not as though copyists or translators always intentionally made errors, but keep in mind every letter was copied and/or translated by hand. You can try this yourself to see how difficult it is to copy a gospel by hand accurately. Try writing on a separate piece of paper an entire gospel from the bible, letter by letter making sure what you write is exactly the same as what is written. Even though you are far more literate and your source of copying is easier to read than what the ancient copyists and translators would have used, you will still make many mistakes. Then have somebody try copying your sloppy handwriting of the gospel exactly word for word in one go, without asking you what you wrote or looking at other documents aside from your handwritten copy. If the 1st copyist of the gospel were to make a mistake, then the 2nd copyist copying the 1st's copy of the gospel would copy the mistake, unless they corrected it realizing it was a mistake. Although the 2nd copyist could also "correct" something that is not a mistake, making a new mistake while not correcting the real mistakes, thereby adding more mistakes. The 3rd copyist would have an even greater dilemma and harder job to do than the previous copyists. Since all were handwritten, every single copy would have been unique, different from the rest in different handwriting. Everyone knows that different types of handwriting can be interpreted in different ways. Depending on who is reading the words they will think different words were written, solely because of the handwriting style. A copyist could also make a mistake by thinking a note in the margins by an earlier copyist was actually a part of the text, so in their copy they would mistakenly add the previous copyist's notes into the scripture. Sometimes alterations were intentionally made to make the texts say what people wanted them to say. It also doesn't help that we don't know who copied and translated these documents, which casts doubt on the reliability of the translations. Let's assume that they were translated from accurate copies without malicious intentions as best as is humanly possible. A translation, no matter how good it is, can never mean the same as the text did in its original form. This is because rhythm, double meaning, idioms, informalization, rhetoric and puns are not translatable. Take "William Shakespeare" for example, who is regarded to be the best English playwright of his time if not all time; according to the popular belief of the majority. If you translate Shakespeare's works into Swahili the translated works will not have the same effect nor the same meaning. Some words simply can't be translated so the character dialogues in his translated stories will be of a different quality, making any plays performed in Swahili have a different plot than the same play would have, had it been done in English. But the English bible we have today was not translated from the original texts, because the originals didn't exist by the time Christianity came to English speaking people. Even if the originals still existed there is another problem because the gospels and epistles were first written in Greek. Jesus and his apostles didn't speak Greek. This means the original New Testament was translated before it was ever written down, so the originals were actually translations, but for the sake of argument let's assume the oral tradition the Greek texts came from were translated correctly, even though when translating from semitic languages such as Hebrew or Aramaic into non-semitic languages like Greek 80% of the meaning is automatically lost. Next they were translated from Greek into Latin, then translated from Latin into German, then translated from German into French, then translated from French into English. Now early Church fathers like Tertullian and Augustine did not know Greek, they relied on Jerome's Latin translation. Which means the leading scholars of the early Christian Church were relying on texts that were translated a minimum of 2 times. Meaning it would be like you reading Shakespere for the first time ever in a Chinese translation, but not a direct Chinese translation from English rather a Chinese translation of the Swahili Shakespeare. Do you think you'd get the same meaning as you would by reading the original English? Today nobody denies that the English bibles are translations. Yet they rarely admit their Bible to be a translation of a translation of a translation of a translation of a translated oral tradition. If you were to translate Shakespeare into French, then take the French Shakespeare and translate it into German, then take the German Shakespeare twice translated and translate it to Latin, then the Latin Shakespeare thrice translated and translate it into Greek, then take the Greek Shakespeare 4 times translated and translate it back into English, you would find that the English Shakespeare that went through so many translations would be very different than the original writings of Shakespeare.

Therefore the Shakespeare that was translated many times would no longer be considered to be the actual words of Shakespeare. The translated Shakespeare compared to the actual words of Shakespeare would be obviously different. You can try this yourself with basic free internet translation tools, or try with an expensive professional translation service. A translation can never be the actual words of the original. Which is why if you are reading this book in a language other than English as the author I can assure you that you are not getting the same meaning as you would if you were reading it in its original English. In fact all types of translations are always mistranslations. This is because languages were never designed to be translatable. No languages have an exact correspondence with the words and grammar of another language to facilitate word for word or literal translations. So there is no such thing as translations rather every translation is an interpretation even if this is not admitted by the translator. Then because languages always evolve we are always in need of updated translations.

One famous Jew Saul, was a anti-Jesus inquisitor going town to town killing the followers of Jesus ruthlessly. Suddenly Saul changes his name to Paul and starts preaching a new religion in the name of Jesus combatting those who preach otherwise, and Paul's alleged letters to churches he founded we get told thousands of years later are divinely inspired scripture despite contradicting themselves and other gospels not written by Paul. It is mind-boggling how a simple letter from a non-prophet known for persecuting the followers of Jesus becomes Divine Revelation. Even letters that genuine prophets like King David or King Solomon wrote are not considered divine revelation but Paul's letters are? That's like getting X number of spam emails from suspicious senders in your inbox and then someone else tells you those are not considered as emails but divine revelation sacrosanct holy scriptures. If a human being is writing a letter then clearly that is not the words of God in the letter, they would be the words of a person. However most Christians believe these letters are divine revelation without even reading them because so many other people they know believe them too. Although democratic methods do not justifiably create divine revelation, so the opinion of the masses regarding something means nothing. Personal opinion does not disqualify divine revelation. Personal opinion cannot make something divine revelation either. Whether you like it, hate it, believe it, or reject it, personal opinion has nothing to do with whether it is the word of God or not. Some non-prophet writing a letter to somebody else can never ever be divine revelation even if it teaches something good and true and accurate. A letter could quote a source of text that is divine revelation but the letter itself is not revelation, it's a piece of human mail. Yet 77%, or 21 out of 27 books of the New Testament of the bibles are letters written from humans to humans. 14 of those letters are attributed to Paul amounting to 52% of the New Testament, although 6 of those 14 letters are forgeries done in Paul's name by unknown people. Of these 14 Pauline epistles, Christian scholars are heavily disputing 6 of them as to whether Paul was the actual author. The epistles Ephesians, Colossians and the 2nd Thessalonians are debated concerning authorship and it is doubtful Paul was the one who wrote them. Aside from textual reasons themselves Paul is thought to have died in 67 CE yet Ephesians was written between 80 and 100 CE, Colossians thought to have been written in 80 CE and 2nd Thessalonians is thought to be written between 80 and 115 CE. So it's rather hard to think Paul wrote decades after he died. While Timothy 1, Timothy 2 and Titus have been declared 100% forgeries by Christian scholars. This is not coming from me, this is according to Christian scholastic intellectuals who go to church and believe in the bible and have studied the language and manuscripts who are recognized biblical experts; they say Timothy 1, Timothy 2 and Titus were NOT written by Paul. Without a doubt about it. They still agree with the doctrines contained in the books but they say Paul did not write it, they wish he did but they publicly admit that he didn't. If you read the letters they say they are written by Paul but they're not, so they are forgeries.

Basically most Christian leaders today take the attitude of *"Well yes Jesus didn't speak Greek. But the only texts we ever got passed down to us, through our sectarian denomination of Christianity, are in Greek. And even though they are dated to hundreds of years after Jesus left earth and are thereby hearsay evidence, they are the only books our denomination has. So therefore if that's all we have then it must be true and authentic because we don't have anything else. So if what we got isn't truly authentic then we got a big problem and the people I learned from were fools or liars and our religion is unproven and invalid, in need of a new prophet. Whereas since I know we cannot be so foolish because I don't feel that stupid, then it simply must be true because otherwise millions of people are damn fools too and I know we all can't be that stupid. Rather it's all the billions of non-Christians that are damned fools."* So rather than be honest as Jesus likely would've taught us these evangelical minded double down on the Greek New Testament and tell blatant lies regarding its reliability and transmission history. Most Christians don't even know that every bible teaches a different religion because each publisher prints according to their specific sectarian beliefs. Yet they refer to "the bible" as if there is only one edition or version, when even the Greek texts that exist have many variations with no two being identical. And then not only do they double down on the Greek New Testament but they triple down and instead of keeping their unscholastic theories privately to themselves, they will go out to preach and invite people to their distorted unproven unverifiable claims about Jesus' teachings. Then they become bigoted and cut off connections to Christian Scholars who as explicit Christians teach exactly what I've written about the gospels. Instead Christians laypeople make their own tiny clubs for biblical adherence as they see fit which sometimes evolve into congregations, denominations, or cults.

So the problem now is what does someone do if they want to learn about what Jesus truly taught?

Firstly one must be aware of the authenticity levels of the information and the unprovability of most information regarding this prophet and previous prophets as well. So patiently bear with me as I explain the historical languages of Jesus and his forerunners in prophethood.

Research from paleolinguists indicates that the Hebrew language didn't even exist at the time Moses received his commandments but came into being approximately 1,000 years after Moses, and the oldest fragment of paleo-Hebrew writing that exists is over 250 years after the earliest possible date Moses is believed to have died. So nobody really knows what language Moses spoke or what language his revelation was in either, and we don't have the Ark of the covenant or any original handwritten documents from Moses to read in order to find out. Although it is reported the original Torah was written by God in Gold lettering on Emerald or Pearl tablets. However everyone knows we don't have the original Mosaic Torah tablets, there are no Torah relics alleged to have been touched by Moses available today. The Jewish Kabbalists even thought 2 whole books were missing from the modern Torah and that the Hebrew alphabet lacked one of the letters that the original Torah was in. Thus the Hebrew language dislocated the Torah and the Hebrew version was missing a good chunk of information due to Hebrew missing letters of the alphabet of the language of the Torah. Likewise Abraham didn't speak Hebrew either but is believed to have spoken "proto-Canaanite", which is a dead language and is the reason why we don't have access to the Scripture called the Suhuf which was given to Abraham. However Abraham's son Ishmael is known to have learned proto-Arabic and married into Arab tribes who spoke proto-Arabic. Also Abraham is known to have spoken to Ishmael in adulthood as well as his wives, so it is most probable that Abraham knew and spoke proto-Arabic. However keep in mind that does not necessarily mean the Suhuf given to Abraham was in proto-Arabic, it could've been but we cannot say for certainty because Abraham could've known other languages besides proto-Arabic; such as "proto-Canaanite" whatever that is. Could "proto-Canaanite" be the same as proto-Arabic? It's possible but obviously if scholars were to say such a thing Jews and Christians would get quite upset because of the serious implications such a discovery would entail. Some Muslim scholars have claimed proto-Arabic was spoken by Noah and some even say it was the original language of Adam, but I do not yet know where those particular scholars got such information from and have not examined its authenticity or reliability. Although historically the language of proto-Arabic is said to have been spoken by Sam the son of Noah. History books relate that Noah partitioned the land of earth and gave his son Sam the land from Syria to Yemen and Sam spoke "natural Arabic"(proto-Arabic) as did his descendants. Whereas biblically all 3 of Noah's sons spoke a different language. (Most Christians don't know this because they believe in the tower of babel language origin story of Genesis 11 and ignore Genesis 10:1, Genesis 10:4-5, Genesis 10:20 and Genesis 10:31-32 which all contradict the tower of babel languages origin story of Genesis 11:1-9.) So historically proto-Arabic is an ancient language spoken by Sam the son of Noah. Now this is very important because it relates directly to Jesus. You see Jesus is known to have raised people from the dead. However Jews still refused to believe in his prophethood despite such miracles and they said it was too easy for Jesus to raise the recently deceased and that they might not even have been truly dead. So the Jews challenged Jesus to raise somebody who had been dead for a very long time, specifically they asked him to resurrect Sam the son of Noah from the dead so they could talk to him. Jesus did this and Sam talked to Jesus and the Jews confirming that Jesus was a prophet of God before going back to being dead. Now Sam did not speak Hebrew because Hebrew did not exist in his lifetime and he didn't speak Aramaic either. My research indicates he spoke proto-Arabic, but you need not accept that opinion. The point is Sam did not speak Hebrew or Aramaic yet was raised from the dead and spoke to Jesus and Jews. Now it could have been a language other than proto-Arabic or it could have been proto-Arabic and even if Sam did speak proto-Arabic that does not necessarily mean Jesus would have, even though they spoke. Because maybe Jesus raised Sam from the dead and he had another guy to translate Sam's language so Sam could be understood, that's possible but then that would risk the point of the miracle if a translator need be relied upon. Also a translator seems unlikely because the Jews specifically asked Jesus to raise Sam from the dead, so it doesn't make sense for them to ask Jesus to raise one they couldn't communicate with. Thus it is most probable they could speak the language Sam spoke and it is a fact that Sam did not speak Hebrew. It could be possible for Sam's reported "natural Arabic" to have been similar enough to ancient Aramaic for them to understand each other but the point I'm making in this lengthy language exposition is that Hebrew was not as prominent during the time of Jesus or other prophets as modern Jews and Christians believe. Whereas leading up to the Babylonian exile the Jews used Aramaic which is a related language to Arabic. To compare them Arabic would be like ancient olyde english vs. modern American slang, they are very similar but clearly distinct enough to be quite different. So again it is possible that Sam's proto-Arabic need not be translated for Jesus and the Jews who knew Aramaic. Although in the holy land itself classical post proto-Arabic was spoken during the time of Jesus. It was an earlier form called Nabataean Arabic. The language of Nabataean Arabic was an offshoot of the Aramaic of the Achaemaenic Empire. The Achaemaenic Empire ruled from China to Greece across the middle east to about where Libya is today, from the years 550 BCE to 330 BCE until Alexander invaded and crippled their kingdom annexing vast portions of it. This Achaemaenic empire is the same as was ruled by Darius I and Cyrus I both of whom are mentioned in the bibles during the Jewish exile in Babylon. The Achaemaenic empire was the empire which conquered the empire that conquered the Jews. Their imperial language was Aramaic. Prophet Ezra allegedly rewrote the Torah, that had been lost, by memory in Aramaic after Jews returned to Jerusalem from Babylon during the reign of Cyrus I, while the Samaritans used proto-Hebrew which eventually became the official language used for the Jewish text as it was translated from Aramaic to Hebrew. However when things got changed into Hebrew that's an entire religion getting translated. Things get lost in translation as well as distorted. When you translate a religion it doesn't quite come out the same, especially when this is done in ancient times where record-keeping itself within one language was dubious due to technology and human errors from handwriting and copying handwriting multiple times over and over throughout generations. So the Jews translated the religion of the prophets into Hebrew even though originally it was not preached or practiced in the Hebrew language. That is a undisputed fact. You need not accept that Sam spoke proto-Arabic or even that Jesus raised him from the dead, but every ancient historian, anthropologist, paleolinguist and archaeologist knows with 100% certainty that the old biblical prophets did not teach in Hebrew and Hebrew was only invented long after the Jews had corrupted the religion their prophets had taught them. While on top of that it is known that Jesus spoke Aramaic and it's assumed he spoke Hebrew for practical religious reasons to accommodate the circumstances of his time due to the Jewish translation of religion into Hebrew but it is not proven that Jesus spoke or knew Hebrew. Whereas after Alexander and the fall of the Achaemaenic empire, their imperial Aramaic turned into Nabataean Arabic and was spoken and written in a very special region. The region Nabataean Arabic was used in consists of the area of Negev between the eastern bank of the Jordan River and the Sinai peninsula. Prior to 85 BCE, when the Romans began to replace Nabatean Arabic with Greek and Latin, the Nabataean Arabic was the main language in the region and archaeological evidence proves it was still used until 356 CE. Whereas Jesus is predicted to have been born somewhere around/between 4 BCE and 6 CE. So it is a real possibility that Jesus spoke

Nabataean Arabic as well as Aramaic, or his Aramaic may have been Nabataean Arabic since Nabataean Arabic was a derivative of Imperial Aramaic. However keep in mind Nabataean Arabic is different than the "classical Arabic", because Nabataean Arabic is a forerunner of classical Arabic. They are similar though. Yet as the Latin and Greek speaking churches conquered the holy land, the ancient Nabataean Arabic went extinct in the region. Hence it began to be said that Jesus spoke Hebrew and only recently has it been made known that Jesus spoke Aramaic of a particular dialect. Whereas for obvious religious reasons it's unlikely the Christian or Jewish world would let any facts that could prove Jesus spoke Arabic (Nabataean Arabic) surface. Since that would lead people to wonder if maybe those Muslims speaking Arabic may actually have some information about Jesus or God or even a connection with the prophetic religion. Thus such findings will likely never be made known, at least as long as the Zionist state of Israel exists, and the world will be told that Jesus was a just a Jew who spoke Hebrew; with the more astute Christians thinking they're smart for knowing Jesus spoke Aramaic too. However the dialect of the Aramaic of

Jesus has been scholastically publicly declared to be "Western Aramaic". That is a big step closer to the truth being known because it limits the possibilities bringing the language of Jesus into more focus. This is because there are only 5 different types of "Western Aramaic" known. The 5 types are, "Western Neo-Aramaic" (which is modern and disqualified because it didn't exist at the time of Jesus), Samaritan Aramaic, Jewish-Palestinian Aramaic, Christian-Palestinian Aramaic, and Nabatean Arabic. Whereas Samaritan Aramaic can be discounted because the Samaritans were their own sect and Jesus would not have grown up with them to pick up their language since he was not a Samaritan. The same applies to Christian-Palestinian Aramaic as well as Jewish-Palestinian Aramaic. Why is that? Because Jesus grew up in Egypt. What type of "Western Aramaic" did Egyptians speak? Nabataean Arabic as did Southern Palestine. So historically speaking there is a very high probability that Jesus may have spoke Nabataean Arabic. However we must remember that baby Jesus did not go to Egypt alone or via spaceship. By all accounts it was a journey over land, meaning those making the journey would've had to speak the language of the places they were traveling through and to in order to blend in as they were trying to do. So Mary the mother of Jesus likely spoke Nabataean Arabic, at least during the journey. Also her uncle Zachariah would've likely spoken Nabataean Arabic because he was a prophet and he had to communicate with the people living in Southern Palestine, the same applies to his son John. Also for what it's worth Nabataean Arabic writings have been found at Qumran, which is the same place those famous "Dead Sea Scrolls" were recovered; so that proves people in various diverse parts of the holy land spoke Nabataean Arabic. Therefore since Mary, Zachariah and John all had a dire religious need to speak Nabataean Arabic then I'm inclined to think they spoke it and by extension Jesus also would've had a similar need, grown up in the region where it was spoken, had relatives who spoke it and would've found it useful to be able to speak it throughout his time on earth.

Also it could be entirely possible that the prophetic language was Nabatean Arabic or proto-Arabic in various forms throughout history. Personally I have no problem with Hebrew, it's just a language, but unfortunately it is not the language of the ancient prophets of God. So that's good and bad news. The bad news is that we don't have the ancient Aramaic texts and don't know what language the original Torah was in or the Scripture called the Zabur given to David for that matter. However in regards to the Zabur given to David we know for certain 3 important details that could indicate a potential candidate for the language it was in. 1. Prophet Solomon kept the Zabur in the same language as it was in during the time of David (his father). 2. Prophet Solomon wrote to and spoke to the Queen of Sheba who subsequently believed in his prophetic religion. 3. This Queen of Sheba by all accounts lived in and came to Solomon from Yemen which is the southwestern portion of the Arabian peninsula. Those are 3 facts everyone agrees upon. The exact time of Solomon's reign is unknown. However it's projected that David reigned from 1010 BCE to 970 BCE and that Solomon reigned from 970 BCE to 931 BCE, again such numbers are just the scholastic projections given today. This projection however falls within Aramaic's extensive existence as a commonly used universal language throughout the middle east region and we have written examples of Aramaic being used at that time, which we don't have for Hebrew. Aramaic was used by the ancient Assyrians who also used Akkadian and Sumerian and are widely believed to have fought against the believers in the Holy land after Moses left Egypt. Aramaic was also used by the Neo-Babylonian Empire which conquered Israel after the reign of Solomon, except they only spoke Akkadian and Aramaic. So we can confidently eliminate Sumerian as a candidate for the prophetic language in the post Moses era. We can eliminate Akkadian as a candidate too because the Achaemaenic Empire which conquered the Neo-Babylonian empire used Aramaic as their imperial language. Whereas since Daniel and Ezra are known to have favored using the Aramaic language instead of the Akkadian and since Yemen is known to have spoken a form of Aramaic, then circumstances would dictate that because Ezra is said to have rewritten the Torah in Aramaic, and the Yemeni people from whom the Queen of Sheba came when she visited Solomon spoke a version of Aramaic, and Jesus spoke a version of Aramaic which may or may not have been Nabataean Arabic, the odds are that Aramaic is the best candidate for the language of the divine revelation of the Zabur given to David as well as the Torah given to Moses. It also makes sense God would keep prophetic messages in a relatively similar language throughout the years for continuity purposes so translation need not occur.

Now <u>when Jesus comes back to earth he is going to speak and some people at that time will understand what he is saying</u>. Whereas ancient Hebrew is a dead language and Aramaic is a dead language. Yet Nabataean Arabic is similar enough to classical Arabic which millions of people still speak today. Thus if we are going to pick a language that Jesus will be speaking when he returns to earth Arabic is scholastically the most likely choice, especially from a Muslim perspective if say in theory they were right about Jesus being one of them. I mean nobody really thinks Jesus is going to come down speaking Chinese or English do they? (Don't feel bad if you did, it's best to find out now than when he comes.) Why then is the high probability of Jesus speaking Nabataean Arabic not published in newspapers and broadcast on TV? Well that's because nothing from the bibles comes from a Nabataean Arabic source. All the alleged Aramaic New Testament bibles today are just translated from Greek into Aramaic in order to console laypeople who learn Jesus never spoke Greek and to trick them into thinking they are reading what Jesus spoke instead of texts whose origins are Greek and thereby disconnected from Jesus. If global headlines said Jesus spoke or possibly spoke an early form of Arabic, then Allah's and Muslims' claims about Jesus and Islam would have to be seriously examined by everyone on the planet who was interested in Jesus. While to accept such a thing like Jesus speaking Nabataean Arabic as true would force Christians to reject the whole New Testament as unreliable, since it's a incomplete copy of copies of copies of copies of compiled Greek translations of an alleged oral Hebrew tradition. Which if further translated from an original Nabataean Arabic speaking Jesus would be admittedly too much translation and thus impossible for ancients to have correctly translated to any degree of accuracy required to justify religious beliefs or practices. Although it's still too much translation anyways, but to add Nabataean Arabic to the list of language transfers would completely sink the Christian's ship because they have never claimed any source of information they have came from a Nabatean Arabic source, so it's too late for them to make something up. Thus they can only indignantly say *"Shutup! It's not possible!"*. It would also completely discredit Paul because Paul taught people in Greek and if Jesus was speaking Nabataean Arabic, or even if we just stick to Aramaic, which we know he was speaking a version of Western Aramaic, then for Paul or any companion of Jesus to teach about Jesus in Greek is foolish and crazy. This is because it's easier to teach what a prophet taught without translating it, while we do know for certain that Jesus didn't speak Greek and that many in the holy land spoke the language he did speak. Why then would Paul, formerly known as Saul, and the companions of Jesus teach Greeks in Greek and write in Greek, instead of in the original language of Jesus to people who would understand that language? It only makes sense if Paul and the authors of the bible were not translating Jesus, but making up their own version of Jesus. I repeat, it makes no sense for Paul or the companions of Jesus to teach and write in Greek when they could've taught in the language Jesus actually spoke in the holy land to people in the holy land, unless the authors of the New Testament were making up stuff about Jesus. Since if they made stuff up then it'd be harder for people who knew Jesus' true teachings to refute them if they had to learn a foreign language to do so. And who best to use for such a purpose than a Jewish enemy of Jesus named Saul to make the Greeks think the Jewish followers were upon the same things they were being taught? Whereas to cover his tracks Saul even changes his name to Paul so if the genuine Jewish followers of Jesus who didn't speak Greek heard that a Paul was preaching about Jesus, they wouldn't know it was Saul and thereby take all efforts necessary to warn the Greeks that it was their archnemesis intentionally corrupting the faith lying to the Greeks. When Christian Biblical Scholars publicly state there are absolutely no original Aramaic gospels or early/ancient/contemporary Greek gospel translations, that's not something they are saying for fun because it damages their faith and makes them seem less academic for being Christian when they know such things. So there is no incentive at all for them to lie and say they don't have anything accurately proven to come from Jesus if they do. Yet because there is significant incentive for Christian ministers and Bible publishers to lie and tell people that their bibles are reliable, they preach such lies and put such fiction in the bible commentaries and then Christians believe it because it's what they want to believe. Then those with Crusader mentalities will say the Christian Biblical Scholars must not have read the bible because the bible commentaries clearly say it's reliable, so all those Biblical Scholars must be fake Christians trying to discredit Christianity and the bible from the inside and they're all paid off by Satan. But Saul or Paul was allegedly beyond such corruption. Some may not express this notion verbally yet still believe it when confronted with Scholastic facts. So there is a gulf between Biblical Scholars and Christian laity who place their trust in ministers, publishers and popular personalities instead of the Biblical experts who refute their religious misconceptions. The easiest way to change a religion is to change the language it's taught in to something different than the language it was originally taught in. Also consider Greek was the language of the enemies of Jesus and his followers. So for those who wanted to safely transmit Jesus' teachings without being harmed if discovered with them, to use Greek would be the absolute worst thing they could do. To use Greek would mean they wanted to be discovered, persecuted and have their literature get destroyed. If a Roman soldier persecuting Christians found Greek scripture versus Aramaic or Hebrew Scripture it'd be far more likely to get destroyed if it was in a language the soldier could read to identify as blasphemous or religious. Whereas Greek was much more popular amongst Roman soldiers than Hebrew or Aramaic was. However we are told that Greek Jesus literature wasn't destroyed, the Hebrew and Aramaic literature was destroyed though, which also happens to be the language(s) it's known Jesus spoke. So you have the modern Biblical New Testament written in the language other than Jesus spoke that could not be read by the people whom Jesus preached to but could only be read by the enemies of Jesus and his followers. This is because those who wrote the Greek Biblical New Testament were actually the enemies of Jesus, their chief being a guy named Saul who changed his name to Paul. Therefore due to religious beliefs and prejudices, it's unlikely the Christian world would ever allow such information or proof about the language of Jesus to become a widely accepted truth. Thus is the problem with religious people, because if the truth means your religious beliefs have no trustworthy connection to God or a prophet then what does one do? Quit their religion? Many cannot bring themselves to do that no matter what. Those types would rather lie or kill than let the truth be told or accepted by others.

To put it in perspective the people who publish bibles today are merely making their own book with their own spin based off of the bibles written in the past, which also had their own spin based on bibles written earlier than that which had their own spin, which were based on writings by people unknown who lied about their names and wrote in a language not spoken by the characters depicted in the stories that are written. Basically the bibles are books that evolve over time as people change them to suit their changing belief systems, but everybody pretends that their bible is original and everyone else's is evolutionary. The advanced one's will prove the other bibles are corrupted but they don't apply the same methodology to their own bibles. Unfortunately the consumers of these bibles don't know how their bibles came to be translated and published but just believe the false advertisement in the appendix, preface or commentary. Christians lie so much about biblical reliability that I remember going to bible study with relatives as a child and looking into my uncle's bible to see written on the first page *"Written by Jesus Christ"*, in what I now guess was his own handwriting. So don't put it past Christians to write something in their own handwriting attributed to Jesus' name when they know he didn't have anything to do with it. My uncle didn't think it was sacrilegious to write that in his bible and neither did many biblical scribes when they composed their texts. Sadly those on the other side of the church pew aisle are so naïve that they are convinced by the conviction of the belief of their preachers who might genuinely believe themselves what was preached to them from a strongly convinced preacher. This means that unfortunately billions of people who think they "believe in Jesus" or "believe in God" don't have an accurate belief that is correct and will be considered disbelievers in the actual Jesus and God, or slanderers of Jesus and God if they publicly or privately share their incorrect beliefs. Technically and linguistically they do "believe in Jesus" and God, but they believe lies and in a Jesus that did not exist and a false version of God. Mainly because of their various bibles, of which no prophet of God ever said they had to believe in, but because their religious leaders say to believe in it they do under false pretenses and in doing so turn their modern leaders into prophets and by extension God without knowing it. This is because the bibles prohibit things God didn't and allows things which God forbid, thus to follow the bibles is to take human authors as their Divine legislator and the worst part is that they don't even know who really wrote those biblical books and they know those texts were not in the language of the prophets of God. So it would be difficult for them to recognize the real Jesus because he doesn't match what they believe him to be. With all this confusion about who Jesus was, what he taught and what we are required to believe about him, we need another prophet to clarify who the prophet Jesus was. Seriously, it's such a mess that we need a prophet of God with divine revelation to let us know just who the prophet Jesus really was because there is so much confusion. It's saddening but true.

Most people only believe Jesus is a prophet because of hearsay evidence anyways, because we heard someone else tell us it was so. None of us today has witnessed a single miracle of Jesus. Therefore we must accept that our beliefs about Jesus will have to come from other than Jesus himself because we have no direct link to this person to communicate directly. Others have realized this throughout history and claimed prophethood themselves and thereby leveled a potentially authentic source of information regarding their information about Jesus. Scholastically the only way we can get authentic information about Jesus today is from a later Prophet who received authentic information directly from God about the past history of Jesus' teachings. Some people such as the first Mormon prophet Joseph Smith, or Mirza Ghulam Ahmed came with clearly dubious nonsensical contradictory claims despite alleging to have divinely transmitted information about Jesus. So then we get an additional problem of false prophet's information about Jesus to add to the mix of Greek unverifiable contradictory hearsay. Yet we do know that Jesus spoke Aramaic. Aramaic doesn't exist today because it evolved into Arabic. Whereas in the 600s CE there was a Arab man named Muhammad bin Abdullah who also claimed prophethood and relayed information about the prophethood of Jesus explaining that the earlier Christians corrupted his true message and that God had sent him with a divine revelation to exonerate Jesus from the lies and reestablish genuine monotheism on earth. This call of Muhammad bin Abdullah led to the spread of Islam, the world's largest religion, and the most widely memorized and most popular book in the world, the Quran which itself claims to be divine revelation from God the Creator of everything. So personally after a life of Christian living and evangelizing I figured given the situation regarding information scarcity about Prophet Jesus then it was worth examining the Quran to see what it actually said, particularly about Jesus. At the least it wouldn't harm me in my search to follow the teachings of Jesus and then after research and prayer on the matter, it became evident that the Quran was authentic revelation so I became a Muslim in order to better adhere to the teachings of Jesus. There is no contradiction between Jesus' authentic teachings and Islam, and much of Jesus' alleged biblical and gospel teachings that are unverifiable also coincide with Islamic teachings too. The reason this is a surprise to many is because Christian politicians in the past waged military warfare and spread many lies during the Crusades that still remain popular amongst fools today. And it is not in the interest of devout but arrogantly ignorant non-scholastic Christian leaders to tell their people the truth about the historical lies about Islam or that the biblical information they preach is not scholastically accurate.

The goal of this compilation of Jesus quotes book is still to better understand Jesus from his own alleged words, so as to clarify the most misrepresented prophet of all time. As all can fairly agree the most important thing about Jesus, regardless of what you think about him, is what he taught so as a hopeful student of the teachings of Jesus I collect these attributed quotations in the hopes that the teachings of Jesus may be known and a source of guidance to all who are blessed to accept prophetic guidance.

So where did I get information about Jesus' teachings for this book and how trustworthy or authentic is it? Firstly even though I've written what I've written about the biblical sources being unreliable that doesn't mean that they are 100% false. They are comparable to a newspaper writing about events thousands of years earlier with no eye-witnesses or ear-witnesses, so basically no journalistic standards whatsoever. However there is a tiny sliver of a chance that some biblical teachings attributed to Jesus could be true despite having gone through so many changes. But how do you know which are and which are not?

To be able to comment on Prophet Jesus' teachings of which the authenticity is not entirely accurate can be religiously risky especially when one knows that one does not know the authenticity of the information. Thus as a Muslim I looked at what Prophet Muhammad taught about teaching about

Jesus and other Israeli prophets from dubious sources of information other than himself or Allah.

Narrated `Abdullah bin `Amr:

The Prophet (ﷺ) said, "*Convey (my teachings) to the people even if it were a single sentence, and tell others the stories of Bani Israel (which have been taught to you), for it is not sinful to do so. And whoever tells a lie on me intentionally, will surely take his place in the (Hell) Fire.*"

Source: Sahih al-Bukhari 3461

Narrated Abu Huraira:

The people of the Book used to read the Torah in Hebrew and then explain it in Arabic to the Muslims. Allah's Messenger (ﷺ) said (to the Muslims). "*Do not believe the people of the Book, nor disbelieve them, but say, 'We believe in Allah and whatever is revealed to us, and whatever is revealed to you.'*"

Source: Sahih al-Bukhari 7362

It was narrated from Jaabir ibn 'Abdullah:

Umar ibn al-Khattaab came to the Prophet with some written material he had got from one of the people of the Book. He read it to the Prophet and he got angry and said: *"Are you confused (about your religion), O son of al-Khattaab? By the One in Whose hand is my soul, I have brought it (the message of Islam) to you clear and pure. Do not ask them about anything, lest they tell you something true and you disbelieve it, or they tell you something false and you believe it. By the One in Whose hand is my soul, if Moses were alive, he would have no option but to follow me."*

Source: Musnad Ahmad (14736); Graded as hasan by al-Albaani

Imam Ahmad also recorded a narration from `Abdullaah bin Thaabit who said:

"Umar came to Allah's Messenger and said; 'O Messenger of Allaah! I passed by a brother of mine from (the tribe of) Qurayzah, so he wrote some comprehensive statements from the Tawrah for me, should I read them to you?' The face of Allaah's Messenger changed (with anger). So I said to him: 'Don't you see the face of Allaah's Messenger?" `Umar said: *'We are pleased with Allaah as our Lord, Islaam as our religion, and Muhammad as our Messenger.'* So the anger of the Prophet subsided, and he said: **"By the One in Whose Hand is Muhammad's soul, if Moses appeared among you and you were to follow him, abandoning me, then you would have strayed.**

Indeed you are my share of the Umam (nations), and I am your share of the Prophets."

Source: Musnad Ahmad (15437, 17871). Graded as "Hasan li ghairihee" by Shaikh al-Albaanee

Furthermore Muslim Scholars amongst the companions of Muhammad and later generations clarified the tight rope act of reporting information from prior prophets, particularly if it's not verified.

Narrated Humaid bin 'Abdur-Rahman that he heard Muawiyya talking to a group of people from Quraish at Al-Madina, and on mentioning Ka'b Al-Ashbar, Muawiyya said:

"He was one of the most truthful of those who used to talk about the people of the Scripture, yet we used to detect certain faults in his information."

Source: Sahih al-Bukhari 7361

Narrated Ubaidullah:

Ibn `Abbas said, "Why do you ask the people of the scripture about anything while your Book (Qur'an) which has been revealed to Allah's Messenger (ﷺ) is newer and the latest? You read it pure, undistorted and unchanged, and Allah has told you that the people of the scripture (Jews and Christians) changed their scripture and distorted it, and wrote the scripture with their own *hands and said, 'It is from Allah,' to sell it for a little gain. Does not the knowledge which has come to you prevent you from asking them about anything? No, by Allah, we have never seen any man from them asking you regarding what has been revealed to you!"*

Source: Sahih al-Bukhari 7363

Imām Shafi'ī said:

"It is well known that the Prophet ﷺ did not permit the narration of falsehood. Thus, the meaning of the Ḥadīth: "Narrate from Banū Isrā'īl," refers to that which is not falsehood. And his statement "There is no sin in it" means that there is no restriction in you narrating from them now. This is because the reports of restriction and blame on narrating from them and looking into their books was in the beginning, then the ruling became relaxed. This is not for everyone, rather only for those that have a deep understanding of the religion and have the ability to distinguish between the truth and falsehood as 'Abdullāh bin 'Amr did when he discovered two loads from the Ahl al-Kitāb and would narrate from them only that which the Sharī'ah permits."

Source: Ramzi Na'na'ah, al-Isrā'īliyyāt wa Atharuha fī Fi Kutub at-Tafsīir

Imām al-Ālusī in his Tafsīr, *Rūh al-Ma'ānī*, commented after mentioning the Ḥadīth of Jābir when he asked the Prophet ﷺ if they could write down some of what they hear from the Ahl al-Kitāb:

"The Prophet ﷺ became angry from his question because the Taurāh which the Jews had during that time was distorted, and it was not the same Taurāh revealed to Moses. Moreover, the people had recently left infidelity. If permission was given in the beginning to refer to the Taurāh and read it, it would have led to a greater calamity."

Ibn Taimiyyah said:

"However, these Isra'īli traditions are quoted as supporting evidence and not as primary sources. These Isra'īli traditions are of three types: first, is authentic as attested by our own sources. Second, is false as attested by our own sources. And third, does not fall within two previous categories, where we can neither judge it to be authentic nor inauthentic. One is allowed to quote from this third type as justified previously above."

Source: Muqaddimah fī Uṣūl at-Tafsīr:

So Islamically there are different ways of utilizing Israeli prophetic reports, depending on intentions and methods. For telling a prophet about an earlier prophet's teachings is almost argumentative and demeaning to the later prophet. Additionally it is extremely dangerous to give a stamp of approval or a stamp of falsehood without proof on anything pertaining to a previous prophet because then you might be sanctioning a religious falsehood or denying a religious truth and to lie about a prophet is heretical disbelief whether you lie by supporting a lie or lie by denying a truth. So I don't want to go to hell by saying anything about Prophet Jesus that isn't accurate. Therefore I must clarify my sources of information and how the following data I've included about Prophet Jesus is to be understood.

Personal religious bias will always play a role in the selection of religious data and no single individual in the modern era is capable of authenticating any portion of biblical text because it is 100% hearsay with no direct links to Jesus nor even the language that Jesus spoke. So first of all know that nobody nowhere has anything written in Jesus' hand nor anything any of Jesus' students have written about him. Therefore anything we get from Jesus is going to be a type of hearsay evidence even if it is from God himself. Of course God himself would be a trustworthy source of information about Jesus yet scholastically speaking that would not be a direct testimony from the subject character in question. So some hearsay evidence is trustworthy, just because it's not Jesus himself doesn't mean its not accurate.

Yet just because people who love Jesus attribute something to Jesus doesn't mean it is accurate either, even if they've done so for thousands of years. In an attempt to be fair and justly balanced I used primarily three categories of data for information about Jesus' teachings and the order in which I use them is from most authentic as in 100% truthfully attributed to least authentic with as low as 65% chance of being true due to modern testing standards of below 65% being failure. Those lower than 65% which I include I only did so if there was supplemental support lending potential legitimacy to the quote being attributed to Jesus. There are biblical quotes of Jesus graded lower than 65% chance of authenticity and even some famous quotes with 0% chance of authenticity which I didn't include, because I decided it was too risky to include them due to their lack of legitimacy despite how popular they are among the masses.

My three sources are as follows:

1. The Quran which I believe to be the literal verbatim speech of God the Creator of the universe who truthfully quoted Jesus.
2. The Hadith which is accurately attributed to God's final prophet Muhammad who

　　　　truthfully quoted Jesus via information
　　　　obtained from God.
　　3. The Greek synoptic biblical gospels from the
　　　　New Testament as translated into English in
　　　　the Modern Literal Version.

Now I will explain the various levels of trustworthiness, reliability and scholastic credibility of the various sources of information.

People of different religions tend to heatedly argue back and forth with each claiming their religion is the only true divine religion and all others are false or corrupted. The problem is most of them always use the same reason for why what they believe is true, their reason being *"because their scriptures said so!"* Usually that ends the argument and no further debate can be considered because no one wants to consider that their beloved scripture may not be entirely divine or true. Of course they are quick to explain why the other's book isn't of divine origins, but they never offer a chance for their own book to be proven false and refuse to hear the other side's argument. Just because someone says the bible is the word of or inspired by God doesn't automatically make it so. Proof needs to be provided, or else why not believe the Hindu, Buddhist or Aztec scriptures just because they say to? In this case we have the Muslim hypothesis that "The Quran is the literal verbatim speech of God", but that's just a hypothesis, if it's not proven then it's just an opinion. The true religion is not a matter of opinion it's a matter of truth and the truth always has proof. In the scientific method there is something called a *"burden of proof"* which means that when a hypothesis is created there is a criteria presented along with it where if A, B and C are true then it means the hypothesis is false. The Quran presents such a *"burden of proof"* for anyone who doubts that it is the word of God. The Quran offers a challenge to those who doubt and gives a criterion which if met then it would mean the Quran is not from God. This is something special that no other book in the world contains. This challenge is significant because it puts the entire religion of Islam on the line. If anyone wants to destroy Islam and make Muslims leave their religion all they would have to do is meet this challenge and every Muslim in the world, including myself, would leave Islam because it would mean the Quran is not from God. This challenge is actually a part of Islam and Muslims are commanded to challenge people, devils and false deities to disprove the Quran. What is this challenge?

In the Quran chapter 11 verses 13 and 14 say:

أَمْ يَقُولُونَ ٱفْتَرَىٰهُ قُلْ فَأْتُوا۟ بِعَشْرِ سُوَرٍ مِّثْلِهِۦ مُفْتَرَيَٰتٍ وَٱدْعُوا۟ مَنِ ٱسْتَطَعْتُم مِّن دُونِ ٱللَّهِ إِن كُنتُمْ صَٰدِقِينَ (١٣)

Or do they say, "He invented it"? Say, "Then bring ten surahs like it that have been invented and call upon [for assistance] whomever you can besides Allah, if you should be truthful." (13)

فَإِلَّمْ يَسْتَجِيبُوا۟ لَكُمْ فَٱعْلَمُوٓا۟ أَنَّمَآ أُنزِلَ بِعِلْمِ ٱللَّهِ وَأَن لَّآ إِلَٰهَ إِلَّا هُوَ فَهَلْ أَنتُم مُّسْلِمُونَ (١٤)

And if they(false gods) do not respond to you - then know that the Qur'an was revealed with the knowledge of Allah and that there is no deity except Him. Then, would you [not] be Muslims? (14)

These verses, respond directly to the claims people had in the past about Muhammad having forged the Quran and it challenges them to prove their claim. If Muhammad, an unlettered man who cannot read or write who worships Allah singularly could forge the Quran then they should call what they worship for help in order so that they can make 10 chapters like it. This is a challenge the Arab pagan critics tried to complete and failed. Ironically people still make the same claim that Muhammad wrote the Quran, or copied it from other sources. What is amazing is that the Quran says disbelievers will say this and if that is true then they can bring 10 chapters like the Quran with the help of anything and everything they worship besides Allah the Creator and thus prove the Quran to be forged. Many who claim the Quran to have been made by Muhammad and not divine revelation don't even know they are mentioned in the Quran and challenged to back up their claim. They don't even have to come up with the 114 chapters of the Quran, only 10 chapters like the Quran are needed for them to prove their point and make every Muslim disbelieve in the Quran and the prophet Muhammad. For over 1400+ years no one has been able to bring 10 chapters like the Quran because they can't make it, yet they foolishly claim that "He forged it". Those who say this should read what they are talking about before they make such a statement, because if someone makes such a statement then the Quran is challenging that person to back it up. The Quran says when those false gods do not help people to make something like 10 chapters of the Quran then we should know that the Quran is divine revelation and that Allah is the only deity deserving of worship.

In Chapter 2 verse 23 of the Quran it says:

وَإِن كُنتُمْ فِى رَيْبٍ مِّمَّا نَزَّلْنَا عَلَىٰ عَبْدِنَا فَأْتُوا۟ بِسُورَةٍ مِّن مِّثْلِهِۦ وَٱدْعُوا۟ شُهَدَآءَكُم مِّن دُونِ ٱللَّهِ إِن كُنتُمْ صَٰدِقِينَ (٢٣)

And if you are in doubt about what We have sent down upon Our Servant [Muhammad], then produce a surah the like thereof and call upon your witnesses other than Allah, if you should be truthful. (23)

    This verse makes the challenge easier reducing it from 10 chapters to just 1 chapter. The shortest chapter in the Quran is chapter 108. It has 3 verses with only 10 words. Only 10 words! That is the challenge. If anyone can produce 10 words like the Arabic Quran then it will disprove Islam, the Quran and the prophet Muhammad to all the Muslims on the planet including myself. Islam would cease to be a religion overnight, all that is required is for a person to produce 10 words like the Quran. It sounds simple right? Well the second word of each verse ends with the Arabic letter form of K while the last letter of the last word of every verse is the Arabic form of R. This is a very specific and rigid structure; does the chapter even make any coherent sense? Let's examine the shortest Quranic chapter to see how easy this challenge is.

Chapter 108 of the Quran:

فَصَلِّ لِرَبِّكَ وَٱنْحَرْ ﴿٢﴾

إِنَّ شَانِئَكَ هُوَ ٱلْأَبْتَرُ ﴿٣﴾

Indeed, We have granted you, [O Muhammad], al-Kawthar. (1) So pray to your Lord and sacrifice [to Him alone]. (2) Indeed, your enemy is the one cut off. (3)

    The word you is referring to Muhammad, to whom this verse was revealed. Remember the Quran is exactly as it was revealed to Muhammad, he did not recite it in the third person, but recited it in exactly the way it was recited to him by the Angel Gabriel, so the reader or reciter is actually put into Muhammad's perspective. The word "We" does not mean Allah is plural or a trinity, but is the English "We" as is used in the royal pronoun form, just the same as any King or Queen would refer to themselves as "We" even though they are just one person. This chapter actually makes quite a lot of sense for having such a rigid structure and is foreboding in that the last verse pronounces he who hates or is an enemy to the prophet Muhammad will be cut off (from future Hope). It's significant that this would be the shortest chapter and the standard for those who want to disprove the Quran or the prophethood of Muhammad, because they are those who hate Muhammad since they reject his prophethood and would be the very people whom the chapter itself discusses. That's no coincidence. In fact this chapter was one of the earliest chapters revealed when Muhammad was in Mecca, during the first 13 years of his 23 years of receiving revelation. When Muhammad's son died in infancy, a hate filled disbeliever taunted Muhammad making fun of him because his infant son died, just like all his sons did, saying he would be "cut off" from posterity and nobody would even know that "Muhammad" ever existed. This chapter of the Quran was a reassurance and retort to his opponent and continues to be a warning against all opponents who fail to produce a chapter like this.

    Not only does the Quran offer a challenge and then make the challenge easier, but it also tells what the results will be for all who try to complete the challenge before they even try. In the verse after the easier challenge in 2:23 the Quran verse 2:24 says:

فَإِن لَّمْ تَفْعَلُوا۟ وَلَن تَفْعَلُوا۟ فَٱتَّقُوا۟ ٱلنَّارَ ٱلَّتِى وَقُودُهَا ٱلنَّاسُ وَٱلْحِجَارَةُ ۖ أُعِدَّتْ لِلْكَـٰفِرِينَ (٢٤)

"But if ye cannot- and of a surety ye cannot- then fear the Fire whose fuel is men and stones,- which is prepared for those who reject Faith."

These are strong words. Immediately after posting a challenge Allah says that all who try will fail. Who would be able to have the confidence to make such a statement unless they knew the results beforehand? Who would know except the All-knowing Creator of All things? Imagine if I claimed my book was the best book that will ever be written and that no one will be able to even bring 10 words that are like it. This would be a very stupid and arrogant challenge for me to make and it would likely be met within 10 minutes and expose the claim as false destroying all my credibility. The pagan Arabs were masters of Arabic, it was their specialty and pride, their poets were the most esteemed of society because of their linguistic abilities. They were the best equipped to meet such a challenge in all of history and they tried to come up with 10 words similar to the Quran in eloquence, sound, content, conciseness, rhetorical devices, grammar and literary form; however they all failed and could not even come close. The Quran also rhymes with various diverse rhyme schemes present throughout. Although don't think that it is some kind of poetry, or rap, because as a former Christian rapper and rap addict I can testify that rap, or poetry, cannot even be compared with the literary achievement that the Quran is. That is how superior the Quran is to music, that you can't even compare the two. All thanks and praises be to God that I was guided away from music and discovered the Quran. Even from an objective point of view, atheist Arab linguists maintain that the Quran is the most advanced piece of Arabic that has ever existed. Everyone who has tried to meet the challenge of the Quran has failed and for over 1450 years people have been trying to meet the challenge to no avail. In the modern era two famous examples of Christians trying to meet this challenge occurred. Evangelical Professor Gary Miller in 1977 tried and became a Muslim after his experience. Reverend Abraham Phillips also tried to disprove the Quran in his thesis for a doctorate degree but he found it impossible to refute and also as a result embraced Islam and became a Muslim. Many failed attempts have been made, most of the challengers just use the Quran and change one word or two trying to pass that off as their attempt since they can't make anything original that can be comparable because only the Quran can be compared to the Quran; that is because it is the only revelation of God we have access to today. However the Quran doesn't just say all challengers will fail, but it says that those who try to disprove the Quran, by accepting the challenge instead of accepting the Quran to be the word of Allah, then such should *"fear the Fire whose fuel is men and stones"*. Again this is a severe warning and who but the creator of Hell would know what the Fire uses as fuel? What a fire it is if stones are its fuel. If you put stones on earthly fire the fire would likely be put out, but the hellfire devours and feeds off of stone idols and people, growing in intensity the more it burns. Meaning the more people in hell the hotter it is and the longer they burn the hotter it gets. It gets hotter and hotter and hotter and hotter and hotter increasing in heat forever. That is the place promised to those who reject the Quran or try to imitate the Quran and fail in replicating it. One would think after reading such a terrible fate awaiting certain people that such a person would be cautious about claiming the Quran is made by man or false. The fact that people burn the Quran saying it's not from God proves that they haven't even read it, because if they did they would know about the challenge in the Quran and try to disprove it by meeting the challenge. If they really wanted to destroy the Quran and Islam then they would bring 10 words like it and it would prove Islam to be false, then presto everyone would burn the Quran and Islam would vanish. They claim this is what they want, but they really just want to cause corruption and mischief to spread throughout the land instigating violent reactions which can be used to justify further violence against Muslims. Their primary goal is to legally kill Muslims and stop Islam from peacefully spreading throughout the world. It's really simple, if you don't believe the Quran is the word of God even though it says it is and that a human(s) authored what none can make 10 words like, then just bring 10 words like it to prove your point. Anyone who doesn't try to do this and says the Quran is not divine revelation must not have read the Quran and therefore they cannot say whether it is divine revelation or not because they don't even know what they are talking about. Ironically such people tend to quote the attempted translations of the meanings of the Quran out of context distorting the meaning yet the Quran quotes their quotes about the Quran. Truly it is amazing to learn from the Quran what people will say about the Quran and then to hear those very people say exactly what the Quran said they would say. The Quran has quoted the enemies of Islam and what they say about the Quran before they were even born. By saying what they say about the Quran they prove it to be true revelation. Also this challenge was given to the Jews and Christians while Muhammad was alive as well, they never met this challenge and it still stands. Yet despite Jews and Christians claiming to have sacred divine revelation or "books inspired by God" they have yet to bring 10 words like the Quran. To this day none have been able to do it. So you know what that means right? That means if you take all the Jewish religious texts and all the Christian religious texts including every bible and alleged Hebrew Torah in the world combining everything all together, in total out of all their texts the Jews and Christians combined don't even have 10 words of divine revelation with them. Jews and Christians may disagree and even some Muslims may not know that Ahl-Kitab have less than 10 words of revelation in their books but that is the Islamic and Scholastic position. Originally Jews and Christians had more in the Suhuf of Abraham, Taurat of Moses, Zabur of David and Injeel of Jesus. However keep in mind that none of those were in Hebrew or Greek which the Old and New Testament consist of. Hebrew did not originate until about 600 BCE and neither Abraham, Moses, or David spoke Hebrew thus the Hebrew Old Testament bible books cannot be the same as the Suhuf, Taurat and Zabur simply because that language didn't exist when the books were revealed. While the New Testament bible books are Greek which is a language not spoken by Jesus and none of those Greek Gospels even portend to be by God but by alleged disciples of Jesus and Paul all of which was written long after Prophet Jesus left earth. For that reason no scholars in academic circles even consider the bibles as historical documents. Yet the Quran refers to Jews and Christians by phrases which mean people of the Scripture and people of the Book. Do you know why? Because they used to have Scripture and they used to have a Book sent by God, thus God honored them for what they used to have. But God also disgraces them with this phrase and challenge as well because by the time the Quran was revealed they didn't even have 10 words.

If someone still doesn't believe the Quran is from God and can't bring a chapter like it then they can ask for help in meeting the challenge of the Quran and don't have to try to meet it all by themselves individually. Quran 17:88 says,

قُل لَّئِنِ ٱجْتَمَعَتِ ٱلْإِنسُ وَٱلْجِنُّ عَلَىٰٓ أَن يَأْتُوا۟ بِمِثْلِ هَـٰذَا ٱلْقُرْءَانِ لَا يَأْتُونَ بِمِثْلِهِۦ وَلَوْ كَانَ بَعْضُهُمْ لِبَعْضٍ ظَهِيرًا (٨٨)

"Say: "If the whole of mankind and Jinns were to gather together to produce the like of this Qur´an, they could not produce the like thereof, even if they backed up each other with help and support.""

This verse instructs Muhammad to say how even if every human who ever existed and all of the species of the Jinn worked together to produce something like the Quran they could never produce anything like it. That may be one of the strongest statements a book can ever contain. Meaning even if Abraham, Moses, Jesus and Muhammad got together they couldn't produce the Quran. What author could have the nerve to make such a claim? If Christians disagree and really are inspired by the "Holy Spirit" and have their prayers answered by Jesus, Mary, or any of their alleged saints then why haven't they been able to come up with something equal to the Quran? It is because their prayers are unanswered and unheard and they are praying to people who cannot benefit them neither in this life or the next and merely get placebo effects and occasional aid from devils just as Hindus do when they pray to false deities. Only the Creator deserves prayers and the Quran could only have come from the Creator. Muhammad was an unlettered man who could not read or write, he did not make the Quran. It was revealed to him during a period of 23 years piece by piece, every time revelation would come he would memorize it and those people he shared it with would also memorize it on the spot and write it down to help with memorization. There is not one contradiction in this entire thing, it's impossible for a normal person to have others memorize what they say for 23 years and not contradict themselves one time. Only for a prophet of God who was receiving divine revelation would this be possible.

Some Muslims wrote verses down on bone or parchment to study and help with memorization, these writings have been found and carbon dated and the verses are exactly the same as the Arabic Quran people read today. This is one difference between Islam and all other religions, Muslims have access to our prophet's main miracle for all to witness and experience 1,450+ lunar years and counting. People didn't believe in Jesus so Allah helped him heal people as a sign and turned the staff of Moses into a serpent as proof that he was sent by the divine. Today no one can experience these signs or witness them firsthand and must just believe what they've been told, but you don't have to believe Muhammad is a prophet based on hearsay, one of his miraculous signs is the Quran and you can experience it today. The Quran was a miracle/sign to prove the prophethood of Muhammad and instruct all of mankind in guidance, this miracle has been perfectly preserved so that today we have the same access to the miracle as those who met Muhammad.

    Despite being known to man for over 1400+ years there is only one version/edition of the Arabic Quran. All over the world ancient manuscripts of the Quran have been found in Russia, Arabia, China, Africa, Europe and India with all of them having the same exact letters as the Arabic Quran we know of today. There are no different versions or editions of Divine Revelation. An Arabic book of the Quran from 646 CE contains the exact same letters, in the same order, as a freshly printed Arabic book of the Quran today and the same as the Qurans printed in any land at any time. But wait just one minute, didn't Muhammad die in 632 CE? How then can the earliest known physical copy of the Quran be dated to 646 CE, 14 years later? Shouldn't it be published earlier in Muhammad's lifetime? Well that would be impossible. How so? Because Muhammad received revelation of the Quran until he died, so if a written book was published in his lifetime and then new verses were revealed to him then there would be a problem with incomplete Qurans and people who found those may think the later verses revealed after such a copy was published may not be part of the Quran since it wouldn't have been included in a copy published before Muhammad died or received that revelation. However can't Christians claim the same about bibles to justify them not existing during the lifetime of Jesus? No. Why not? Because Jesus never read the bibles or taught it to people and nothing in it was written during his lifetime. In comparison Muhammad taught the Quran and told people to write it down during his lifetime. A full compendium of every verse just wasn't compiled or published in his lifetime. Publicly Muhammad would recite the Quran to the masses on a daily basis as did all the other Muslims, when giving speeches, praying 5 times a day in congregation, talking or just as a hobby/good deed. Every Ramadan Muhammad would recite all that had been revealed of the entire Quran up to that point publicly to the masses during the taraweeh prayer. After Muhammad died, it was known that no more verses of the Quran would be revealed by Allah since the prophet was gone and only prophets can receive revelation and Muhammad was the final prophet. Then the first Khalifh Abu Bakr ordered the complete Quran be organized into book form to be published. All of the Quran had already been written before Muhammad died but all the written verses just weren't collected in one written book. Thousands of people had memorized the whole Quran but the written pieces were the private property of the individual Muslims who had written them down. In order to publish the written book format of the Quran all these written pieces had to be collected. Also since the publishing of the Quran effected the whole Muslim world no individual wanted to just do it on their own because the consequences of making any error were too great and publishing costs were high during the 600s CE. To mass produce a book you needed quite a bit of money, the types that governments have and an Islamic State initially wasn't going to publish the first ever full written copy of the Quran because that was such an important religious deed the state figured it should make sure nothing goes wrong with such a project. Yet keep in mind the Islamic

State was run by the companions of Muhammad, it wasn't a foreign anti-prophetic state like Pharaonic Egypt or the Roman Empire, the first 4 Khalifhs were not only the best friends of Muhammad but the first was his father in-law, as was the second and the third had married 2 of Muhammad's daughters (one at a time) while the 4th was his cousin and married Muhammad's favorite daughter. So when the Islamic State worked on the written Quran project it wasn't some "shoddy state project" as we think of them today. Think of it as if it were Solomon composing the Zabur that was given to David in written form. Nobody would view Solomon as "some corrupt government official" who is unqualified to publish the revelation given to Prophet David. We'd agree Prophet Solomon would be the best one for the job after David himself, so rulership doesn't always mean anti-religious or unreligious; sometimes good rulers can do great things for religion. The criteria for publication of the Quran was extremely strict. Zaid ibn Thabit was chosen for the task primarily because he was known to have heard the full Quran recited to him by Muhammad during the last Ramadan before Muhammad's death. Regarding the compilation of the Quran in its complete written form, not just any Muslim was able to say what the Quran said. A Muslim couldn't just come with a piece of paper and say it's a verse from the Quran and have it published in the book. They had to have heard it directly from Muhammad's mouth, AND they had to have written it down in the presence of Muhammad AND recited it to Muhammad, to verify they knew how to pronounce it correctly and knew it exactly accurate 100%. Also aside from hearing it from Muhammad, writing it in his presence and reciting it to Muhammad, a person needed two trustworthy pious witnesses who could testify that person had heard, written and recited that particular verse or letter of the Quran during the lifetime of Muhammad to him/her directly before that person was qualified to testify to what a single letter of the Quran to be published said. Now Zaid bin Thabit had to have more than just 1 person who met this criteria for every letter of the Quran before he could compile the full written book, he needed a minimum 2 people who met this criteria for every letter, along with the 4 witnesses who could testify for those 2 people that they heard X letter from Muhammad, wrote it in his presence and recited X letter of the Quran to Muhammad. Every single letter in the written Quran had to have been written down at least twice in the presence of Muhammad by 2 different individuals with 4 different witnesses to that or else it would not be included in the Quran. Meaning every letter to be put into the written book format of the Quran needed a minimum of 6 people to testify it had come from Muhammad's mouth, was written in his presence and accurately recited/verified by Muhammad. This criteria strict as it was did not cause authentic verses to be excluded. Why then was it done if in theory this strict criteria could have resulted in unabrogated authentic verses of the Quran not getting into the written version? For the sake of literary authenticity. Afterall you can't just say X is the word of God taught to us by a prophet of God, you gotta prove that 100%. If you can't prove your book is truly from God via a prophet then there is no reason to believe in it at all. If X book is something which all people "need to believe in" this book needs to be proven to have come from the sources which it really came from. It's hard enough for people to believe in prophets, so the least a believer must do is prove that what they are telling people to believe in actually came from their prophet as they claim. Also if you can't prove it then there is no justified reason for you to believe in it either, you'd just be blindly following what non-prophets told you without proof that it actually goes back to a prophet. The companions of Muhammad knew this and knew they needed to have an undisputable method for authentically preserving the teachings of the final Messenger of God because if they didn't then the religion of God would be lost and a "final messenger" means humanity cannot afford to screw it up and fail to keep the authentic information scholastically preserved. To not be able to prove the information that is preached after the final messenger of God is gone really is from the final messenger of God is to delegitimize the true faith and to fail the test of life and give everybody a valid excuse to disbelieve in and disobey God. If the companions of Muhammad didn't painstakingly preserve the prophetic teachings and prove that they did so then everyone to come after them would not have to believe in or obey God and they would get blamed by God for every sin every person did after Muhammad died. They didn't want such blame from God so they decided to get super-scholastic and prove that the information they are passing on to people really is from Muhammad as they claim. If they didn't they knew they would go to hell because Muhammad told them it was their duty to preserve the true religion after he died and that God wasn't sending any more prophets to fix things if they failed. Thus the companions of Muhammad were put in a spot where they could either be the best of people if they succeeded in preserving the prophetic faith, when so many other peoples had failed, or they could be the worst for dooming everyone else to come after them if they didn't scholastically preserve and prove they preserved the authentic teachings of God's final prophet including God's final revelation, the Quran. Hence the companions of Muhammad knew they either preserved the Quran 100% or they would go to hell forever and whether you believe that would've happened to them or not, they did believe that and that's a fact. They knew the consequences of making mistakes and this is why Zaid ibn Thabit took so long to do the job and said how he wished someone else did it because for him it'd be easier to move a mountain than to bear the burden of the responsibility of publishing God's book in written form since the risk of making a mistake was so great and he didn't want to have that responsibility which the other companions forced upon him. All the Muslims were afraid of making a mistake unintentionally when the Quran was to be published. I mean just take my books for example, you've probably noticed hundreds of errors, spelling or grammatical or worse, and that's all from me with my own stuff. So for a religious person to be burdened with publishing God's book is extremely hard to do, not impossible but it's perhaps the most stressful job one can have in life. A single spelling error and you go to hell forever, how would you like to publish a book like that considering all books at that time were written by hand? Thus all the Muslims gave the job to Muhammad's companion Zaid ibn Thabit. Thankfully for him and us he succeeded with perfection. When he finished thousands of companions testified that his written compilation was 100% complete and accurate. This book was completed within 2 years after Muhammad's death, before Abu Bakr died about 2 years after Muhammad. This copy was kept with the Khalifh Abu Bakr, the Khalifh Umar kept it after Abu Bakr died, then Uthman bin Affan possessed it as Khalifh. Uthman bin Affan decided to make more than one copy and sent the various copies throughout the Muslim world. It is this Uthmanic copy that was published for the masses in 646 CE,

14 years after the death of Muhammad. But what about Abu Bakr's copy? Well that doesn't have the dots. In Arabic the dots are diacritical marks that help one easily identify the letters since many letters in Arabic use the same root shape with only context or dots distinguishing them. For example in english the letters, i and t both use the same exact root shape but the i has a dot and the t has dash. If the i wasn't dotted and the t wasn't dashed then one could mistake the two letters and misunderstand the text if you didn't know the letters from context or the english language well. The same applies to the letters l, d, P, R, and b, they all look so similar sharing the l root shape that without the loops it'd be hard to identify each letter. In Arabia during the prophet's time nobody used the dots because they were that advanced linguistically because they lived in a desert and had nothing else to do but get good at language. However Arabs and Arabia changed and since Islam was spreading to non-Arab lands where people could misunderstand the Quran if it wasn't dotted then Uthman included the dots so nobody could ever possibly make a mistake. The dots were added to the Quran in Uthman's time, though they existed in some of the individual written copies before that. Adding dots didn't

change a thing regarding pronunciation nor meaning, but it just closed the door for misinterpretation. Uthman then gathered the companions of Muhammad and showed them his copy and Abu Bakr's and they confirmed they were identical to what everyone knew was the Quran. Uthman then said how he planned to burn the undotted copy because someone in the future might come and see the undotted copy and then wrongfully claim the Uthmanic copy did the dots incorrectly and then do their own dots incorrectly and get believed by ignorant people and thus the Quran could in theory be changed as long as that undotted copy remained. Because a thousand years later who is to say whether the dot should be above or below the line when all those who heard the verse from Muhammad directly are dead? Hence realizing the theoretical danger of the undotted copy for future generations and evil/ignorant people the companions agreed to burn Abu Bakr's copy though it was identical to Uthman's because it didn't have the dots, and if they simply added the dots in then future generations might say or learn somehow that they added the dots to Abu Bakr's copy years later and then accuse them of changing the Quran putting dots in the wrong places. To add the dots to Abu Bakr's copy years later would be forgery since Abu Bakr was dead, it could no longer then be called "Abu Bakr's copy" if it had the dots. So they couldn't just add dots to "Abu Bakr's Quran copy" because that would be a type of forgery but if they left it intact and undotted then foolish or evil people might reject Uthman's correct copy that leaves no room for misunderstanding. Thus Abu Bakr's copy was burned and replaced with the Uthmanic Quranic script in 646 CE. It was exactly the same, it was just non-Arab friendly and fool friendly. This way you didn't need to be a master in Arabic to read it in Arabic correctly. The Quran was already memorized by the masses, the written copy was initially just a copy for safety reasons in case all those who memorized the full Quran died out. Over time to help with memorization of the Quran, copies were distributed to the masses as they are today. However then people started translating them. This phenomenon of translation could lead to trouble down the road, if the Arabic is neglected or the translations get considered equal or 100% the same as the Arabic Quran. However there is a benefit in the translations of the Quran in that some non-Arabs can get some of it's message, like me.

Yet there is still a danger of losing the Arabic if the translations come to be treated in an extreme fashion as the trend seems to be going towards. However because Muslims pray in Arabic and memorize the Quran in Arabic then the danger is much reduced. Anyways that in a nutshell explains why and how the oldest written copy of the Quran which exists today was published in 646 CE while Muhammad died in 632 CE and the first written copy was published between 632-634 CE. One could in theory allege Uthman changed the Quran but nobody ever said this against Uthman during his lifetime, the following Khalifh Ali didn't say it either and thousands of Muslims memorized the Quran prior to Uthman's edition so it wasn't as though it was only a written copy. Plus original scraps of undotted copies of the Quran exist and were discovered in modern time with the verses exactly the same as the dotted Uthmanic script, they just don't have the dots but contextually it means the same. For example if I wrote "i did it" but didn't dot the i's and someone else came and said that it's supposed to be "t dtd tt", anyone who knows english would know that the claim "the dots are wrong" is foolish. So that's where theoretically one might think there is a tiny chance Uthman could've changed the meaning via the dots but if you know Arabic you know it is too hard to do and get away with. I've even seen english books written in the 1700s where the t is used for both t and f and you still understand contextually what is t and what is f even though the letters are messed up due to "wrong dots". So the dot difference is theoretical, but even if it weren't, since thousands of Muslims memorized the full Quran and never contested the dotted Uthmanic script during that era, nor have any ever contested it greatly implies no changes were made. Scholastically if one persists as a skeptic they still must concede that since 646 CE all Muslims have been united and had the same exact Quran without even a dot being changed. So none can ever claim the written Quran has been changed from 646 CE onwards, even if they think it was changed before that, which no Muslim believes it was. The written copies were meant to be backups primarily, just in case the world no longer has Muslims who have memorized the full Quran. Now people claim "the bible" is the same and just as authentic or historical. But answer me this? 1. Has a single Christian in all of history ever memorized any full bible in it's original language including the original pronunciation (including the length which vowels are elongated and the spaces where the reader takes breaths when reading)? Seriously ask a Christian *"When you read the bible out loud at which points in the verses did Jesus or his companions teach you to take a breath while reading the bible?"* Because Muhammad and the companions of Muhammad taught the Muslims when to take a breath when they "speak the words of God". Afterall doesn't it make sense that if God is going to send you "God's word" to read and verbalize then God is going to tell you at which spots to pause for breath? God does know you gotta breathe right? You can't just breathe in the middle of the word or sentence because that can change the whole meaning of the verse. Allah told Muhammad when to breathe when reciting the Quran. Do Christians actually think God doesn't care when they breathe when speaking God's word out loud? Why would God care when you breathe? Because God's book is unlike any other and if you read God's book aloud there are rules for breathing because it's a special book. That's one thing that makes God's book special and unique in that there are rules for breathing when reading it aloud. Do Christians not think the word of God is special and unique or were they not "guided unto all truth" and "taught all things" as the bible says Jesus said the "Holy Spirit/Comforter/Holy Prophet" would do who would "speak only what he hears"? 2. Can Christians prove with physical documentation that the bible in their hand today is dot for dot exactly the same as the one that they don't even allege existed 14 years after the departure of Jesus? But more importantly, 3. Did Jesus recite the New Testament to people during his lifetime, have it written down in his lifetime and have it recited to him in his lifetime and then have a minimum of 2 written copies of every verse in the New Testament that existed before he left earth? AND have 2 witnesses to witness each letter of the New Testament, meaning 4 trustworthy pious witnesses can testify for every letter in the New Testament that "Mark", "Matthew", "Luke", "John" and "Paul" and the rest wrote? Making a minimum of 6 total trustworthy pious witnesses who are companions of Jesus that approve of every verse in the New Testament and testify that Jesus taught it? Hell no! Paul and Luke even according to Christians never even met Jesus, heard him or saw what he looked like. Paul didn't even believe in the religion of Jesus while Jesus was on earth, according to his own admission. Thus Paul is scholastically disqualified from saying a single word about Jesus, even if what he said was true, which it's not and is contradictory to Jesus, his disciples, other Christians(some whom Paul killed as Saul) and Paul's other versions of Jesus. The same applies to the books of the Hebrew bible and/or "Old Testament". None are traceable back to Moses and Moses, David and Solomon didn't even speak or write Hebrew. So the bible is not only scholastically inauthentically transcribed but it's not even in the same language the prophets to whom such writings are alleged to have come from spoke. Just on that fundamental point alone, that the New Testament is written in a language Jesus never spoke and that the Old Testament is written in a language Abraham, Ishmail, Isaac, Jacob, Joseph, Noah, Job, Jonah, Adam, Moses, David, Solomon, Lot, Seth, Enoch and most biblical characters never spoke disqualifies them as authentic religiously useable texts. Forget translations, copies, forgeries, lack of chains of transmission. The books are in different languages than the prophets they purport to teach us about, hence they could never be from those prophets and could never be the divine revelation given to those prophets. There is absolutely zero connection between the biblical prophets and the biblical texts.

A newspaper article written today has as much likelihood to have been written by Moses as the bible. Yet who would dare claim Moses is writing articles for the modern media outfits? This is how farfetched the claim of Jews and Christians are when they say that the books they read and preach today are the Taurat that was revealed to Moses or the Zabur revealed to David or the Suhuf revealed to Abraham (though most Jews/Christians don't even know about that book to even claim such a thing). Likewise it's more reasonable to think Jesus wrote Mein Kempf than it is to think the New Testament is the Injeel that was revealed to Jesus. Yet some people consider the Quran comparable to the bible? That's ludicrous insanity. Scholastically the bible is invalid and belongs in the fiction genre of libraries and bookstores. This is why the notion of Christian and Jewish "scholars" is an academic insult, it's an insult not a joke, but an insult, because scholastically speaking to believe in scholastic academia's methods of authenticity means to disbelieve in the authenticity of the alleged literary foundations of Judaism and Christianity. Nobody with academic integrity or credentials claims the bibles have any connection with the prophets described in them. Not a single scholastic link exists. Zeus and Hercules have as much of a connection with the bible as Moses and Jesus do. Just because the bible has information about Moses and Jesus putting words in their mouth doesn't mean it has any connection to them at all. It's truly disgusting when religious scholastic minds examine the bible and then get told it's holy, sacred scripture, authentic or the "inspired word of God". It's utterly depressing to know of the deception Christians and Jews are under and the sheer lack of scholasticism amongst them regarding their claims. With Christians/Jews their claims about their texts is mainly all talk and tradition which contradicts genuine scholastic authenticity. Every "Scholar" they claim supports them is one of their own who just has a diploma, likely from a diploma mill that lacks academic credentials in the non-religious universe. Sadly though people think Muslims are just like Christians/Jews because we say we got a book from God too when scholastically our books are incomparable. It's the same claim but 2 totally different things, though non-Muslim non-Christian non-Jews tend to unjustly judge the Quran the same as they do "the bible". Muslims beg them to just read the Quran knowing they will see the difference but since the bible is so damn long and

Christians/Jews also say "Just read it then you'll see." they tend to arrogantly refuse not knowing you can read the whole Quran in a few hours. The bible may take years to read but the full Quran can be read within 1 day's time. The bible is nothing like the Quran it even addresses the reader in a different direct "God to reader" perspective while the bible is a boring contradictory historical monologue. Ironically evil cartoonish villains are known for monologues. In literary terms the bible has an "evil speech style" whereas God is not known to have ever monologued. In literary terms the Quran is unlike every other book, especially regarding style, worth of content/wisdom per length, historical authenticity and proof of preservation.

However isn't it possible that somehow the Quran was corrupted in between Muhammad and us today? So that "our Quran" isn't the real Quran or couldn't the Quran be destroyed and lost and then someone invents a new one and tricks all the Muslims into thinking it was the same Quran as the original even though it wasn't? Imagine if we all agreed to destroy every book in the world, deleting every digital, audio and written copy by fire and/or other methods so that no book that we know of today existed in physical format. Within less than 24 hours mankind would be able to reprint the Quran from scratch without referencing any physical copies and have it turn out exactly the same as the original because millions have it entirely memorized in its original Arabic, no other book could be recovered as quickly as fully if at all. This is a vital detail because if God sends a final prophet with a final revelation then that revelation has to be available, if it's not then people will not know how they are supposed to conduct themselves and will have an excuse for not living the way God desires them to. If you had no chance to know what God wanted from you then you would have had no chance to do what God wanted. In that case God would have no legal recourse to punish you if you had no chance to know the laws which you were supposed to obey. For someone to say that nothing today is divine revelation, it means that they think it's impossible to know what God's rules are for us, therefore it would be impossible for someone to go to hell no matter how evil they were, or what bad things they did. Obviously thinking that the evil mass-murdering, thieving, adulterous, disbelieving people will not be punished is preposterous. Thus the divine revelation must exist and every religious text other than the Quran and Sunnah has been proven to be corrupted and changed from its original, as has been demonstrated with the analysis of the bibles. Some might say that "the bible" hasn't been corrupted (pretending there is only 1 version), but even they will agree that if all digital, audio and written bibles were destroyed then "the bible" would be lost forever. Now if something can potentially be lost then that is not the final divine revelation, because the final divine revelation cannot be potentially lost by definition. By default that would make the Quran the only candidate for being the final divine revelation. Not only is it the only candidate, but it also says that it is the final divine revelation which will be preserved from distortion and corruption, which time has proven that claim to be true. The Quran is also the only religious Scripture that is impossible to be changed or lost. So many people have the Quran memorized completely in Arabic that it would be easier to change the mathematical numbers than to change the Quran. It'd be easier to get people to forget or not think the sun and moon existed than to change the Quran. Little kids who can't even ride a bicycle have memorized the entire Quran in

Arabic. Do you know how this is possible? Because Allah said in the Quran 54:17,

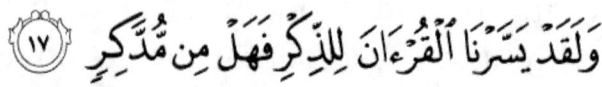

"*And We have indeed made the Quran easy to understand and remember, then is there any that will remember (or receive admonition)?*"

It's simply because the Quran said it was easy to remember and because it's true then it is. There is no other explanation one can have to say why a book which claims to be from God which says it is easy to remember is also the most memorized book in the history of all mankind in the original Arabic language which it was revealed in, being remembered by people who don't even know the meaning of the Arabic. If any book at all can be called "easy to remember" it's the Quran, it is the easiest to remember of all books. For example Ibn Shihab Al-Zuhri is reported to have memorized the entire Quran when he was 7 years old in only 8 days. 8 days for a 7 year old to memorize all 114 chapters of the Quran. Such things even take place in modern times with Rukkayatu Fatahu Umar being a 3 year old girl in Nigeria who memorized the entire Quran in 2013 CE. She was 3 years old! For a 3 year old in modern times to memorize a religious book of 114 chapters in length, totaling 600 pages in Arabic, is practically a miracle itself. Oh and keep in mind she was a 3 year old Nigerian and Arabic is not the common language in Nigeria, so most likely she didn't even know the meaning of the Arabic she memorized unless she also memorized the meanings in Nigerian or another language if she didn't know Arabic. Typically it's hard to memorize things in a language you don't understand but not so with the Quran. What other 600 page religious book which has been on earth for thousands of years can be memorized by a modern 3 year old child in a language they don't even know? So when Allah says in the Quran how he has made it easy to understand and remember those aren't just words, it's miraculously easy to remember the Quran. It's not just some empty claim that any book could make. No book on the planet can even come close to being as easy to remember as the Quran. The Quran is also the most popular and widely read book of all time. Christians falsely dispute this and say "the bible" is but they are pretending that there is only one edition of a bible and ignoring the fact that different languages constitute a different book and that until very recently only priests were allowed to even possess a bible, let alone read one; under legal punishment. If any bible set any record it's for being the most misunderstood least divine book of all time with the largest discrepancy between owners/readers. Out of all books that are bought or believed in "the bible" is the least read and least followed. Basically if you consider the popularity of "the bible" it is technically the least impactful book known to man of all recorded history, any divine book if as widely known as the bible would've had much greater impact and created a much better world. Yet despite these facts Christians lie about the bible being the best-selling most popular book of all time just as they tell their kids that Santa Claus magically visits every child in the world on Christmas despite Santa Claus never ever coming to non-Christian countries or even being portrayed there as existing. Christians live in a massively conspiratorially constructed superficial bubble or echo-chamber where their mythical lies are repeated so much they get believed to be self-evident common sense truths which they think are universally accepted without opposition except by idiotic evil non-Christian fools. Understandably this book may stunningly overdose some people with a fact check so much so they may not even read this far. Those people who quit reading because they can't handle the truth are not worthy of learning the Quotes of Prophet Jesus because it is known that they would reject and distort his true teachings before they ever accepted them. Even amongst Christendom the various denominations disagree on what bible they are even supposed to use. So any and every individual bible edition is vastly less popular than the one 1400+ year old singular edition of the Arabic Quran, so why do Christians lie to their people about the popularity of "the bible"? Why don't their bible publishers and leaders tell the truth and say the Arabic Quran is the most popular book of all time?

Once more to illustrate how translations are never the same as the original take this book I've written as an example. As the author I can say with certainty that no person will ever be able to translate this book correctly conveying 100% of the meanings I intended because only I and God know what I meant when I wrote something. You don't and will never know what I meant when I used every word, so to translate all of my words into another language you would need to know exactly what I meant to say with each word in order to translate all my words correctly. Thus I am the only person who will ever be qualified to translate my book 100% correctly. Others could try but they could never claim to have accurately translated my book because they don't know what I really meant, they could only guess. So anyone who tried to translate this book would be changing the book with their own ideas of my intended meanings and any translation that's not done by me personally would not really be "my book", but someone else's interpretation of my English book in another language. Whereas this also applies to the biblical books too, only Jesus is qualified to translate Jesus. In theory if the gospels were written by actual companions of Jesus, which they weren't, then they still would be corrupting his teachings by translating them into Greek since they wouldn't know if Jesus would've translated himself the way Christians allege they have done. The same applies to Paul's letters which get translated. The same even applies to hadith and the Quran. Translations done by 2nd parties can never be 100% the same thing as the original. But again remember the biblical books aren't translations of the original sources, they are translations of translations of translations and only God knows how messed up they've gotten. Just as a fish cannot translate a human neither can a human translate God. By saying a translation is divine revelation then you are saying the translator was divine. To say a translation is "*the word of God*" it means you consider the translator to be God since it is their words you are referencing and not God's words even if they were translating God's words, which typically isn't the case anyways. Truly if you have revelation of God get translated the only way it can be considered revelation is if God translated it himself. Simply claiming a translator was "inspired" doesn't count, just as nobody could say God inspired them to translate my book because accurate translations are not possible unless they are done by the original author themself. So the common claim that the biblical passages are the "inspired word of God" is false for so many reasons. That a translation is done by a human is enough proof that translations are not divine revelations or 100% accurate because humans don't know every word in a language. God knows every word and knows the best word to use to convey the correct meaning, humans don't and thus can never ever translate another human 100% correctly, let alone God the Creator of the Universe. Honestly nobody can even translate me 100% accurately so it is impossible that anybody could translate God 100% accurately. That's why some Islamic Scholars passed legal rulings saying because the Quran is Arabic it is actually not permissible to print a translation of the Quran without also including the Arabic alongside the translation. There is great wisdom in this. For instance how can someone know that the translation is accurate if the translator didn't show the reader the text they translated? This would amount to having blind faith in the translator. As a result of the religious books of other faiths being translated without the original text accompanying it, today the original texts are no longer accessible and adherents to such religions must simply hope their translations are accurate because they no longer possess the original revelation in its original language. Negligence caused them to lose the original divine revelation and thereby lose their way, become deviant and be led astray. Sometimes people modernize translations then claim it's what was originally translated by someone else. So, when some Muslim scholars give a ruling saying how Quran translations must have the Arabic alongside, it's for a very important reason. Usually Muslim strictness is for safety reasons, it's not to make things difficult. From my very limited experience the most reliable attempted English translation of the meanings of the Quran I've read thus far is either Saheeh International or the version by Dr. Muhsin Khaan, and Taqi-ud-Deen Hilaali, but even they have some errors in that they incorrectly associate the Injeel with the word Gospel and Zabur with the word Psalms. Yet that grievous sacreligious error stems from the translators forgetting we can only call God's revelations what God has said we can call them. The Injeel and Zabur are exactly that and can only be called that unless God says otherwise. Likewise one cannot add the English word "Holy" to the title of a non-english book under any circumstances unless God himself made a multi-lingual label for his book. The reason it is so important that the Quran remains in its original Arabic is because the previous revelations and their meanings were lost in translation. Concerning the bibles, the originals of the gospels, epistles and Jewish books don't exist.

There are thousands of different translations of the bibles today, which means thousands of different gospels of "Matthew" and the rest. In reality there would only have been one gospel, today there are thousands of different translations of the gospel of "Matthew" and that is just counting the English translations. The original words of that gospel could never have had thousands of different meanings so these translations we know of today could not possibly even be considered comparable to the original. The original gospel doesn't exist, so how can someone translate what doesn't exist? Simply put they can't, instead they translate translations which most falsely allege are copies of the copies of the originals in the same language as the original. Yet even if such spurious hopes were true, even then the process of biblical copying, ignoring and denying the fact of translation distortion, caused the gospels to become diluted through each translation of the Greek(translations, not copies) and the modern translations bear nearly no resemblance to the originals. This is why another prophet and further divine revelation was needed because the original revelations previously sent had been lost and the translations corrupted with the copies miscopied. A bible is not the revelation God gave Moses, David and Jesus as the Quran is the revelation God gave Muhammad. Instead the Old and New Testaments of the bibles would be comparable to a weak or fabricated hadith collection in which only translations are available and the original statements in the original language is unknown and the chain of narrators only includes Person C without anyone else in the chain listed for Persons A, B, D, E or F except it is known that the authors of the biblical books in reality aren't even Person C but are actually anonymous authors whose writings get changed with every new printing of their books. Sadly Christians are led to believe that the authors of their texts are eyewitnesses and that what they consider to be an eyewitness account of an alleged student of a prophet is divine revelation instead of a news report. The problem is the Judeo-Christian definition of divine revelation is wrong. A **divine revelation is the verbatim speech of God revealed to a Messenger of God transmitted from that Messenger to us**. Neither Moses, David nor Jesus taught or endorsed any bible thus it cannot be divine revelation by definition, but since neither Jews nor Christians want to admit they don't have divine revelations they change the definition of revelation into being whatever they have and/or believe is an instruction manual for salvation. The Quran is the uncreated **Arabic speech of Allah** that was **revealed to the Prophet Muhammad** both **in word and in meaning**. The Ahl-Kitab(People of the book/Jew and Christians) have lost their Kitabs but they are still called Ahl-Kitab in Islam because they are descendants of those given Kitabs and a Kitab of Allah is a very big thing to have been given, even if one has lost it tis still an honor to have once been given one. Also it's a type of shame for them and reminder to us that they're a people originally given books from Allah yet look at their evil and distance from Allah.

I mentioned hadith in the previous paragraph which leads me to explain my second source of information about Jesus, which is the hadith of prophet Muhammad. Both the Hadith and the Quran are revelation but there are differences between them. For those unfamiliar with what a Hadith is, it comprises a statement, action or approval/forbiddance of the prophet Muhammad. Basically the Quran is a book from Allah and the Hadith contains everything that Muhammad taught aside from the Quran. We need the Hadith to explain the Quran correctly according to prophetic understanding. Yet since the era of the prophet ended so long ago how do we know the Hadith we quote is actually from the prophet? This can be verified with what is called the science of hadith.

A hadith's Isnad or chain of narrators may be like this: "**Person E heard from Person D who heard** *from Person C who was told by Person B that Person A said*: When I was eating dinner with the prophet, after he had finished eating a piece of gourd he had selected with his right hand, of which gourd was his favorite food, I saw Muhammad smile so much his molar teeth were visible and heard him say:"_____". This chain of narrators is called the isnad. Imam Abdullah Ibn Mubarak said regarding the isnad: **"The isnad is part of the religion: had it not been for the isnad, whoever wished to would have said whatever he liked."** While Imam Ash-Shafi'i said in regards to the isnad: *"Whoever attempts to seek and learn hadith without an isnad he is like one who gathers wood at night in the darkness. He picks up wood, not knowing there is a serpent inside."* Now the Jewish and Christian books do not have any isnads at all, not for even 1 biblical verse. So the isnad is a special proof of authentic information Islam has, which all other faiths and texts of other religions do not have. No other religion can prove that the information they teach today attributing it to X person is the exact same material that was actually taught by X person in the past many years ago. Other faiths say to "trust in God and their texts", Muslims trust in God but scientifically prove their religious texts are trustworthy. You trust the material that's from God or his prophets only after it's been proven to really come from God or his prophets. If it's not proven you can't treat it as though it's prophetic, even if it is, because the prophets taught us to follow only what was proven to have truly come from God and forbid us from the sinful blind-following of non-prophets.

There is a methodology for authentication and it is historically scientific. Because of the intellectual honesty of Muslim scholars, the hadiths have various classifications. Islamic scholars admit that not everything people say about Muhammad is true. There are hadiths which have been forged and fabricated, or are doubtful. Muslim scholars have preserved them, as well as those which are true. There are even books by Muslim scholars devoted to lies people said about Muhammad detailing who started the lie and why it is a lie. There are also books by Muslim scholars who say: it appears this hadith is true and seems like something Muhammad would do but we cannot prove it. Then there are classes of hadith which have been proven to be 100% true. No other religion has such intellectual honesty where they say what's true and what's false and what can't be verified; every other religion just says, *"everything we're telling you is true, just trust us"*. A Muslim scholar will tell you if what he is saying has not been proven as well as how strong a religious opinion is. Even non-Muslim scholars have said that Muslims should be proud of their hadith tradition because it is beyond scholastic comparison and no other religion has anything comparable to it. A legal or religious ruling can only be based upon authentic information. Weak(da'eef) or doubtful hadiths by themselves cannot be used to justify doing or not doing something. For a hadith to be classified as sahih or authentic it has to meet a high level of criteria. Usually there must be two separate chains of narration confirming the same tradition. Meaning there must have been more than one witness to the event in question unless it were something specific, such as something that only his wife could witness, but then that has to be mentioned if there is only one chain. The chain must be entirely reliable throughout, meaning all the narrators must have been able to have actually learned from each other and been in the same place at the same time in their lives. Sometimes you will find that person E will say they heard from person D but person D died before person E was born, so it would have been impossible for person E to have learned from person D, or perhaps persons D and E while both alive at the same time and in the same city they may never have actually been able to communicate with each other and share information, these details must be made known and those types of things affect the grade of a hadith. Those in the chain of narration and the scholars must know the biographies of every single person in the chain of each narration, knowing what they did with their life, who they learned from and who they taught, what their morals were like, if they were honest or forgetful and must make sure they are all of reputable character. You cannot just accept a narration at face value, you have to know exactly who these narrators actually were and what they and their memories were like. You cannot just say "I heard from so and so who heard from so and so", when discussing something the prophet Muhammad said or did, you have to know if "so and so #1" is trustworthy and reliable and you have to know if "so and so #2" is trustworthy and reliable and so on and so forth for the whole chain of narrators for each and every hadith. This is a serious scientific intellectual processing method which is actually inconvenient, however it's the only way to be certain that information is authentic. The authentically proven sound hadith are scholastically more reliable than any bible. The science of hadith is so precise that it even requires critical thinking talents just to contemplate and it overwhelmed me when I first learned about it. I felt like a total fool when I first learned about hadith and realized I could not really prove most of what I thought I knew and considered true. May God help us to have correct comprehension, give us understanding, guide us to the truth and make us of those who accept and follow it until we die.

Different scholars have slightly different criteria for grading hadith but some basic principles are:

1. The chain of narration, from Muhammad to the final narrator, must be connected in such a way that every single person in the chain has himself heard or received this narration from the person he is narrating from.

2. All the narrators in the chain must be upright, meaning that they must be:

    a) Muslim

    b) Of the age of puberty

    c) Sane

    d) Not an open sinner

e) Free from bad habits

3. All the narrators must possess the ability to preserve the hadith precisely letter for letter.

4. The hadith should not contradict other hadiths which have come from more reliable narrators.

5. There are no other hidden weaknesses in the hadith or isnad – such as a hidden gap in the chain of narration.

Upon the absence of any one of the above 5 conditions, the hadith immediately is classed as Weak (*da'if*). But if all of the conditions are met with the third (preservation) being of a lower degree, then it is classed as Sound/Good (*hasan*). A hadith is classed as rigorously verified to be 100% true and Authentic (*sahih*) if it meets the previous 5 conditions and has a high degree of preservation.

In regards to Imam Bukhari's criteria for a hadith he was one of many who strictly would refuse to accept something as being authentic unless he knew of 2 separate isnads for a hadith. So his criteria was even stricter than they needed to be. Basically he required 2 authentic hadiths before he'd consider what either one of them taught as being true.

However Imam Bukhari lived a few generations after Muhammad, were Muslims always so strict about verifying whether something someone said about Muhammad was true or false? Yes. There are many examples to demonstrate this but for brevity since this is a book pertaining to Jesus and not hadith, I will limit myself to mentioning the famous case of the incident which occurred between Abu Musa Al-Ash'ari and Umar bin Khattab. The background context of this incident is important, this took place only a few years after the death of Muhammad. At most within 13 years of his death because Umar was the Khalifh at the time this took place. Umar became Khalifh 2 years after Muhammad and ruled for 10 years, before dying about 13 years after Muhammad died. The incident was reported by Abu Musa Al-Ash'ari himself who says what in English means:

"I sought permission to see Umar and I did not have permission after three times. Hence, I left. He called me and said: 'Abdullah, have you found it hard to wait at my door? You better know that people may find it hard to wait at your door.' I said: 'No. I have sought permission three times and I did not obtain it; so I returned, as we have been ordered to do so.' **He said: 'Whom have you heard this from?' I said: 'From the Prophet.' He then**

said to me: 'Have you heard from the Prophet what we have not heard? You will either support your statement with further evidence or I will certainly punish you.' I left him and went to the masjid where I found a member of the Ansar. *I asked them about the case, and they said: 'Is this to be doubted?' I told them what Umar said to me.* They said: 'Then the best way is that the youngest among us should go with you as witness.' Thus, Abu Saeed al-Khudri came with me to Umar and told him: 'We accompanied the Prophet when he went to Saad ibn Ubadah. When he arrived, he offered the greeting of peace, 'Assalam alaikum', but no permission was given to him. He repeated his greeting a second time and a third, but no permission was given. He then said: 'We have done what we can.' Then he left. Saad came fast after him, and said: 'Messenger of God! By Him who has sent you with the message of the truth, every time you said the greeting I heard it and replied. But I only wanted that you offer more greetings to me and to my household.' **Abu Musa then said (to Umar): 'By God I am worthy of trust** when it comes to reporting the Prophet's Hadith.' **Umar said: 'Certainly. I only wanted to ascertain the matter.'**"

    This incident occurred between the companions of Muhammad shortly after he had died. None of them ever lied about Muhammad, since they became Muslims, to suspect a Muslim of lying about Muhammad at that time was to accuse them of disbelief because Muhammad himself taught that those who lie about him should prepare for their place in the hellfire. Whereas Abu Musa (which was his nickname, Abdullah was his real name) was a well known trustworthy person. Yet Umar the ruler of the Muslims at that time threatened to physically harm him, a fellow student of prophet Muhammad, with punishment for acting upon what he said he heard Muhammad teach him with his own two ears. Umar himself never even actually doubted Abu Musa but he did not want Muslims to think they could just say "Muhammad said X" and have it get believed without corroborating evidence as would be legally required in a court of law when giving testimony about what somebody had said. Legally Muslims who had lived with Muhammad were not allowed to even say what he taught them unless they could prove that he actually taught them what they claimed Muhammad taught them. Amongst the companions of Muhammad it was legally a punishable offense to just say "*Muhammad told me so*" the early generations of Muslims had to prove it, and this was even though they all knew that they had seen and heard Muhammad in the flesh.

Obviously this is a very serious process of information verification that is the legal standard used throughout the world in courts today. Today many even sarcastically say "*Gee you don't have to make it a federal case*" when you ask for proof about something to back up what they say. Well for Muslims when it comes to saying that Muhammad said or taught something, it was always a federal case; literally. For someone known to have met Muhammad, for them to say something about Muhammad without proving what they said was true was considered to be a crime. If they couldn't prove what they claimed was true they would be convicted as criminals. The early Muslims took it as a matter of law to prove what they said about Muhammad was true because to have false information about a prophet of God circulate was too great a risk. To not have such strict requirements would imperil the entire religion. Without government policy making strict criteria for quotations and attributing teachings to prophets then there is no way to preserve the prophetic faith. The Jewish state was conquered by the Babylonians and their scriptures lost and corrupted, the Christians were persecuted for nearly 400 years before the heretical Christians took over Rome and caused the collapse of the Roman empire with sectarian infighting prior to Constantine establishing a conglomeration of heretical Greek texts as Scripture that is still fine-tuned and edited until today. Ironically 30 years after the Roman Empire became officially Catholic, the Germanic Arians sacked Rome in 410, 455 and 546 CE destroying the Western Roman Empire while those Christians who broke off from the Catholic church as "Orthodox" formed the Byzantine empire, subsequently conquered by the Muslim Ottoman empire. It's ironic because the early Catholic Church leaders preached that God would cause the Roman empire to prosper and expand since it had made what they considered "*the truth*" the official religion. To which non-Catholic Christians will say that Rome fell because they chose the wrong version of Christianity and not theirs, to which I say even if there is a right form of Christianity there is no right form of the bible because the corrupters were the compilers of the bible. It was not the case that the bible was made and then Christianity was corrupted as many Christians believe/hope, Christianity was corrupted the minute Jesus miraculously left Earth and it is proven to have been corrupted hundreds of years before the first edition of the bible was compiled. Rather Rome declined as it unified upon greater error and downgraded from paganism to Christianity. The point is that the task of preserving prophetic teachings from ancient times until today requires a strict government body sponsoring the prophetic faith and scrupulous scholastic students for generations and generations until widespread publishing became possible. If you are absent the support of ancient governments, then the text will be lost to history forever. And not only did the followers of Jesus not have the necessary government support, they on the contrary had violent Government persecution for hundreds of years. Verification of prophetic teachings and credentials of all the teachers in-between the student and the prophet is obligatory. Is it a pain in the butt to do? Yes. But it must be done or else people will be able to change the religion with ease and without even being detected. Scholastically speaking there is no other way than this way. So this is "*the way to know what really happened in the past*", it has to have been a legal crime by the State to not prove the past true from now all the way up to the past event one is referencing. One can only be able to prove the past if those past generations took this precaution in the past, unfortunately not every community has cared to diligently preserve the truth of their present while they were alive knowing that one day it would be the past. However this was the Muslim practice and standard after the prophet Muhammad. Umar declared the first principles for hadith to be:

1. The report should be literally faithful.

2. Every Hadith narrated should carry with it the name of the narrator and the chain of narrators.

3. The narrators must be of proven faith and integrity.

4. In judging the veracity of a report the occasion and circumstances involved should be taken into consideration.

5. The report cannot be repugnant/contradictory to Quran.

6. The report should be rational.

It still remains the legal religious standard but over time some Muslims became lax and then people said stuff without fully proving it and some made stuff up. This is when hadith qualities began to differ. For the first 3 generations there were only authentic hadiths and the isnads or chains of narrators were short. Such as Abu Musa's chain was a direct personal connection to Muhammad and he would be person A with Umar being person B. Yet when time passes and people get added on to that chain later then it can cause problems if those later people aren't considered trustworthy or reliable. This is because an unreliable person can relate something that's proven to be true and is 100% authentic, however because of their personal lack of credibility it tarnishes the trustworthiness of the information itself. A good example of this is the internet. If you say "*I learned on the internet....*" it's only natural that people are skeptical about such information just because of the source you learned it from even though the information may be completely trustworthy. Thus as a result of more links in the chains of narrators being added through time and the criteria that each chain in the link of narration has to be known as a reliable source, some hadith which were and are 100% true and authentic cannot in our modern day be labeled or classified as 100% authentic because our chain of information may not be 100% reliable or preserved to a high degree of precision. This is also because the principles of the science of hadith have evolved to be more strict to ensure authenticity, today the criteria is stricter because there is more information in the chain and the liars have evolved their lies as well. Anyone who sees a physical chain can understand this, in that 2 links are hard to separate from each other yet a chain with many links can easily be broken. As a result, today some hadith which are not classified as 100% true could be true, but legally we cannot say that they are because of the strict criteria of proving the truth. But don't get the wrong idea. There are thousands of authentic hadith who's chain is rock-solid 100% reliable and true who have been precisely preserved to a high degree. I'm just saying this because some people may incorrectly think that a "Good" or "Weak" hadith is automatically false because it's not labeled as Sahih or authentic. It is incorrect to think this. However legally from a religious perspective, even though a "Good" or "Weak" hadith may contain true information, such information alone cannot be used to justify a religious belief or action. What this means is that if someone says "*in X hadith it says.....*" and X hadith is classified as weak then the hadith could be true but you can't use that to justify believing or doing what it teaches. The hadith's grade would not be high enough to pass the test of usability. It's interesting information to ponder, or speculate about, but it's not very useful, in a practical sense. Unfortunately some Muslims don't understand this legal standard and they do things thinking it's okay to do because they learned it from a hadith of Muhammad. Whereas they forget that a "Weak" hadith means "It might NOT be true", so it's for safety reasons that one only follows 100% authentic information. It's a foolproof system, where if you can't prove it to be true then you can't legally use it as a religious proof, or else you'd be a fool. Such a method may seem strict but it's safe and legally necessary, because God will ask us why we believed what we believed and why we did what we did and you don't want to be basing your religion on something that "might be true". If it was that important to know or practice then God would've preserved such information with 100% authenticity. There is so much authentic information that one can live an entire lifetime without learning it all, so in general it is dangerous and needless to look into weak hadith. According to academic standards a weak hadith is at best what Christians hope and claim their biblical quotations about Jesus are, and that is even though they are disconnected without any isnad and mistranslated and don't even qualify to be counted on the same level of authenticity grade as a weak hadith from Muhammad. So truly the best a Christian can hope for from their texts amounts to material that Muslims don't even consider actionable or useable if it were attributed to Muhammad. In reality most of what Christians have would be considered Mawdu or fabricated narrations. So when a Christian comes to a Muslim and proudly claims "Jesus said: such and such" it is a depressing laughable matter because of the nerve they have in their unknown unscholastic claims. Where do we even start to explain the difference between saying what Allah said and/or what Muhammad said when Muslims bring a quote and what Christians say Jesus said? Most commoner laypeople don't know the difference and such confusion leads to vast depressing misunderstandings.

Everyone who studies Quran and Hadith, whether they believe in Islam or not, agrees that it is exactly letter for letter the same today as what Muhammad originally disseminated. There were only about 1,060 companions of Muhammad who reported hadith. Of which 500 of those 1,060 only reported 1 hadith. So 47% of the people who met Muhammad and reported hadith from him only adds up to 500 hadith statements, however the total number of authentic hadith is more because the other 560 sahabah who reported hadith reported more than just 1 hadith. Whereas you don't need to have a photogenic memory to accurately remember and report 1 hadith from Muhammad, so it's not as though every Sahabah who reported hadith was a genius master at memorization. 500 Sahabis only reported a single hadith. Some reported 2, some reported more than 2, some reported more than 10, while some companions of Muhammad reported 20+ hadith and seven noteworthy individuals reported more than a thousand each, although to be fair even these companions have some repeats amongst them where they both reported the same incident from their perspective. The companions in the thousand + reported club are Abu Hurairah, Abdullah bin Umar, Anas bin Malik, Aisha bint Abi Bakr, Abdullah ibn Abbas, Jabir bin Abdullah and Abu Said Al Khudri. The vast majority of the hadith were written down by the Sahabah during the lifetime of Muhammad. The individual man who reported the most hadith was Abu Hurairah. The woman who reported the most was Aisha (Muhammad's wife).

I hope such will suffice for a crash course introduction to the science of hadith which is the secondary source of information I used for quotes from Prophet Jesus who Muslims also consider to be the last living Sahabi. My third source of information for this book about Jesus is the synoptic gospels that are not to be confused with the Injeel, as they are all Greek and written hundreds of years after Jesus left earth with no chain of narration, nor copyist or translator identification. Thus it is with reluctance that I even use the biblical sources because of their wild nature of non-scholasticism and the major unknowns regarding them. I didn't include the apocrypha gospels because for thousands of years Christians said they were heretical and upon examining them I agree they are even more blasphemous than their reputation suggest. Therefore since the apocrypha gospels are relatively ignored by Christians I decided to stick to the popular sources and extract the most authentic. Anyways I hope you forgive me for such a long introduction to the subject and appreciate why such a large disclaimer was needed to put the Greek Synoptic biblical gospels in their appropriate categorization prior to mentioning the few quotes that Christian Scholars say are potentially credibly attributed to Jesus.

When quoting biblical gospel teachings of Jesus I deferred to the line-by-line scholastic grading of the gospels done by the multi-denominational Christian Biblical Scholars of the Jesus Seminar in the 1980s. Regarding the particular English bible translation, I used the Modern Literal Version. The reason I used this version is because according to the publisher's website:

> *The MLV is not owned by a publishing company, a government, foundation, bible society or a church. The largest Bible project in English history, over a million proofreaders. Open Source as in you (yes, you) can submit any correction that is not "Thus saith the Greek." We want "Error-free." If you find anything not Koine Greek, which is denominational in 'anyway shape or form' we will remove it. The MLV project is dedicated to the ending of 600 years of error, the traditions of men, to produce error-free textbooks and the end of making a 'bible' for profit.*
>
> *The MLV is open source, all can participate. No English Bible translation on this planet allowed all religious groups to participate, most never allowed one single word from your particular religious*

> group to enter 'their' bible. So far the only ones who have never (to our knowledge) helped with the MLV are: Jehovah Witnesses, Hebrew Roots, Christian Scientist and the Mormons.
>
> We have had the greatest Greek Scholars ever on this planet and proofreaders with a 6th grade education and 2nd English speakers all contribute. We can never thank those enough, ones living and ones dead for their contributions to end 600 years of error in English translation and Koine Greek books."

It is because at MLV they seem to be less prejudiced and more sincere in trying to accurately translate in an unbiased manner. Of course if they were truly academic they would realize that Greek itself is a major red flag regarding the religion of Aramaic speaking Jesus and would search for alternative sources for Jesus data. Though alas God guides who he wills to see what they are destined to see. Regarding Christian texts Open Source is a step in the correcting direction, it's still completely abhorrent to think anyone anywhere can interpret scripture into another language as long as they have evidence supporting their translation claim. Its only because Christians for the past 600 years, have done such a bigoted corrupted job of translating the bibles that they finally resorted to Open Source translations. The true interpretation and translation criteria of divine revelation requires God to do that work or a prophet of God to do so. Anything which is without prophetic guidance is not going to be reliable or trustworthy because language rules change regarding religious terminology. Religion gives different words different definitions that the ordinary language doesn't. So if you aren't God or the God-sent prophet you cannot correctly translate revelation. That applies to Quran too which is why any translation always must have a disclaimer that it is a flawed attempt of interpretive commentary.

Regarding the authenticity or grade of the biblical Jesus quotes the grading system utilized a weighted average to ensure every scholar's input was valued rather than a democratic majority voting system that would have meant the minority scholastic opinion would be ignored. Thus far in my opinion it is the best attempt Christians have set forth to use semi-scholastic methods when discussing their alleged scriptures which scholastically cannot be considered revelation since they were authored by non-prophets without a doubt. The Jesus Seminar had four categories or grade levels for biblical sayings attributed to Jesus, they are as follows:

1. Red (75%+ possibility Jesus said it.)
2. Pink (50%-75% possibility Jesus said it.)
3. Gray (25%-50% possibility Jesus said it.)
4. Black (0%-25% possibility Jesus said it.)

The color red was chosen as the strongest grade level because around 1854 a red letter edition of the bible was attempted by Louis Klopsch where he tried to print a bible with the words of Jesus while on earth to be in the color of blood. Later bible editions however included everything in red as long as it was attributed to Jesus without any regard as to the authenticity, it was merely an ascetic visual style. When the critical Red letter edition of the Jesus Seminar came out many Christians were furious anything attributed in the bible to Jesus could be scholastically graded as anything less than 100% truly attributed. So in response they started publishing masses of "Red letter" bibles with everything Jesus allegedly said in Red to try to confuse people regarding the Red grade category of the Scholastic analysis with what they wanted people to believe. So in hindsight Red was probably not the best color to choose because of the trickery it enabled by other non-scholastic red letter editions but alas people that are that dishonest would still find other ways to lie about what Jesus said even if other colors were chosen. Yet Christian Scholars themselves have said that not everything in the bible attributed to Jesus' mouth is true. Shockingly many things were given black grades with 82% being proven as falsely attributed to Jesus, especially all the contradicting information of the post-resurrection material and nearly everything in the gospel of John. In fact some of the inauthentic non-biblical heretical Gnostic gospels have more accurate information about Jesus than the biblical gospel of John does, according to the Scholars, despite gnostic gospels being excluded from the bible. Yet John 3:16 is what most Christians live and die upon as their summation of faith. Despite the mistranslations of the word begotten being corrected and removed in recent years and the contradiction of John 3:13 which refutes the Old Testament claims of Elijah and Enoch going to heaven thus making John 3:13 a proof the speech is heretical and impossible to have come from Jesus. As well as the numerous claims of Israel being God's firstborn son and Solomon being God's firstborn son and many other sons being attributed to God in the Old Testament but regardless anyway you dice it, Christian Scholars admit that John 3:16 is not even authentic despite it being the favorite most popular bible quote for Christians around the world. Yet just because the favorite quote of Christians is fraudulent doesn't mean everything is, despite it all being in a foreign Greek language. So even though scholastically and from an Islamic perspective the Greek gospels have less than 10 words of divine revelation, some information in them can still be true. Whereas due to Christian sensitivities being outraged at what their own Scholars say and them most likely refusing what any Christian-turned Muslim would say about the bible grading then I have respectfully deferred to the Jesus Seminar's grading system of authenticity. For those quotes Christian Scholars have said have less than 50% chance of being authentically from Jesus, I felt it too risky to mention them due to their dubious nature despite how much I liked or disliked them. Especially when you have 50+ Christian Scholars from all denominations saying that there is less than 50% chance its true then only a fool would put those words into Jesus' mouth. If he did say them I'm not going to go to hell for neglecting to mention it, because I'm not denying the possibility I'm just not reporting everything due to the low possibility. Yet on the other hand if I reported it and Jesus didn't say it then I would be going to hell because I'd be lying about a prophet. So for my soul it is much safer to have a 50% cut-off limit when compiling these quotes according to the grading system as done by the Jesus Seminar and utilizing as a translation the open source less bigoted translators of the MLV bible. Therefore I have not cited any Gray or Black graded gospel quotes. Regarding the numerous non-biblical Gospels often labeled apocrypha, I have not included them because of the problems with grading their authenticity, which as far as I know nobody has done yet and with the problem that they are also in languages Jesus never spoke. If I was truly being scholastic then we would discard everything other than the language Jesus spoke and even stuff that is hearsay evidence from either God or other prophets. This is because Jesus said what Jesus said and what others say about him are what others say even if what others said is true academically it is not a direct quote from the primary source of information. Many students perhaps remember those DBQ (Document Based Questions) on history exams, well academically we have no documents from Jesus so there technically isn't even any material to make a book of Jesus quotes or teachings. Thus the peculiar name for this book is "The Collection of Quotes Credited to Prophet Jesus" because this book does not contain a single quote directly from Jesus' mouth or handwriting himself. Instead it is all what others have said about what Jesus said, whether it is Allah, or Muhammad, or Greek biblical gospels, then it is all still a non-primary source other than Jesus doing the speaking in Jesus' namesake. I clarify this so there isn't confusion about what this book is or isn't. We don't have anything from Jesus directly, nobody does. So either we academically dismiss Jesus or look to other hearsay evidences for information. Out of love for this Prophet I decided to compose this from what is found to be most authentic from a Muslim perspective of 100% Quran, and varying grades of hadith from Muhammad and including the limited Christian Greek data restricting myself to including only that which is 50% or more likely to have been said by Jesus, listing the Christian Scholars authenticity grade of each such quote. Now after having patiently endured this lengthy explanation of my intentions and information sources I hope you are prepared for "The Collection of Quotes Credited to Prophet Jesus".

QURAN QUOTES OF GOD ATTRIBUTED TO PROPHET JESUS

Quran 3:33-60

۞ إِنَّ ٱللَّهَ ٱصْطَفَىٰٓ ءَادَمَ وَنُوحًا وَءَالَ إِبْرَٰهِيمَ وَءَالَ عِمْرَٰنَ عَلَى ٱلْعَٰلَمِينَ (٣٣) ذُرِّيَّةًۢ بَعْضُهَا مِنۢ بَعْضٍ ۗ وَٱللَّهُ سَمِيعٌ عَلِيمٌ (٣٤) إِذْ قَالَتِ ٱمْرَأَتُ عِمْرَٰنَ رَبِّ إِنِّى نَذَرْتُ لَكَ مَا فِى بَطْنِى مُحَرَّرًا فَتَقَبَّلْ مِنِّىٓ ۖ إِنَّكَ أَنتَ ٱلسَّمِيعُ ٱلْعَلِيمُ (٣٥) فَلَمَّا وَضَعَتْهَا قَالَتْ رَبِّ إِنِّى وَضَعْتُهَآ أُنثَىٰ وَٱللَّهُ أَعْلَمُ بِمَا وَضَعَتْ وَلَيْسَ ٱلذَّكَرُ كَٱلْأُنثَىٰ ۖ وَإِنِّى سَمَّيْتُهَا مَرْيَمَ وَإِنِّىٓ أُعِيذُهَا بِكَ وَذُرِّيَّتَهَا مِنَ ٱلشَّيْطَٰنِ ٱلرَّجِيمِ (٣٦) فَتَقَبَّلَهَا رَبُّهَا بِقَبُولٍ حَسَنٍ وَأَنۢبَتَهَا نَبَاتًا حَسَنًا وَكَفَّلَهَا زَكَرِيَّا ۖ كُلَّمَا دَخَلَ عَلَيْهَا زَكَرِيَّا ٱلْمِحْرَابَ وَجَدَ عِندَهَا رِزْقًا ۖ قَالَ يَٰمَرْيَمُ أَنَّىٰ لَكِ هَٰذَا ۖ قَالَتْ هُوَ مِنْ عِندِ ٱللَّهِ ۖ إِنَّ ٱللَّهَ يَرْزُقُ مَن يَشَآءُ بِغَيْرِ حِسَابٍ (٣٧) هُنَالِكَ دَعَا زَكَرِيَّا رَبَّهُۥ ۖ قَالَ رَبِّ هَبْ لِى مِن لَّدُنكَ ذُرِّيَّةً طَيِّبَةً ۖ إِنَّكَ سَمِيعُ ٱلدُّعَآءِ (٣٨) فَنَادَتْهُ ٱلْمَلَٰٓئِكَةُ وَهُوَ قَآئِمٌ يُصَلِّى فِى ٱلْمِحْرَابِ أَنَّ ٱللَّهَ يُبَشِّرُكَ بِيَحْيَىٰ مُصَدِّقًۢا بِكَلِمَةٍ مِّنَ ٱللَّهِ وَسَيِّدًا وَحَصُورًا وَنَبِيًّا مِّنَ ٱلصَّٰلِحِينَ (٣٩) قَالَ رَبِّ أَنَّىٰ يَكُونُ لِى غُلَٰمٌ وَقَدْ بَلَغَنِىَ ٱلْكِبَرُ وَٱمْرَأَتِى عَاقِرٌ ۖ قَالَ كَذَٰلِكَ ٱللَّهُ يَفْعَلُ مَا يَشَآءُ (٤٠) قَالَ رَبِّ ٱجْعَل لِّىٓ ءَايَةً ۖ قَالَ ءَايَتُكَ أَلَّا تُكَلِّمَ ٱلنَّاسَ ثَلَٰثَةَ أَيَّامٍ إِلَّا رَمْزًا ۗ وَٱذْكُر رَّبَّكَ كَثِيرًا وَسَبِّحْ بِٱلْعَشِىِّ وَٱلْإِبْكَٰرِ (٤١) وَإِذْ قَالَتِ ٱلْمَلَٰٓئِكَةُ يَٰمَرْيَمُ إِنَّ ٱللَّهَ ٱصْطَفَىٰكِ وَطَهَّرَكِ وَٱصْطَفَىٰكِ عَلَىٰ نِسَآءِ ٱلْعَٰلَمِينَ (٤٢) يَٰمَرْيَمُ ٱقْنُتِى لِرَبِّكِ وَٱسْجُدِى وَٱرْكَعِى مَعَ ٱلرَّٰكِعِينَ (٤٣) ذَٰلِكَ مِنْ أَنۢبَآءِ ٱلْغَيْبِ نُوحِيهِ إِلَيْكَ ۚ وَمَا كُنتَ لَدَيْهِمْ إِذْ يُلْقُونَ أَقْلَٰمَهُمْ أَيُّهُمْ يَكْفُلُ مَرْيَمَ وَمَا كُنتَ لَدَيْهِمْ إِذْ يَخْتَصِمُونَ (٤٤) إِذْ قَالَتِ ٱلْمَلَٰٓئِكَةُ يَٰمَرْيَمُ إِنَّ ٱللَّهَ يُبَشِّرُكِ بِكَلِمَةٍ مِّنْهُ ٱسْمُهُ ٱلْمَسِيحُ عِيسَى ٱبْنُ مَرْيَمَ وَجِيهًا فِى ٱلدُّنْيَا وَٱلْءَاخِرَةِ وَمِنَ ٱلْمُقَرَّبِينَ (٤٥) وَيُكَلِّمُ ٱلنَّاسَ فِى ٱلْمَهْدِ وَكَهْلًا وَمِنَ

ٱلصَّٰلِحِينَ (٤٦) قَالَتْ رَبِّ أَنَّىٰ يَكُونُ لِى وَلَدٌ وَلَمْ يَمْسَسْنِى بَشَرٌ ۖ قَالَ كَذَٰلِكِ ٱللَّهُ يَخْلُقُ مَا يَشَآءُ ۚ إِذَا قَضَىٰٓ أَمْرًا فَإِنَّمَا يَقُولُ لَهُۥ كُن فَيَكُونُ (٤٧) وَيُعَلِّمُهُ ٱلْكِتَٰبَ وَٱلْحِكْمَةَ وَٱلتَّوْرَىٰةَ وَٱلْإِنجِيلَ (٤٨) وَرَسُولًا إِلَىٰ بَنِىٓ إِسْرَٰٓءِيلَ أَنِّى قَدْ جِئْتُكُم بِـَٔايَةٍ مِّن رَّبِّكُمْ ۖ أَنِّىٓ أَخْلُقُ لَكُم مِّنَ ٱلطِّينِ كَهَيْـَٔةِ ٱلطَّيْرِ فَأَنفُخُ فِيهِ فَيَكُونُ طَيْرًۢا بِإِذْنِ ٱللَّهِ ۖ وَأُبْرِئُ ٱلْأَكْمَهَ وَٱلْأَبْرَصَ وَأُحْىِ ٱلْمَوْتَىٰ بِإِذْنِ ٱللَّهِ ۖ وَأُنَبِّئُكُم بِمَا تَأْكُلُونَ وَمَا تَدَّخِرُونَ فِى بُيُوتِكُمْ ۚ إِنَّ فِى ذَٰلِكَ لَـَٔايَةً لَّكُمْ إِن كُنتُم مُّؤْمِنِينَ (٤٩) وَمُصَدِّقًا لِّمَا بَيْنَ يَدَىَّ مِنَ ٱلتَّوْرَىٰةِ وَلِأُحِلَّ لَكُم بَعْضَ ٱلَّذِى حُرِّمَ عَلَيْكُمْ ۚ وَجِئْتُكُم بِـَٔايَةٍ مِّن رَّبِّكُمْ فَٱتَّقُوا۟ ٱللَّهَ وَأَطِيعُونِ (٥٠) إِنَّ ٱللَّهَ رَبِّى وَرَبُّكُمْ فَٱعْبُدُوهُ ۗ هَٰذَا صِرَٰطٌ مُّسْتَقِيمٌ (٥١) ۞ فَلَمَّآ أَحَسَّ عِيسَىٰ مِنْهُمُ ٱلْكُفْرَ قَالَ مَنْ أَنصَارِىٓ إِلَى ٱللَّهِ ۖ قَالَ ٱلْحَوَارِيُّونَ نَحْنُ أَنصَارُ ٱللَّهِ ءَامَنَّا بِٱللَّهِ وَٱشْهَدْ بِأَنَّا مُسْلِمُونَ (٥٢) رَبَّنَآ ءَامَنَّا بِمَآ أَنزَلْتَ وَٱتَّبَعْنَا ٱلرَّسُولَ فَٱكْتُبْنَا مَعَ ٱلشَّٰهِدِينَ (٥٣) وَمَكَرُوا۟ وَمَكَرَ ٱللَّهُ ۖ وَٱللَّهُ خَيْرُ ٱلْمَٰكِرِينَ (٥٤) إِذْ قَالَ ٱللَّهُ يَٰعِيسَىٰٓ إِنِّى مُتَوَفِّيكَ وَرَافِعُكَ إِلَىَّ وَمُطَهِّرُكَ مِنَ ٱلَّذِينَ كَفَرُوا۟ وَجَاعِلُ ٱلَّذِينَ ٱتَّبَعُوكَ فَوْقَ ٱلَّذِينَ كَفَرُوٓا۟ إِلَىٰ يَوْمِ ٱلْقِيَٰمَةِ ۖ ثُمَّ إِلَىَّ مَرْجِعُكُمْ فَأَحْكُمُ بَيْنَكُمْ فِيمَا كُنتُمْ فِيهِ تَخْتَلِفُونَ (٥٥) فَأَمَّا ٱلَّذِينَ كَفَرُوا۟ فَأُعَذِّبُهُمْ عَذَابًا شَدِيدًا فِى ٱلدُّنْيَا وَٱلْـَٔاخِرَةِ وَمَا لَهُم مِّن نَّٰصِرِينَ (٥٦) وَأَمَّا ٱلَّذِينَ ءَامَنُوا۟ وَعَمِلُوا۟ ٱلصَّٰلِحَٰتِ فَيُوَفِّيهِمْ أُجُورَهُمْ ۗ وَٱللَّهُ لَا يُحِبُّ ٱلظَّٰلِمِينَ (٥٧) ذَٰلِكَ نَتْلُوهُ عَلَيْكَ مِنَ ٱلْـَٔايَٰتِ وَٱلذِّكْرِ ٱلْحَكِيمِ (٥٨) إِنَّ مَثَلَ عِيسَىٰ عِندَ ٱللَّهِ كَمَثَلِ ءَادَمَ ۖ خَلَقَهُۥ مِن تُرَابٍ ثُمَّ قَالَ لَهُۥ كُن فَيَكُونُ (٥٩) ٱلْحَقُّ مِن رَّبِّكَ فَلَا تَكُن مِّنَ ٱلْمُمْتَرِينَ (٦٠)

Indeed, Allah chose Adam and Noah and the family of Abraham and the family of 'Imran over the worlds - (33) Descendants, some of them from others. And Allah is Hearing and Knowing. (34) [Mention, O Muhammad], when the wife of 'Imran said, "My Lord, indeed I have pledged to You what is in my womb, consecrated [for Your service], so accept this from me. Indeed, You are the Hearing, the Knowing." (35) But when she delivered her, she said, "My Lord, I have delivered a female." And Allah was most knowing of what she delivered, "And the male is not like the female. And I have named her Mary, and I seek refuge for her in You and [for] her descendants from Satan, the expelled [from the mercy of Allah]." (36) So her Lord accepted her with good acceptance and caused her to grow in a good manner and put her in the care of Zechariah. Every time Zechariah entered upon her in the prayer chamber, he found with her provision. He said, "O Mary, from where is this [coming] to you?" She said, "It is from Allah. Indeed, Allah provides for whom He wills without account." (37) At that, Zechariah called upon his Lord, saying, "My Lord, grant me from Yourself a good offspring. Indeed, You are the Hearer of supplication." (38) So the angels called him while he was standing in prayer in the chamber, "Indeed, Allah gives you good tidings of John, confirming a word from Allah and [who will be] honorable, abstaining [from women], and a prophet from among the righteous." (39) He said, "My Lord, how will I have a boy when I have reached old age and my wife is barren?" The angel said, "Such is Allah; He does what He wills." (40) He said, "My Lord, make for me a sign." He Said, "Your sign is that you will not [be able to] speak to the people for three days except by gesture. And remember your Lord much and exalt [Him with praise] in the evening and the morning." (41) And [mention] when the angels said, "O Mary, indeed Allah has chosen you and purified you and chosen you above the women of the worlds. (42) O Mary, be devoutly obedient to your Lord and prostrate and bow with those who bow [in prayer]." (43) That is from the news of the unseen which We reveal to you, [O Muhammad]. And you were not with them when they cast their pens as to which of them should be responsible for Mary. Nor were you with them when they disputed. (44) [And mention] when the angels said, "O Mary, indeed Allah gives you good tidings of a word from Him, whose name will be the Messiah, Jesus, the son of Mary - distinguished in this world and the Hereafter and among those brought near [to Allah]. (45) He will speak to the people in the cradle and in maturity and will be of the righteous." (46) She said, "My Lord, how will I have a child when no man has touched me?" [The angel] said, "Such is Allah; He creates what He wills. When He decrees a matter, He only says to it, 'Be,' and it is. (47) And He will teach him writing and wisdom and the Torah and the Injeel (48) And [make him] a messenger to the Children of Israel, [who will say], 'Indeed I have come to you with a sign from your Lord in that I design for you from clay [that which is] like the form of a bird, then I breathe into it and it becomes a bird by permission of Allah. And I cure the blind and the leper, and I give life to the dead - by permission of Allah. And I inform you of what you eat and what you store in your houses. Indeed in that is a

sign for you, if you are believers. (49) And [I have come] confirming what was before me of the Torah and to make lawful for you some of what was forbidden to you. And I have come to you with a sign from your Lord, so fear Allah and obey me. (50) Indeed, Allah is my Lord and your Lord, so worship Him. That is the straight path." (51) But when Jesus felt [persistence in] disbelief from them, he said, "Who are my supporters for [the cause of] Allah?" The disciples said, "We are supporters for Allah. We have believed in Allah and testify that we are Muslims [submitting to Him]. (52) Our Lord, we have believed in what You revealed and have followed the messenger Jesus, so register us among the witnesses [to truth]." (53) And the disbelievers planned, but Allah planned. And Allah is the best of planners.
(54) [Mention] when Allah said, "O Jesus, indeed I will take you and raise you to Myself and purify you from those who disbelieve and make those who follow you [in submission to Allah alone] superior to those who disbelieve until the Day of Resurrection. Then to Me is your return, and I will judge between you concerning that in which you used to differ. (55) And as for those who disbelieved, I will punish them with a severe punishment in this world and the Hereafter, and they will have no helpers." (56) But as for those who believed and did righteous deeds, He will give them in full their rewards, and Allah does not like the wrongdoers.

(57) This is what We recite to you, [O Muhammad], of [Our] verses and the precise [and wise] message. (58) Indeed, the example of Jesus to Allah is like that of Adam. He created Him from dust; then He said to him,(the word) "Be," and he was. (59) The truth is from your Lord, so do not be among the doubters. (60)

Quran 19:2-38

ذِكْرُ رَحْمَتِ رَبِّكَ عَبْدَهُ زَكَرِيَّا (٢) إِذْ نَادَىٰ رَبَّهُ نِدَاءً خَفِيًّا (٣) قَالَ رَبِّ إِنِّي وَهَنَ الْعَظْمُ مِنِّي وَاشْتَعَلَ الرَّأْسُ شَيْبًا وَلَمْ أَكُن بِدُعَائِكَ رَبِّ شَقِيًّا (٤) وَإِنِّي خِفْتُ الْمَوَالِيَ مِن وَرَائِي وَكَانَتِ امْرَأَتِي عَاقِرًا فَهَبْ لِي مِن لَّدُنكَ وَلِيًّا (٥) يَرِثُنِي وَيَرِثُ مِنْ آلِ يَعْقُوبَ ۖ وَاجْعَلْهُ رَبِّ رَضِيًّا (٦) يَا زَكَرِيَّا إِنَّا نُبَشِّرُكَ بِغُلَامٍ اسْمُهُ يَحْيَىٰ لَمْ نَجْعَل لَّهُ مِن قَبْلُ سَمِيًّا (٧) قَالَ رَبِّ أَنَّىٰ يَكُونُ لِي غُلَامٌ وَكَانَتِ امْرَأَتِي عَاقِرًا وَقَدْ بَلَغْتُ مِنَ الْكِبَرِ عِتِيًّا (٨) قَالَ كَذَٰلِكَ قَالَ رَبُّكَ هُوَ عَلَيَّ هَيِّنٌ وَقَدْ خَلَقْتُكَ مِن قَبْلُ وَلَمْ تَكُ شَيْئًا (٩) قَالَ رَبِّ اجْعَل لِّي آيَةً ۚ قَالَ آيَتُكَ أَلَّا تُكَلِّمَ النَّاسَ ثَلَاثَ لَيَالٍ سَوِيًّا (١٠) فَخَرَجَ عَلَىٰ قَوْمِهِ مِنَ الْمِحْرَابِ فَأَوْحَىٰ إِلَيْهِمْ أَن سَبِّحُوا بُكْرَةً وَعَشِيًّا (١١) يَا يَحْيَىٰ خُذِ الْكِتَابَ بِقُوَّةٍ ۖ وَآتَيْنَاهُ الْحُكْمَ صَبِيًّا (١٢) وَحَنَانًا مِّن لَّدُنَّا وَزَكَاةً ۖ وَكَانَ تَقِيًّا (١٣) وَبَرًّا بِوَالِدَيْهِ وَلَمْ يَكُن جَبَّارًا عَصِيًّا (١٤) وَسَلَامٌ عَلَيْهِ يَوْمَ وُلِدَ وَيَوْمَ يَمُوتُ وَيَوْمَ يُبْعَثُ حَيًّا (١٥) وَاذْكُرْ فِي الْكِتَابِ مَرْيَمَ إِذِ انتَبَذَتْ مِنْ أَهْلِهَا مَكَانًا شَرْقِيًّا (١٦) فَاتَّخَذَتْ مِن دُونِهِمْ حِجَابًا فَأَرْسَلْنَا إِلَيْهَا رُوحَنَا فَتَمَثَّلَ لَهَا بَشَرًا سَوِيًّا (١٧) قَالَتْ إِنِّي أَعُوذُ بِالرَّحْمَٰنِ مِنكَ إِن كُنتَ تَقِيًّا (١٨) قَالَ إِنَّمَا أَنَا رَسُولُ رَبِّكِ لِأَهَبَ لَكِ غُلَامًا زَكِيًّا (١٩) قَالَتْ أَنَّىٰ يَكُونُ لِي غُلَامٌ وَلَمْ يَمْسَسْنِي بَشَرٌ وَلَمْ أَكُ بَغِيًّا (٢٠) قَالَ كَذَٰلِكِ قَالَ رَبُّكِ هُوَ عَلَيَّ هَيِّنٌ ۖ وَلِنَجْعَلَهُ آيَةً لِّلنَّاسِ وَرَحْمَةً مِّنَّا ۚ وَكَانَ أَمْرًا مَّقْضِيًّا (٢١) ۞ فَحَمَلَتْهُ فَانتَبَذَتْ بِهِ مَكَانًا قَصِيًّا (٢٢) فَأَجَاءَهَا الْمَخَاضُ إِلَىٰ جِذْعِ النَّخْلَةِ قَالَتْ يَا لَيْتَنِي مِتُّ قَبْلَ هَٰذَا وَكُنتُ نَسْيًا مَّنسِيًّا (٢٣) فَنَادَاهَا مِن تَحْتِهَا أَلَّا تَحْزَنِي قَدْ جَعَلَ رَبُّكِ تَحْتَكِ سَرِيًّا

(٢٤) وَهُزِّىٓ إِلَيْكِ بِجِذْعِ ٱلنَّخْلَةِ تُسَٰقِطْ عَلَيْكِ رُطَبًا جَنِيًّا (٢٥) فَكُلِى وَٱشْرَبِى وَقَرِّى عَيْنًا ۖ فَإِمَّا تَرَيِنَّ مِنَ ٱلْبَشَرِ أَحَدًا فَقُولِىٓ إِنِّى نَذَرْتُ لِلرَّحْمَٰنِ صَوْمًا فَلَنْ أُكَلِّمَ ٱلْيَوْمَ إِنسِيًّا (٢٦) فَأَتَتْ بِهِۦ قَوْمَهَا تَحْمِلُهُۥ ۖ قَالُواْ يَٰمَرْيَمُ لَقَدْ جِئْتِ شَيْـًٔا فَرِيًّا (٢٧) يَٰٓأُخْتَ هَٰرُونَ مَا كَانَ أَبُوكِ ٱمْرَأَ سَوْءٍ وَمَا كَانَتْ أُمُّكِ بَغِيًّا (٢٨) فَأَشَارَتْ إِلَيْهِ ۖ قَالُواْ كَيْفَ نُكَلِّمُ مَن كَانَ فِى ٱلْمَهْدِ صَبِيًّا (٢٩) قَالَ إِنِّى عَبْدُ ٱللَّهِ ءَاتَىٰنِىَ ٱلْكِتَٰبَ وَجَعَلَنِى نَبِيًّا (٣٠) وَجَعَلَنِى مُبَارَكًا أَيْنَ مَا كُنتُ وَأَوْصَٰنِى بِٱلصَّلَوٰةِ وَٱلزَّكَوٰةِ مَا دُمْتُ حَيًّا (٣١) وَبَرًّۢا بِوَٰلِدَتِى وَلَمْ يَجْعَلْنِى جَبَّارًا شَقِيًّا (٣٢) وَٱلسَّلَٰمُ عَلَىَّ يَوْمَ وُلِدتُّ وَيَوْمَ أَمُوتُ وَيَوْمَ أُبْعَثُ حَيًّا (٣٣) ذَٰلِكَ عِيسَى ٱبْنُ مَرْيَمَ ۚ قَوْلَ ٱلْحَقِّ ٱلَّذِى فِيهِ يَمْتَرُونَ (٣٤) مَا كَانَ لِلَّهِ أَن يَتَّخِذَ مِن وَلَدٍ ۖ سُبْحَٰنَهُۥٓ ۚ إِذَا قَضَىٰٓ أَمْرًا فَإِنَّمَا يَقُولُ لَهُۥ كُن فَيَكُونُ (٣٥) وَإِنَّ ٱللَّهَ رَبِّى وَرَبُّكُمْ فَٱعْبُدُوهُ ۚ هَٰذَا صِرَٰطٌ مُّسْتَقِيمٌ (٣٦) فَٱخْتَلَفَ ٱلْأَحْزَابُ مِنۢ بَيْنِهِمْ ۖ فَوَيْلٌ لِّلَّذِينَ كَفَرُواْ مِن مَّشْهَدِ يَوْمٍ عَظِيمٍ (٣٧) أَسْمِعْ بِهِمْ وَأَبْصِرْ يَوْمَ يَأْتُونَنَا ۖ لَٰكِنِ ٱلظَّٰلِمُونَ ٱلْيَوْمَ فِى ضَلَٰلٍ مُّبِينٍ (٣٨)

[This is] a mention of the mercy of your Lord to His servant Zechariah (2) When he called to his Lord a private supplication. (3) He said, "My Lord, indeed my bones have weakened, and my head has filled with white, and never have I been in my supplication to You, my Lord, unhappy. (4) And indeed, I fear the successors after me, and my wife has been barren, so give me from Yourself an heir (5) Who will inherit me and inherit from the family of Jacob. And make him, my Lord, pleasing [to You]." (6) [He was told], "O Zechariah, indeed We give you good tidings of a boy whose name will be John. We have not assigned to any before [this] name." (7) He said, "My Lord, how will I have a boy when my wife has been barren and I have reached extreme old age?" (8) [An angel] said, "Thus [it will be]; your Lord says, 'It is easy for Me, for I created you before, while you were nothing.' " (9) [Zechariah] said, "My Lord, make for me a sign." He said, "Your sign is that you will not speak to the people for three nights, [being] sound." (10) So he came out to his people from the prayer chamber and signaled to them to exalt [Allah] in the morning and afternoon. (11) [Allah] said, "O John, take the Scripture with determination." And We gave him judgement [while yet] a boy (12) And affection from Us and purity, and he was fearing of Allah (13) And dutiful to his parents, and he was not a disobedient tyrant. (14) And peace be upon him the day he was born and the day he dies and the day he is raised alive. (15) And mention, [O Muhammad], in the Book [the story of] Mary, when she withdrew from her family to a place toward the east. (16) And she took, in seclusion from them, a screen. Then We sent to her Our Angel, and he represented himself to her as a well-proportioned man. (17) She said, "Indeed, I seek refuge in the Most Merciful from you, [so leave me], if you should be fearing of Allah." (18) He said, "I am only the messenger of your Lord to give you [news of] a pure boy." (19) She said, "How can I have a boy while no man has touched me and I have not been unchaste?" (20) He said, "Thus [it will be]; your Lord says, 'It is easy for Me, and We will make him a sign to the people and a mercy from Us. And it is a matter [already] decreed.' "

(21) So she conceived him, and she withdrew with him to a remote place. (22) And the pains of childbirth drove her to the trunk of a palm tree. She said, "Oh, I wish I had died before this and was in oblivion, forgotten." (23) But he called her from below her, "Do not grieve; your Lord has provided beneath you a stream. (24) And shake toward you the trunk of the palm tree; it will drop upon you ripe, fresh dates. (25) So eat and drink and be contented. And if you see from among humanity anyone, say, 'Indeed, I have vowed to the Most Merciful abstention, so I will not speak today to [any] man.' "
(26) Then she brought him to her people, carrying him. They said, "O Mary, you have certainly done a thing unprecedented. (27) O sister of Aaron, your father was not a man of evil, nor was your mother unchaste."
(28) So she pointed to him. They said, "How can we speak to one who is in the cradle a child?" (29) [Jesus] said, "Indeed, I am the servant of Allah. He has given me the Scripture and made me a prophet. (30) And He has made me blessed wherever I am and has enjoined upon me prayer and zakah as long as I remain alive (31) And [made me] dutiful to my mother, and He has not made me a wretched tyrant. (32) And peace is on me the day I was born and the day I will die and the day I am raised alive." (33) That is Jesus, the son of Mary - the word of truth about which they are in dispute. (34) It is not [befitting] for Allah to take a son; exalted is He! When

He decrees an affair, He only says to it, "Be," and it is. (35) [Jesus said], "And indeed, Allah is my Lord and your Lord, so worship Him. That is a straight path." (36) Then the factions differed [concerning Jesus] from among them, so woe to those who disbelieved - from the scene of a tremendous Day. (37) How [clearly] they will hear and see the Day they come to Us, but the wrongdoers today are in clear error. (38)

Quran 43:59-65

إِنْ هُوَ إِلَّا عَبْدٌ أَنْعَمْنَا عَلَيْهِ وَجَعَلْنَٰهُ مَثَلًا لِّبَنِىٓ إِسْرَٰٓءِيلَ (٥٩) وَلَوْ نَشَآءُ لَجَعَلْنَا مِنكُم مَّلَٰٓئِكَةً فِى ٱلْأَرْضِ يَخْلُفُونَ (٦٠) وَإِنَّهُۥ لَعِلْمٌ لِّلسَّاعَةِ فَلَا تَمْتَرُنَّ بِهَا وَٱتَّبِعُونِ ۚ هَٰذَا صِرَٰطٌ مُّسْتَقِيمٌ (٦١) وَلَا يَصُدَّنَّكُمُ ٱلشَّيْطَٰنُ ۖ إِنَّهُۥ لَكُمْ عَدُوٌّ مُّبِينٌ (٦٢) وَلَمَّا جَآءَ عِيسَىٰ بِٱلْبَيِّنَٰتِ قَالَ قَدْ جِئْتُكُم بِٱلْحِكْمَةِ وَلِأُبَيِّنَ لَكُم بَعْضَ ٱلَّذِى تَخْتَلِفُونَ فِيهِ ۖ فَٱتَّقُوا۟ ٱللَّهَ وَأَطِيعُونِ (٦٣) إِنَّ ٱللَّهَ هُوَ رَبِّى وَرَبُّكُمْ فَٱعْبُدُوهُ ۚ هَٰذَا صِرَٰطٌ مُّسْتَقِيمٌ (٦٤) فَٱخْتَلَفَ ٱلْأَحْزَابُ مِنۢ بَيْنِهِمْ ۖ فَوَيْلٌ لِّلَّذِينَ ظَلَمُوا۟ مِنْ عَذَابِ يَوْمٍ أَلِيمٍ (٦٥)

Jesus was not but a servant upon whom We bestowed favor, and We made him an example for the Children of Israel. (59) And if We willed, We could have made [instead] of you angels succeeding [one another] on the earth. (60) And indeed, Jesus will be [a sign for] knowledge of the Hour, so be not in doubt of it, and follow Me. This is a straight path. (61) And never let Satan avert you. Indeed, he is to you a clear enemy. (62) And when Jesus brought clear proofs, he said, "I have come to you with wisdom and to make clear to you some of that over which you differ, so fear Allah and obey me. (63) Indeed, Allah is my Lord and your Lord, so worship Him. This is a straight path." (64) But the denominations from among them differed [and separated], so woe to those who have wronged from the punishment of a painful Day. (65)

Quran 5:78

لُعِنَ ٱلَّذِينَ كَفَرُوا۟ مِنۢ بَنِىٓ إِسْرَٰٓءِيلَ عَلَىٰ لِسَانِ دَاوُۥدَ وَعِيسَى ٱبْنِ مَرْيَمَ ۚ ذَٰلِكَ بِمَا عَصَوا۟ وَّكَانُوا۟ يَعْتَدُونَ (٧٨)

Cursed were those who disbelieved among the Children of Israel by the tongue of David and of Jesus, the son of Mary. That was because they disobeyed and [habitually] transgressed. (78)

Quran 61:14

يَٰٓأَيُّهَا ٱلَّذِينَ ءَامَنُوا۟ كُونُوٓا۟ أَنصَارَ ٱللَّهِ كَمَا قَالَ عِيسَى ٱبْنُ مَرْيَمَ لِلْحَوَارِيِّـۧنَ مَنْ أَنصَارِىٓ إِلَى ٱللَّهِ ۖ قَالَ ٱلْحَوَارِيُّونَ نَحْنُ أَنصَارُ ٱللَّهِ ۖ فَـَٔامَنَت طَّآئِفَةٌ مِّنۢ بَنِىٓ إِسْرَٰٓءِيلَ وَكَفَرَت طَّآئِفَةٌ ۖ فَأَيَّدْنَا ٱلَّذِينَ ءَامَنُوا۟ عَلَىٰ عَدُوِّهِمْ فَأَصْبَحُوا۟ ظَٰهِرِينَ (١٤)

O you who have believed, be supporters of Allah, as when Jesus, the son of Mary, said to the disciples, "Who are my supporters for Allah?" The disciples said, "We are supporters of Allah." And a faction of the Children of Israel believed and a faction disbelieved. So We supported those who believed against their enemy, and they became dominant. (14)

Quran 61:5-9

وَإِذْ قَالَ مُوسَىٰ لِقَوْمِهِ يَٰقَوْمِ لِمَ تُؤْذُونَنِى وَقَد تَّعْلَمُونَ أَنِّى رَسُولُ ٱللَّهِ إِلَيْكُمْ ۖ فَلَمَّا زَاغُوٓا۟ أَزَاغَ ٱللَّهُ قُلُوبَهُمْ ۚ وَٱللَّهُ لَا يَهْدِى ٱلْقَوْمَ ٱلْفَٰسِقِينَ (٥) وَإِذْ قَالَ عِيسَى ٱبْنُ مَرْيَمَ يَٰبَنِىٓ إِسْرَٰٓءِيلَ إِنِّى رَسُولُ ٱللَّهِ إِلَيْكُم مُّصَدِّقًا لِّمَا بَيْنَ يَدَىَّ مِنَ ٱلتَّوْرَىٰةِ وَمُبَشِّرًۢا بِرَسُولٍ يَأْتِى مِنۢ بَعْدِى ٱسْمُهُۥٓ أَحْمَدُ ۖ فَلَمَّا جَآءَهُم بِٱلْبَيِّنَٰتِ قَالُوا۟ هَٰذَا سِحْرٌ مُّبِينٌ (٦) وَمَنْ أَظْلَمُ مِمَّنِ ٱفْتَرَىٰ عَلَى ٱللَّهِ ٱلْكَذِبَ وَهُوَ يُدْعَىٰٓ إِلَى ٱلْإِسْلَٰمِ ۚ وَٱللَّهُ لَا يَهْدِى ٱلْقَوْمَ ٱلظَّٰلِمِينَ (٧) يُرِيدُونَ لِيُطْفِـُٔوا۟ نُورَ ٱللَّهِ بِأَفْوَٰهِهِمْ وَٱللَّهُ مُتِمُّ نُورِهِۦ وَلَوْ كَرِهَ ٱلْكَٰفِرُونَ (٨) هُوَ ٱلَّذِىٓ أَرْسَلَ رَسُولَهُۥ بِٱلْهُدَىٰ وَدِينِ ٱلْحَقِّ لِيُظْهِرَهُۥ عَلَى ٱلدِّينِ كُلِّهِۦ وَلَوْ كَرِهَ ٱلْمُشْرِكُونَ (٩)

And [mention, O Muhammad], when Moses said to his people, "O my people, why do you harm me while you certainly know that I am the messenger of Allah to you?" And when they deviated, Allah caused their hearts to deviate. And Allah does not guide the defiantly disobedient people. (5) And [mention] when Jesus, the son of Mary, said, "O children of Israel, indeed I am the messenger of Allah to you confirming what came before me of the Torah and bringing good tidings of a messenger to come after me, whose name is Ahmad." But when he came to them with clear evidences, they said, "This is obvious magic." (6) And who is more unjust than one who invents about Allah untruth while he is being invited to Islam. And Allah does not guide the wrongdoing people. (7) They want to extinguish the light of Allah with their mouths, but Allah will perfect His light, although the disbelievers dislike it. (8) It is He who sent His Messenger with guidance and the religion of truth to manifest it over all religion, although those who associate others(in worship) with Allah dislike it. (9)

Quran 5:109-118

﴿ يَوْمَ يَجْمَعُ ٱللَّهُ ٱلرُّسُلَ فَيَقُولُ مَاذَآ أُجِبْتُمْ ۖ قَالُوا۟ لَا عِلْمَ لَنَآ ۖ إِنَّكَ أَنتَ عَلَّامُ ٱلْغُيُوبِ (١٠٩) إِذْ قَالَ ٱللَّهُ يَٰعِيسَى ٱبْنَ مَرْيَمَ ٱذْكُرْ نِعْمَتِى عَلَيْكَ وَعَلَىٰ وَٰلِدَتِكَ إِذْ أَيَّدتُّكَ بِرُوحِ ٱلْقُدُسِ تُكَلِّمُ ٱلنَّاسَ فِى ٱلْمَهْدِ وَكَهْلًا ۖ وَإِذْ عَلَّمْتُكَ ٱلْكِتَٰبَ وَٱلْحِكْمَةَ وَٱلتَّوْرَىٰةَ وَٱلْإِنجِيلَ ۖ وَإِذْ تَخْلُقُ مِنَ ٱلطِّينِ كَهَيْـَٔةِ ٱلطَّيْرِ بِإِذْنِى فَتَنفُخُ فِيهَا فَتَكُونُ طَيْرًۢا بِإِذْنِى ۖ وَتُبْرِئُ ٱلْأَكْمَهَ وَٱلْأَبْرَصَ بِإِذْنِى ۖ وَإِذْ تُخْرِجُ ٱلْمَوْتَىٰ بِإِذْنِى ۖ وَإِذْ كَفَفْتُ بَنِىٓ إِسْرَٰٓءِيلَ عَنكَ إِذْ جِئْتَهُم بِٱلْبَيِّنَٰتِ فَقَالَ ٱلَّذِينَ كَفَرُوا۟ مِنْهُمْ إِنْ هَٰذَآ إِلَّا سِحْرٌ مُّبِينٌ (١١٠) وَإِذْ أَوْحَيْتُ إِلَى ٱلْحَوَارِيِّۦنَ أَنْ ءَامِنُوا۟ بِى وَبِرَسُولِى قَالُوٓا۟ ءَامَنَّا وَٱشْهَدْ بِأَنَّنَا مُسْلِمُونَ (١١١) إِذْ قَالَ ٱلْحَوَارِيُّونَ يَٰعِيسَى ٱبْنَ مَرْيَمَ هَلْ يَسْتَطِيعُ رَبُّكَ أَن يُنَزِّلَ عَلَيْنَا مَآئِدَةً مِّنَ ٱلسَّمَآءِ ۖ قَالَ ٱتَّقُوا۟ ٱللَّهَ إِن كُنتُم مُّؤْمِنِينَ (١١٢) قَالُوا۟ نُرِيدُ أَن نَّأْكُلَ مِنْهَا وَتَطْمَئِنَّ قُلُوبُنَا وَنَعْلَمَ أَن قَدْ صَدَقْتَنَا وَنَكُونَ عَلَيْهَا مِنَ ٱلشَّٰهِدِينَ (١١٣) قَالَ عِيسَى ٱبْنُ مَرْيَمَ ٱللَّهُمَّ رَبَّنَآ أَنزِلْ عَلَيْنَا مَآئِدَةً مِّنَ ٱلسَّمَآءِ تَكُونُ لَنَا عِيدًا لِّأَوَّلِنَا وَءَاخِرِنَا وَءَايَةً مِّنكَ ۖ وَٱرْزُقْنَا وَأَنتَ خَيْرُ ٱلرَّٰزِقِينَ (١١٤) قَالَ ٱللَّهُ إِنِّى مُنَزِّلُهَا عَلَيْكُمْ ۖ فَمَن يَكْفُرْ بَعْدُ مِنكُمْ فَإِنِّىٓ أُعَذِّبُهُۥ عَذَابًا لَّآ أُعَذِّبُهُۥٓ أَحَدًا مِّنَ ٱلْعَٰلَمِينَ (١١٥) وَإِذْ قَالَ ٱللَّهُ يَٰعِيسَى ٱبْنَ مَرْيَمَ ءَأَنتَ قُلْتَ لِلنَّاسِ ٱتَّخِذُونِى وَأُمِّىَ إِلَٰهَيْنِ مِن دُونِ ٱللَّهِ ۖ قَالَ سُبْحَٰنَكَ مَا يَكُونُ لِىٓ أَنْ أَقُولَ مَا لَيْسَ لِى بِحَقٍّ ۚ إِن كُنتُ قُلْتُهُۥ فَقَدْ عَلِمْتَهُۥ ۚ تَعْلَمُ مَا فِى نَفْسِى وَلَآ أَعْلَمُ مَا فِى نَفْسِكَ ۚ إِنَّكَ أَنتَ عَلَّامُ ٱلْغُيُوبِ (١١٦) مَا قُلْتُ لَهُمْ إِلَّا مَآ أَمَرْتَنِى بِهِۦٓ أَنِ ٱعْبُدُوا۟ ٱللَّهَ رَبِّى وَرَبَّكُمْ ۚ وَكُنتُ عَلَيْهِمْ شَهِيدًا مَّا دُمْتُ فِيهِمْ ۖ فَلَمَّا تَوَفَّيْتَنِى كُنتَ أَنتَ ٱلرَّقِيبَ عَلَيْهِمْ ۚ وَأَنتَ عَلَىٰ كُلِّ شَىْءٍ شَهِيدٌ (١١٧) إِن تُعَذِّبْهُمْ فَإِنَّهُمْ عِبَادُكَ ۖ وَإِن تَغْفِرْ لَهُمْ فَإِنَّكَ أَنتَ ٱلْعَزِيزُ ٱلْحَكِيمُ (١١٨)

[Be warned of] the Day when Allah will assemble the messengers and say, "What was the response you received?" They will say, "We have no knowledge.

Indeed, it is You who is Knower of the unseen" (109) [The Day] when Allah will say, "O Jesus, Son of Mary, remember My favor upon you and upon your mother when I supported you with the Pure Spirit and you spoke to the people in the cradle and in maturity; and [remember] when I taught you writing and wisdom and the Torah and the Injeel; and when you designed from clay [what was] like the form of a bird with My permission, then you breathed into it, and it became a bird with My permission; and you healed the blind and the leper with My permission; and when you brought forth the dead with My permission; and when I restrained the Children of Israel from [killing] you when you came to them with clear proofs and those who disbelieved among them said, "This is not but obvious magic." (110) And [remember] when I inspired to the disciples, "Believe in Me and in My messenger Jesus." They said, "We have believed, so bear witness that indeed we are Muslims [in submission to Allah]." (111) [And remember] when the disciples said, "O Jesus, Son of Mary, can your Lord send down to us a table [spread with food] from the heaven? [Jesus] said," Fear Allah, if you should be believers." (112) They said, "We wish to eat from it and let our hearts be reassured and know that you have been truthful to us and be among its witnesses." (113) Said Jesus, the son of Mary, "O Allah, our Lord, send down to us a table [spread with food] from *the heaven to be for us a festival for the first of us and the last of us and a sign from You. And provide for us, and You are the best of providers." (114) Allah said, "Indeed, I will send it down to you, but whoever disbelieves afterwards from among you - then indeed will I punish him with a punishment by which I have not punished anyone among the worlds." (115) And [beware the Day] when Allah will say, "O Jesus, Son of Mary, did you say to the people, 'Take me and my mother as deities besides Allah?'" He will say, "Exalted are You! It was not for me to say that to which I have no right. If I had said it, You would have known it. You know what is within myself, and I do not know what is within Yourself. Indeed, it is You who is Knower of the unseen. (116) I said not to them except what You commanded me - to worship Allah, my Lord and your Lord. And I was a witness over them as long as I was among them; but when You took me up, You were the Observer over them, and You are, over all things, Witness. (117) If You should punish them - indeed they are Your servants; but if You forgive them - indeed it is You who is the Exalted in Might, the Wise. (118)*

Hadith Quotes Attributed to Prophet Jesus

Narrated Abu Huraira:

The Prophet said, "Jesus, seeing a man stealing, asked him, 'Did you steal?', He(the thief) said, 'No, by Allah, besides Whom there is none who has the right to be worshipped' Jesus said, 'I believe in Allah and suspect my eyes."

Source: Sahih al-Bukhari 3444

Imam Malik related from Yahya ibn Said that Jesus ibn (son of) Maryam encountered a pig on the road. Jesus said to it:

"Go in peace."

Somebody asked, "Do you say this to a pig?"

Jesus said, *"I fear lest I accustom my tongue to evil speech."*

Source: Muwatta Imam Malik

Yahya related from Imam Malik that he had heard that Jesus ibn (son of) Maryam used to say:

"O Banu Israil! You must drink pure water and the green things of the land and barley bread. Beware of wheat bread, for you will not be grateful enough for it."

Source: Muwatta Imam Malik

Malik related that he heard that Jesus ibn (son of) Maryam used to say:

"Do not speak much without the mention of Allah for you will harden your hearts. A hard heart is far from Allah, but you do not know. Do not look at the wrong actions of people as if you were lords. Look at your wrong actions as if you were slaves. Some people are afflicted by wrong action and some people are protected from it. Be merciful to the people of affliction and praise Allah for His protection."

Source: Muwatta Imam Malik

Narrated Al-Harith Al-Ash'ari:

that the Messenger of Allah (ﷺ) said: "Indeed Allah commanded John bin(son of) Zakariyya with five commandments to abide by, and to command the Children of Isra'il to abide by them. But he was slow in doing so. So Jesus said: 'Indeed Allah commanded you with five commandments to abide by and to command the Children of Isra'il to abide by. Either you command them, or I shall command them.' So John said: 'I fear that if you precede me in this, then the earth may swallow me, or I shall be punished.' So he gathered the people in Jerusalem, and they filled [the Masjid] and sat upon its balconies. So he said: 'Indeed Allah has commanded me with five commandments to abide by, and to command you to abide by.

The first of them is that you worship Allah and not associate anything with him. The parable of the one who associates others with Allah is that of a man who buys a servant with his own gold or silver, then he says to him: "This is my home and this is my business so take care of it and give me the profits." So he takes care of it and gives the profits to someone other than his master. Which of you would live to have a servant like that?

And Allah commands you to perform Salat(prayer), and when you perform Salat(prayer) then do not turn away, for Allah is facing the face of His worshipers as long as he does not turn away.

And He commands you with fasting. For indeed the parable of fasting, is that of a man in a group with a sachet containing musk. All of them enjoy its fragrance. Indeed the breath of the fasting person is more pleasant to Allah than the scent of musk.

And He commands you to give charity. The parable of that, is a man captured by his enemies, tying his hands to his neck, and they come to him to beat his neck. Then he said: "I can ransom myself from you with a little or a lot" so he ransoms himself from them.

And He commands you to remember Allah. For indeed the parable of that, is a man whose enemy quickly tracks him until he reaches an impermeable fortress in which he protects himself from them. This is how the worshiper is; he does not protect himself from Ash-Shaitan except by the remembrance of Allah.'"

Source: Jami Tirmidhi 2863 Grade: Sahih

It has been reported that Mary mother of Jesus said, "In the days I was pregnant with Jesus, whenever there was someone in my house speaking with me, I would hear Jesus praising God inside me. Whenever I was alone and there was no one with me, I would converse with him and he with me, while he was still in my womb."

Source: Sirat al Sayyid al Masih by Abu al Qasim ibn Asakir pg. 30 #6

Jesus said:

"Blessed is he who guards his tongue, whose house is sufficient for his needs and who weeps for his sins."

Source: Kitab al Zuhd w al Raqa'ia by Ibn Mubarak pg.40-41 #124

Jesus said:

"Do not talk much without the mention of God, lest your hearts grow hard; for the hard heart is far from God, but you do not know. Do not examine the sins of people as though you were lords but examine them, rather as though you were servants. Men are of two kinds: the sick and the healthy. Be merciful to the sick and give thanks to God for health."

Source: al Zuhd by Ibn Mubarak pg. 44 #135

Jesus said:

"If it is a day of fasting for one of you let him anoint his head and beard and wipe his lips so that people will not know that he is fasting. If he gives with the right hand, let him hide this from his left hand. If he prays, let him pull down the door curtain, for God apportions praise as He apportions livelihood."

Source: al Zuhd by Ibn Mubarak pg 48 #150

Gabriel met Jesus and said to him,

"Peace be upon you, Spirit of God."

"And upon you be peace, Spirit of God." Jesus said.

Then Jesus asked, "O Gabriel, when will the hour come?" Gabriel's wings fluttered and he replied, "The questioned knows no more about this than the questioner. It has grown heavy in the heavens and the earth; it will only come upon you suddenly." Or else he said, "Only God will reveal it when it is time."

Source: al zuhd by Ibn Mubarak pg. 77 #228

Whenever the Hour was mentioned in the presence of Jesus, he would cry and say:

"It is not fitting that the son of Mary should remain silent when the Hour is mentioned in his presence."

Source: al Zuhd by Ibn Mubarak pg 77-78 #229

Jesus said to his students:

"Do not take wages from those whom you teach except such wages as you gave me. Salt of the earth, do not become corrupt. Everything when it becomes corrupt can be treated with salt, but if salt is corrupted it has no remedy. Know that you possess two traits of ignorance: laughter without [cause for] wonder, and morning nap without wakefulness."

Source: al Zuhd by Ibn Mubarak pg. 96 #283

Jesus said to his students: "Just as kings have left wisdom to you, so you should leave the world to them."

Source: al Zuhd by Ibn Mubarak pg. 96 #284

Jesus said *"Son of Adam, if you do a good deed, try to forget it, for it abides with Him who will not forget it."* He then recited a verse *"We do not neglect the reward of him who does a good deed."* afterwards saying *"If you commit an evil deed, let it remain before your eyes."*

Source: al Zuhd by Ibn Mubarak pg. 101 #301

Jesus said: *"O disciples seek the love of God by your hatred of sinners, seek to be near Him by [doing] that which distances you from them; and seek His favor by being angry with them."*

They said, "Spirit of God, whose company then shall we keep?"

Jesus replied: *" Keep the company of him whose sight reminds you of God, whose speech increases your knowledge, whose deeds make the afterlife desirable."*

Source: al Zuhd by Ibn Mubarak pg. 121 #355

Jesus used to tell his followers:

"Takes places of worship to be your homes, houses to be stopping places. Eat from the plants of the wilderness and escape from this world in peace."

Source: al Zuhd by Ibn Mubarak pg 198 #563

Jesus said:

"For the patient man, misfortune soon results in ease; for the sinner ease soon results in misfortune."

Source: al Zuhd by Ibn Mubarak pg 222 #627

Jesus said:

"There are four [qualities] which are not found in one person without causing wonder: silence, which is the beginning of worship; humility before God; an ascetic attitude toward the world; and poverty."

Source: al Zuhd by Ibn Mubarak pg. 222 #629

Jesus said:

"Strive for the sake of God and not for the sake of your bellies. Look at the birds coming and going! They neither reap nor plough and God provides for them. If you say, 'Our bellies are larger than the bellies of birds,' then look at these cattle, wild or tame, as they come and go, neither reaping nor plowing and God provides for them too. Beware the excesses of the world, for the excesses of the world are an abomination in God's eyes."

Source: al Zuhd by Ibn Mubarak pg. 291 #848

Jesus was asked, "Spirit and Word of God, who is the most seditious of men?"

Jesus replied: *"The scholar who is in error. If a scholar errs, a host of people will fall into error because of him."*

Source: al Zuhd by Ibn Mubarak pg 520 #1474

Prophet John son of Zachariah met Jesus and said, "Tell me what it is that draws one near to God's favor and distances one from God's wrath?"

Jesus said, *"Avoid feeling anger."*

John asked, "What arouses anger and what makes it recur?"

Jesus replied, *"Pride, fanaticism, haughtiness, and magnificence."*

John said, "Let me ask you another." Jesus said, "Ask what you will." John said, "Adultery, what creates it and what makes it recur?"

Jesus said:

"A glance, which implants in the heart something that makes it veer excessively towards amusement and self-indulgence, thus increasing heedlessness and sin. Do not stare at what does not belong to you, for what you have not seen will not make you wiser and what you do not hear will not trouble you."

Source: al Zuhd by Ibn Mubarak appendix page 12 #44

Jesus was asked by his students "Tell us, which man is the most devoted to God?"

Jesus replied: *"He who labors for the sake of God without seeking the praise of mankind."*

Again they asked "Which man offers sincere counsel for the sake of God?"

Jesus replied: *"He who begins by fulfilling his duties toward God before his duty to men [and prefers] the duties to God to the duties of men. When faced with two choices, worldly matters and matters of the afterlife, he begins with what concerns the afterlife and then turns his attention to this world."*

Jesus used to say:

"Love of paradise and fear of hell beget patience in adversity and draw the servant away from worldly comfort."

Source: al Zuhd by Ibn Mubarak appendix pg 46 #175

Jesus stood by a grave with his students and said while a dead man was lowered into the grave:

"You were once in a place narrower than this in your mother's wombs. If God wishes to expand [His mercy], He does so."

Source: al Zuhd by Ibn Hanbal pg 93 #301

Jesus said:

"*Make frequent mention of God the Exalted, also of His praise and glorification, and obey Him. It suffices for one of you when praying, and if God is truly pleased with him, to say: 'O God, forgive my sins, reform my way of life, and keep me safe from hateful things, O my God.*"

Source: al Zuhd by Ibn Hanbal pg.93 #302

Jesus said:

"*Blessed is the Believer, and then again blessed, for God watches over his progeny after his death.*"

Source: al Zuhd by Ibn Hanbal pg 93 #304

Jesus was asked, "Prophet of God, why do you not get yourself a donkey to ride upon for your needs?"

Jesus replied: "*I am more honorable in God's sight than that he should provide me with something which may distract me from Him.*"

Source: al Zuhd by Ibn Hanbal pg 94 #309

Jesus said to his students, "*Truly I say to you, you desire neither this world nor the next.*"

They said, "Prophet of God, explain this matter to us, for we used to think that we desired one of them."

Jesus said, "Had you desired this world, you would have obeyed the Lord of the world, who holds the keys of its treasures in His hands. Had you desired the other world, you would have obeyed the Lord who owns it, and He would have given it to you. But you want neither the one nor the other."

Source: al Zuhd by Ibn Hanbal pg 94-95

Jesus said:

"Why do I not observe in you the best of worship?"

They said, "What is the best of worship Spirit of God?"

Jesus said, "Humility before God."

Source: al Zuhd by Ibn Hanbal pg 95 #312

Jesus said:

"Place your treasures in heaven, for the heart of man is where his treasure is."

Source: al Zuhd by Ibn Hanbal pg 95 #313

Once the disciples lost track of Jesus then found him walking on water. One of them said, "Prophet of God, shall we walk toward you?"

Jesus said, "Yes."

As the disciple walked toward Jesus he sank.

Jesus said: "*Strech forth your hand, you man of little faith. If the son of Adam had a grain or atom's weight of faith, he would walk upon water.*"

Source: al Zuhd by Ibn Hanbal pg 96 #315

Jesus was asked, "How can you walk on water?"

Jesus replied, "Through certainty of faith."

He was told, "We too have certain faith."

Jesus asked, "*Do you believe stones, mud, and gold are all equal in your sight?*"

They replied, 'No'

Jesus said, "*They are all the same in my sight.*"

Source: al Zuhd p. 99 #331

Jesus used to say: "*Charity does not mean doing good to him who does good to you, for this is to return good for good. Charity means that you should do good to him who does you harm.*"

Source: al Zuhd pg. 96 #317

Jesus met prophet John and said, "Admonish me." John said, "Avoid feeling anger." Jesus said, "This I cannot do." John said, "Do not own any wealth." Jesus said, "As for this, it is possible."

Source: al Zuhd pg 97 #322

Jesus said:

"O Disciples, which of you can build a house upon the waves of the sea?"

They said, "Spirit of God, who can do that?"

Jesus said:

"Beware the world and do not make it your abode."

Source: al Zuhd by Ibn Hanbal pg 98 #325

Jesus used to say:

"Truly I say to you, to eat wheat bread, to drink pure water, and to sleep upon dunghills with the dogs more than suffices him who wishes to enter Paradise."

Source: al Zuhd by Ibn Hanbal pg 98 #326

Jesus said:

"It is of no use to you to come to know what you did not know, so long as you do not act in accordance with what you already know. Too much knowledge only increases pride if you do not act in accordance with it."

Source: al Zuhd by Ibn Hanbal pg. 98 #327

Jesus said:

"Time revolves around three days: a yesterday which has passed away and during which you have been admonished, a today which supplies your needs, and a tomorrow in which you do not know what is in store for you. All matters revolve around three things: a thing whose rightness has become apparent to you and which you must follow, a thing whose evil has become apparent to you and which you must shun, and a thing which appears uncertain to you and which you must defer to God."

Source al Zuhd by Ibn Hanbal pg. 98 #328

Jesus said:

"Console me, for my heart is soft and I hold myself in low esteem."

Source: al Zuhd by Ibn Hanbal pg. 98 #329

Jesus said:

"Whoever has learned, acted and imparted knowledge-he is the one who is called great in the kingdom of heaven."

Source: al Zuhd by Ibn Hanbal pg. 98-99 #330

A man said to Jesus, "Teacher of goodness, teach me something that you know and I do not, that benefits me and does you no harm."

Jesus asked, "What would that be?" the man said, "How can a servant be truly pious before God?"

Jesus replied: *"The matter is easy. You must truly love God in your heart and work in His service, exerting all your effort and strength, and be merciful toward the people of your race as you show mercy to yourself."*

He said, "Teacher of goodness, who are the people of my race?"

Jesus replied:

"All the children of Adam. And that which you do not wish done to you, do not do to others. In this way you will be truly pious before God."

Source: al Zuhd by Ibn Hanbal pg.99 #332

Jesus used to frequently prepare food for his followers then call them to eat and say:

"This is what you must do for the poor."

Source al Zuhd by Ibn Hanbal pg. 99 #333

Jesus said:

"In truth I say to you, those among you who sorrow most in misfortune are the most attached to this world."

Source al Zuhd by Ibn Hanbal pg. 100 #338

The disciples said, "O Jesus, who are 'the friends of God almighty upon whom no fear shall come nor shall they grieve?'"

Jesus replied, *"They are the ones who look into the heart of this world while the rest of mankind looks at its surface, who look forward to the end of the world while the rest of mankind looks at the fleeting present. They kill of the world what they fear might kill them and abandon what they know will abandon them. Hence, what once they considered of much worldly account they now consider negligible. When they make mention of it, this is only in passing, and their joy at what they gain from it is sadness. They reject every chance of worldly gain and disdain every chance of worldly glory without just cause. For them, the world is grown old and tattered but they do not renew it. It has fallen into ruin around them, but they do not rebuild it. It has died in their hearts but they do not resurrect it. They destroy it in order to rebuild their afterlife with it. They sell it in exchange for that which lasts. They reject it and are thus the truly happy in it. They look at its people, fallen dead and disfigured upon the earth, and renew the mention of death and kill the mention of life. They love God and the mention of God, seeking His light and shining through His light. Wonders are related of them and they relate wondrous things. The Book of God is known through them and they act in accordance with it. The Book of*

God makes mention of them and they make mention of the Book. Knowledge of the Book comes through them and through it they themselves acquire knowledge. They expect no gain greater than what they have gained, no peace other than what they hope for, no fear other than what they shun."

Source al Zuhd pg. 100-101 #339

Prophet John and Jesus met. John said, "Ask God's forgiveness for me, for you are better than me."

Jesus replied, *"You are better than me. I pronounced peace upon myself, whereas God pronounced peace upon you.(before you were born when announcing the news of your birth)"*

Source: al Zuhd by Ibn Hanbal pg 122 #392

A man committed adultery and was brought to Jesus. Jesus ordered them to stone him and said:

"But no one should stone him who has committed what he has committed." They let the stones fall from their hands, all except for Prophet John son of Zachariah.

Source: al Zuhd by Ibn Hanbal pg 124 #402

Jesus said:

"What God loves most are the Strangers."

He was asked, "Who are the strangers?"

Jesus replied, "*Those who flee [the world] with their faith[intact]. They shall be gathered together with Jesus on the Day of Resurrection.*"

Source: al Zuhd by Ibn Hanbal pg. 124 #402

Jesus said:

"*Slaves of this world, instead of dispensing alms, be merciful to those whom you treat unjustly.*"

Source al Zuhd by Ibn Hanbal pg. 141 #466

Jesus said:

"*Leave the people alone. Be at ease with people and ill at ease with yourself. Do not seek to earn their praises or merit their rebuke. Perform what you have been commanded to do.*"

Source: al Zuhd by Ibn Hanbal pg 142 #467

After raising a man from the dead, the man's wife told Jesus, "Blessed is the belly that carried you and the breasts from which you fed."

So Jesus replied, "*Blessed is he whom God has taught His Book and who dies without having become haughty.*"

Source al-Zuhd by Ibn Hanbal pg 142-143 #470

Jesus said:

"The greatest sin is love of the world. Women are the ropes of Satan. Wine is the key to every evil."

Source: al-Zuhd by Ibn Hanbal pg. 143 #472

Jesus used to say, "*Love of the world is the root of all sin. Worldly wealth is a great sickness.*"

He was asked, "What is that sickness?"

Jesus said, "*Its owner cannot avoid pride and self-esteem.*"

He was asked, "Suppose he avoided this?"

Jesus replied, "*The cultivation of wealth distracts man from the mention of God.*"

Source al-Zuhd by Ibn Hanbal pg. 143 # 473

Jesus said to his disciples:

"*O disciples, do not cast pearls before swine, for the swine can do nothing with them. Do not impart wisdom to one who does not desire it, for wisdom is more precious than pearls and whoever rejects wisdom is worse than a swine.*"

Source: al-Zuhd by Ibn Hanbal pg 144 #477

Jesus said:

"*If you desire to devote yourselves entirely to God and to be the light of the children of Adam, forgive those who have done you evil, visit the sick who do not visit you, be kind to those who are unkind to you, and lend to those who do not repay you."*

Source: al-Zuhd by Ibn Hanbal pg. 144-145 #480

Jesus said to his students:

" I would have you eat barley bread and escape from the world in safety and peace. Truly I say to you, the sweetness of this world is the bitterness of the world beyond, and the bitterness of this world is the sweetness of the world beyond. The true worshipers of God are not those who live in comfort. Truly I say to you, the most evil among you in act is a scholar who loves this world and prefers it to right conduct. Could he do so, he would have all people act the way he does."

Source: al-Zuhd by Ibn Hanbal pg. 145 #482

Jesus used to say:

"I preach to you so that you may learn. I do not preach to you so that you may grow conceited."

Source: al-Zuhd by Ibn Hanbal pg. 145 #483

Jesus said:

"Satan accompanies the world. His deceit accompanies wealth. His seductiveness accompanies caprice. His ultimate power accompanies the appetites."

Source: al-Zuhd by Ibn Hanbal pg. 146 #487

Jesus used to say:

"O disciples, do not seek the world by destroying yourselves; seek your salvation by abandoning what is in the world. Naked you came into the world and naked you shall depart. Do not seek what sustenance tomorrow may bring, but let each day's sustenance suffice and tomorrow will bring its own concerns. Pray God to bring you sustenance day by day."

Source: al-Zuhd by Ibn Hanbal pg. 146 #488

Jesus came upon a group of people who were crying. Jesus asked, "Why are these people crying?"

He was told, "They are afraid of their sins."

Jesus said, *"Abandon them and you will be forgiven."*

Source: al Bayan wa al Tabyin by al-Jahiz 1:399 and 3:167

Jesus was insulted by a group of Jews. Everytime they spoke evil Jesus replied with good. He was asked, "Will you answer them with good each time they speak evil?"

Jesus said, *"Each person spends of what he owns."*

Source: al Bayan by al Jahiz 2:177

Jesus was seen leaving the house of a prostitute, when asked what he was doing there Jesus replied:

"It is the sick that a physician visits."

Source: al Bayan by al Jahiz 3:140

Jesus said:

"The world is Satan's farm, and its people are his plowmen."

Source: al Bayan by al Jahiz 3:140-141

Jesus said:

"Woe unto you, slaves of this world! How your practices contradict your principles, and your whims your reason! Your words are a remedy which cures disease, but your actions are a disease which defies cure. You are not like the vine which has fine leaves, tasty fruit, and is easy to reach, but are in truth like the acacia tree, which has few leaves, many thorns, and is difficult to reach! Woe unto you, slaves of this world! You have placed good works beneath your feet, [thinking] that they can be attained by whoever so wishes and have placed this world above your heads, [thinking] that it cannot be reached. You are neither pious slaves nor worthy freemen. Woe unto you, wage-earners of sin! You take your wages and spoil the work. You shall meet with

what you most fear, for the Taskmaster will soon see the work you have spoilt and the wages you have taken. Woe to you, debtors of evil! You begin with gifts before discharging your debt, you volunteer to perform what is superfluous but do not perform what you have been commanded to do. The owner of the debt will not accept gifts until his debt has been discharged."

Source: al Bayan by al Jahiz 3:157

Jesus said:

"You work for this world, where you are provided for without working; whereas you do not work for the afterlife, where you will not be provided for except by working."

Source: al Bayan by al Jahiz 3:166

Jesus said:

"It is a sign of how trivial the world is to God that only in the world is He disobeyed, and only by forsaking the world can His bounty be attained."

Source: al Bayan by al Jahiz 3:166

Jesus said:

"Man is created into this world in four stages, in three of which he feels secure and in the fourth of which he is ill disposed and fears that God will forsake him. In the first stage, he is born in three darknesses: the darkness of the belly, the darkness of the womb, and the darkness of the placenta. God provides for him in the darkness of the cavity of the belly. When he is brought out from the darkness of the belly, he falls upon milk which he does not advance toward on foot or leg, or obtain with his hand or move strongly toward, but he is forced to it and rewarded with it until flesh and blood grows upon him. Weaned from milk, he falls upon the third stage: food provided by his parents, who earn it either lawfully or unlawfully. When his parents die, people take pity on him, one person feeding him, another giving him drink, another sheltering him, and another clothing him. When he falls upon the fourth stage and has grown strong and erect and has become a man, he fears that he will not be provided for, so he attacks people, betrays their trust, robs their belongings, and carries away their wealth, fearing that God Almighty might forsake him."

Source: al-Mahasin wa al-Addad by al Jahiz pg 82-83

Jesus was asked, "Which of your deeds is the best?" Jesus replied:

"Leaving alone that which does not concern me."

Source: Kitab Kitman al-Sirr by al Jahiz 1:162

Jesus said to his followers:

"If people appoint you as their heads, be like tails."

Source: Uyun al-Akhbar by Ibn Qutayba 1:266

Jesus met a man and asked him, "What are you doing?" The man said, "I am devoting myself to God." Jesus asked, "Who is caring for you?" The man said, "My brother." Jesus said, "Your brother is more devoted to God than you are."

Source: Uyun by Ibn Qutayba 1:327

Jesus said:

"Till when do you describe the road to travelers by night while you yourselves remain behind with the perplexed? Only a little religious knowledge suffices, but many should be your deeds."

Source: Uyun by Ibn Qutayba 2:127

Jesus said:

"The most hateful of scholars to God is one who is fond of backbiting, who likes to occupy a seat of honor in an assembly, to be invited to feasts, and to have sacks of food emptied for him. Truly I say to you, such men have obtained their wages in this world, and God shall multiply their punishment on the Day of Judgment."

Source: Uyun by Ibn Qutayba 2:127

Jesus said:

"He who speaks without mentioning God is merely babbling. He who reflects without self-admonition is merely heedless. He who is silent without reflecting is merely wasting time."

Source: Uyun by Ibn Qutayba 2:178

Jesus said to his companions:

"If you are truly my brothers and friends, accustom yourselves to the enmity and hatred of men. For you shall not obtain what you seek except by abandoning what you desire. You shall not possess what you love except by tolerating what you hate."

Source: Uyun by Ibn Qutayba 2:268

Jesus said:

"You will not commit adultery as long as you avert your eyes."

Source: Uyun by Ibn Qutayba 4:84

Jesus said:

"As God is my witness, the world has not dwelt in the heart of a servant without his heart attaching itself to three things in it: labor, whose burden is never alleviated; poverty, which cannot be surmounted, and hope, which cannot be fulfilled. The world is both a pursuer and a thing pursued. It pursues him who seeks the afterlife until his term of life comes to an end, whereas the afterlife pursues him who seeks this world until death comes and seizes him by the neck."

Source: Kitab al Qana'a wa al Ta'affuf in Mawsu'at Rasa'il by Ibn abi al Dunya 1:68 #162

Jesus said:

"The heart of a believer cannot really support the love of both this world and the next, just as a single vessel cannot really support both water and fire."

Source: Kitab Dhamm al Dunya in Mawsu'at Rasa'il by Ibn abi al Dunya 2:44 #76

A man once accompanied Jesus saying, "I want to be with you and be your companion." They set forth and reached the bank of a river where they sat down to eat. They had with them three loaves of bread. They ate two loaves and a third remained. Jesus then rose and went to the river to drink. When he returned he did not find the third loaf, so he asked the man: "Who took the loaf?", The man replied, "I do not know."

Jesus set forth with the man and saw a doe with two of her young. Jesus called one of the two, and it came to him. Jesus slaughtered it, roasted some of it and ate with his companion. Then he said to the young deer, "Rise, by God's leave." The deer rose and left. Jesus then turned to his companion and said, "I ask you in the name of Him who showed you this miracle, who took the loaf?" The man replied, "I do not know."

The two of them then came to a body of water in a valley. Jesus took the man by the hand and they walked upon the water. When they had crossed over, Jesus said to him, "I ask you in the name of Him who showed you this miracle, who took the loaf?" The man replied, "I do not know."

They then came to a waterless desert and sat down upon the ground. Jesus began to gather some earth and sand, then said, "Turn to gold, by God's leave." And it did so. Jesus divided the gold into three portions and said, "A third for me, a third for you, and a third for whoever took the loaf." The man said, "It was I who took the loaf." Jesus said, "The gold is all yours." Jesus then left him.

Two men came upon the man in the desert with the gold and wanted to rob and kill him. He said to them, "Let us divide it into three portions among us, and send one of you to town to buy us some food to eat." One of them was sent off, and then said to himself, "Why should I divide the gold with those two? Rather I shall poison the food and have the gold to myself." He went off and did so.

Meanwhile the two who stayed behind said to each other, "Why should we give him a third of the gold? Instead, let us kill him when he returns and divide the money between the two of us." When he returned they killed him, ate the food and died. The gold remained in the desert with the three men dead beside it. Jesus passed by, found them in that condition and said to his companions, *"This is the world. Beware of it."*

Source: Kitab Dhamm al dunya in Mawsu'at Rasa'il by ibn Abi al Dunya 2:49 #87

Jesus said:

"Truly I say to you, just as a sick man looks at food and does not enjoy it because he is in pain, so a lover of this world does not enjoy worship or appreciate its delights because of his love for this world. Truly I say to you, if a beast of burden is left unridden and undisciplined, it grows headstrong and changes its character. So also if the heart is not softened by mention of death and the strain of worship, it grows hard and callous. Truly I say to you, if a water skin is not torn or withered it may hold honey. So also if the heart is not torn by desires, defiled

by avarice, or hardened by luxury, it can be a vessel of wisdom."

Source: Kitab Dhamm al dunya in Mawsu'at Rasa'il by Ibn abi Dunya 2:52 #90

Jesus was asked, "Why do you not acquire a house to shelter you?"

Jesus replied:

"Let us be satisfied with the ruins of those who came before us."

Source: Kitab Dhamm al Dunya in Mawsu'at Rasa'il by ibn Abi Dunya 2:68 #129

Jesus said:

"The world existed and I was not in it, and it shall exist and I shall not be in it. All I have are my days which I am now living. If I sin in them, I am indeed a sinner."

Source: Kitab Dhamm al Dunya in Mawsu'at Rasa'il by ibn Abi Dunya 2:105 # 216

Jesus said:

"It is a mark of the ascetics in this world that they shun the company of any companion who does not desire what they desire."

Source: Kitab Dhamm al Dunya in Mawsu'at Rasa'il by ibn Abi Dunya 2:109 #225

Jesus said:

"You work for a petty world and you ignore the great afterlife, and upon you all death shall pass."

Source: Kitab Dhamm al Dunya in Mawsu'at Rasa'il by ibn Abi Dunya 2:129-130 # 236

Jesus said:

"He who seeks worldly things is like the man who drinks sea water: the more he drinks the more thirsty he becomes until it kills him."

Source: Kitab Dhamm al Dunya in Mawsu'at Rasa'il by ibn Abi Dunya 2:146 #342

Jesus said:

"O Disciples, be ascetics in this world and you will pass through it without anxiety."

Source: Kitab Dhamm al Dunya in Mawsu'at Rasa'il by ibn Abi Dunya 2:146 #344

Jesus said:

"Woe to you evil scholars! For the sake of a despicable world and a calamitous desire, you squander the kingdom *of paradise and forget the terror of the Day of Judgement."*

Source: Kitab Dhamm al Dunya in Mawsu'at Rasa'il by ibn Abi Dunya 2:158 #377

Jesus looked at Satan and said, *"Here is the pillar of the world. It is to the world that he went out, and it is the world that he demanded. I do not share anything of it with him, not even a stone to place beneath my head. Nor will I laugh much in it until I have left it."*

Source: Kitab Dhamm al Dunya in Mawsu'at Rasa'il by ibn Abi Dunya 2:168 #409

Satan passed by Jesus while he was reclining his head upon a stone and said, "So, then, Jesus, you have been satisfied with a stone in this world!"

Jesus removed the stone from beneath his head, threw it at him, and said, *"Take this stone, and the world with it! I have no need of either."*

Source: Kitab Dhamm al Dunya in Mawsu'at Rasa'il by ibn Abi Dunya 2:168 #410

Jesus said:

"O disciples, be satisfied with what is vile in this world while your faith remains whole and sound, just as the

people of this world are satisfied with what is vile in religion while their world remains whole and sound."

Source: Kitab Dhamm al Dunya in Mawsu'at Rasa'il by ibn Abi Dunya 2:179 #449

Jesus said:

"God likes His servant to learn a craft whereby he can become independent of people, and God hates a servant who acquires religious knowledge and then adopts it as a craft."

Source: Kitab Dhamm al Dunya in Mawsu'at Rasa'il by ibn Abi Dunya 2:95 #316

Jesus was asked:

"Show us an act by which we may enter paradise."

Jesus said: *"Do not speak at all."*

They said "We cannot do this."

Jesus replied: *"Then speak only good."*

Source: Kitab al Samt wa Adab al Lisan by Ibn Abi Dunya pg. 215 #46

Jesus said:

"He who lies much loses his beauty, he who constantly quarrels with men loses his sense of honor, he who

worries much grows sick in body; and he whose character is nasty tortures himself."

Source: Kitab al Samt wa Adab al Lisan by Ibn Abi Dunya pg. 276-277 #133

Jesus said:

"Among the greatest of sins in the sight of God is that a servant of God should say, 'God knows' and God knows it is not so."

Source: Kitab al Samt wa Adab al Lisan pg.608-609 #727

Jesus was asked about sincere counsel. He said:

"If two matters arise before you, one of which concerns you and the other of which concerns God, begin with the matter that concerns God."

Source: al Salat wa Maqasidiha by Al Tirmidhi 119

Jesus said:

"Multiply what fire cannot consume."

He was asked, "And what is that?"

Jesus replied, "Good works."

Source: al Fadil by abu abbas al Mubarrad pg. 35

Jesus used to say:

"If you find yourselves in need of people, eat in moderation and walk to the side."

Source: al Kamil by abu abbas al Mubarrad 1:210

Jesus said:

"He whom God honors from among his worshippers must be honored by all His creation."

Source: Tarikh Iftitah al Andalus by Abu Bakr ibn Qutiyya pg. 60

Jesus told the Israelites:

"Do not reward a wrongdoer with wrongdoing, for this will nullify your virtue in God's sight."

Source: Tanbih al Ghafilin by Abu al Layth al Samarqandi pg. 75

Jesus said:

"What avails the blind man if he carries a lamp that only others can see by? And what avails the darkened house if the lamp is placed on its roof? And what avails you who speak words of wisdom but do not act upon them?"

Source: Tanbih al Ghafilin by Abu Layth Samarqandi pg. 156

Jesus said:

"The merciful in this world is the one who will be shown mercy in the next world."

Source: al Sa'ada wa al Is'ad by Abu Hasan al Amiri pg. 311

Jesus said:

"None of you can come to true belief until he no longer cares to be praised for his worship of God almighty and no longer cares to partake of the goods of this world."

Source: Qut al Qulub by Abu Talib al Makki 1:256

Jesus said, *"The lover of God loves hardship."*

And it is related that he once came upon a large group of worshipers who had shriveled up from worshiping, like worn-out waterskins. "Who are you?" Jesus asked. "We are worshipers." They answered. So Jesus asked, "Why do you worship?" They replied, "God put the fear of hell in us, and we were afraid." So Jesus said: *"It is incumbent upon God to save you from what you fear."* Then Jesus passed on and came to others who were even more worshipful. Jesus asked, "Why do you worship?" They replied, "God gave us a longing for paradise and what He has prepared there for His friends. This is what we hope for." So Jesus said, *"It is incumbent upon God to give you what you hope for."*

Then he passed them by and came upon others who were worshipping and said, "Who are you?" They said, "We are lovers of God. We worship Him not out of fear of hell or longing for paradise, but out of love for Him and to His greater glory." So Jesus said, "*You are truly the friends of God, and it is with you that I was commanded to live.*" And Jesus resided among them.

It is also reported he said to the first two groups, "*It is a created thing you fear, and a created thing you love,*" and to the third group, "*You are truly the nearest to God.*"

Source: Qut al Qulub by abu Talib al Makki 2:56

Jesus said:

"*O disciples, I have laid the world down flat upon its belly for your sake and made you sit upon its back. Only two groups vie with you for its mastery: kings and devils. As for devils, seek support against them in patience and prayer. As for kings, leave their world to them and they will leave the other world to you.*"

Source: al Basa'ir wal Dhakha'ir by Abu Hayyan al Tawhidi 1:23

Jesus said:

"Even if God Almighty had not decreed torment for sinning against Him, it would [nonetheless] be fitting that He should not be disobeyed, out of gratitude for His bounty."

Source: al Basa'ir wal Dhakha'ir by Abu Hayyan al Tawhidi 2:423

Jesus said:

"Every man slain shall be avenged on the Day of Judgement except the man slain by the world, which shall avenge itself upon him."

Source: al Basa'ir wal Dhakha'ir by Abu Hayyan al Tawhidi 7:147

Jesus preached to the Israelites so they wept and began to tear their clothes. Jesus said:

"What sin have your clothes committed? Turn instead to your hearts and reprove them."

Source: al Basa'ir wal Dhakha'ir by Abu Hayyan al Tawhidi 7:226

Jesus said to his disciples:

"The sign that you shall use to recognize each other as my followers is your affection for one another." Additionally Jesus said to his disciple Yashu,

"As for the Lord, you must love Him with all your heart. Then you must love your neighbor as yourself."

Jesus was asked, "Show us, Spirit of God, what difference there is between these two loves so that we may prepare ourselves for them with clarity of vision."

Jesus replied:

"You love a friend for you own sake and you love your soul for the sake of your Lord. If you take good care of your friend you are doing so for your own sake, but if you give your soul away, you do so for the sake of your Lord."

Source: Risala fi al Sadaqa wa al Sadiq by Abu Hayyan al Tawhidi pg. 64

Jesus said:

"The likeness of this world to the next is like a man who has two wives: if he pleases one, he arouses the other's resentment."

Source: Ihya by al Ghazali 3:18

Jesus was asked:

"Why are the old more attached to the world than the young?"

Jesus answered:

"Because they have tasted of this world what the young have not."

Source: Muhadarat al Udaba by Al Raghib al Isfahani 1:525

Jesus said:

"Let him who thinks God is slow with His bounty beware! For God might be angry and open wide to him the bounties of the world."

Source: al Hikma by Abu ali Miskawayh pg. 156

Jesus said:

"Do you desire the world for the sake of virtuous deeds? It is more virtuous for you to forsake the world."

Source: al Hikma by Abu ali Miskawayh pg. 192

Jesus said:

"He who acts without counsel acts in vain."

Source: Hilyat al Awliya by Abu Nuaym al Isbahani 5:237

Jesus said:

"Talk much to God, talk little to people."

He was asked, "How do we talk much to God?"

Jesus answered:

"Converse with Him in solitude, pray to Him in solitude."

Source: Hilyat al Awliya by Abu Nuaym al Isbahani 6:195

Jesus said:

"O Israelites, Moses forbade you to commit adultery and he did well to forbid it. I forbid you even to contemplate it, for he who contemplates it without acting upon it is like an earthenware house in which a fire is lit: even though it does not burn, it becomes charred from the smoke. O Israelites, Moses forbade you to swear by God falsely, and he did well to forbid it. I forbid you to swear by God at all, be it falsely or truly."

Source: Hilyat al Awliya by Abu Nuaym al Isbahani 8:145-146

Jesus said:

"O man of learning, learn of knowledge what you do not know and teach the ignorant what you have learned."

Source: Adab al Dunya wa al Din by Abu Hasan al Mawardi pg. 67

Jesus said:

"Beware of glancing at women and glancing again, for this sows lust in the heart, seduction enough for him who does it."

Source: Adab al Dunya wa al Din by Abu Hasan al Mawardi pg. 294

Jesus was asked:

"Until what age is it seemly to acquire knowledge?"

Jesus answered, *"As long as life itself is seemly."*

Source: Jami Bayan al Ilm by al Qurtubi 1:96

Jesus said:

"O reciters and scholars, how can you go astray after acquiring knowledge, or how can you be blind after acquiring knowledge, or how can you be blind after acquiring eyesight, and all for the sake of a despicable world and base desires? Woe to you in this world, and woe to this world from you."

Source: Jami Bayan al Ilm by al Qurtubi 1:190

Jesus said:

"Do not be saddened by what people say about you. If what they say is false it would be like a good deed that you have not performed. If true, it would be like an evil deed whose punishment has been prematurely exacted."

Source Bahjat al Majalis by al Qurtubi 1:405

Jesus said:

"How many trees there are but not all bear fruit! How many fruits there are but not all are good to eat! How many sciences there are but not all are useful!"

Source: Ihya by al Ghazali 1:38

Jesus said:

"To dispense wisdom to other than those worthy of it is to do it an injustice, and to bar it from those worthy of it is to do them an injustice. Be like the gentle physician who applies medication to the place of illness."

Source: Ihya by al Ghazali 1:43

Jesus said:

"The scholars of evil are like a rock which has fallen into the mouth of a river: it neither drinks the water nor allows the water to pass to the crops. The scholars of evil are also like the channels of a sewer: their exterior is white plaster and their interior is foul; or like tombs which are grand on the outside and full of dead bones inside."

Source: Ihya by al Ghazali 1:66

Jesus said:

"How can someone be considered a man of learning if he deliberately travels down the road of this world while his destination is the afterlife? And how can someone be considered a man of learning if he desires speech in order to relay it to others rather than to act upon it?"

Source: Ihya by al Ghazali 1:67

Jesus said:

"One who acquires knowledge but does not act in accordance with it is like a woman who commits adultery in secret and becomes pregnant, and her shame is known to all. So, also he who does not act in accordance with his knowledge shall be shamed by God before all men on the Day of Judgement."

Source: Ihya by Ghazali 1:69

Jesus said:

"Blessed is he who abandons a present desire for the sake of an absent, invisible promise."

Source: Ihya by al Ghazali 3:64

Jesus said:

"Piety is $9/10^{ths}$ silence and $1/10^{th}$ fleeing from people."

Source: Ihya by al Ghazali 3:107

Jesus said:

"Woe to the man of this world! How he dies when he leaves it and all that is in it behind him! How the world deceives him yet he still trusts it! How it lets him down, yet he still has faith in it! Woe to the deceived! How the world showed them what they hate! How those things they loved have forsaken them! How they have encountered what they have been threatened with! Woe to him who makes the world his concern and sin his pursuit! How soon his sin will be revealed!"

Source: Ihya by al Ghazali 3:200

Jesus said:

"O scholars of evil! You fast and pray and give alms but do not do what you order others to do, and you preach what you do not practice. Wretched indeed is your judgement! You repent in word and false hope, but you act according to your whims. What does it avail you if you keep your skins clean while your hearts are sullied? In truth I say to you do not be like the sieve through which the tasty flour falls while the residue is left behind, for so are you when you pass judgment with your mouths but malice is left behind in your hearts. Slaves of the world, how can a man attain the other world when his lust for this world is unceasing, his desire for it unsatisfied? In truth I say to you, your hearts weep because of your deeds. You have placed the world under your tongues and the deed under your feet. In truth I say *to you, you have corrupted your afterlife, since the good of this world is dearer to you than the good of the next. Who among men is more lost than you are, if only you knew! Woe to you! How long will you continue to describe the road for travelers by night and take up your stations among men who are bewildered as though you were calling upon the people of this world to leave the world to you? Go slow! Go slow! Woe to you, what does it avail the dark house if the lantern is placed on the roof while the inside is dark and desolate? Likewise will it be no avail to you if the light of wisdom is in your mouths while inside you all is desolate and void. Slaves of the world, but not indeed like pious slaves nor like honorable freemen! The world is about to pull you out by the roots, throw you down upon your faces, and grind your noses into the dust. It will then seize you by your forelocks because of your sins and propel you from behind until it delivers you naked and alone to the King and Judge, who shall acquaint you with your sins and then punish you for your evil deeds."*

Source: Ihya by al Ghazali 3:258-259

Jesus said:

"Seeds grow in a plain but not among rocks. So also, wisdom flourishes in the heart of a humble man but not in the heart of the proud. Do you not see how the man

who flaunts his head to the ceiling will dash it, while he who lowers his head shelters and protects it?"

Source: Ihya by al Ghazali 3:336

Jesus said: *"You shall not attain what you desire except by suffering what you do not desire."*

Source: Ihya by al Ghazali 4:61

Jesus asked the Israelites:

"Where does seed grow?"

They answered, *"In the soil."*

Jesus said:

"Truly I say to you, wisdom grows only in a soil-like heart."

Source: Ihya by al Ghazali 4:347

The disciples asked Jesus, "Spirit of God, is there anyone on earth now who is like you?"

Jesus answered:

"Yes, he whose speech is a mention of God, whose silence is contemplation of God and whose every glance derives a lesson, such a man is like me."

Source: Ihya by al Ghazali 4:411

Jesus said:

"Have no care for tomorrow's gain. If tomorrow is one of your appointed times, your gain will come with your appointed time. If it is not, have no care for the appointed times of others."

Source: Ihya by al Ghazali 4:442

Jesus said to Prophet John son of Zachariah:

"If a man makes mention of you and speaks the truth, give thanks to God. If he is lying, multiply your thanks for God will increase the register of your good deeds without exertion from you."

Source: al Tibr al Masbuk by al Ghazali pg. 21

Jesus said:

"Earthly life consists of three days: a yesterday over which you have no control, a tomorrow which you do not know whether you will attain, and a today which you should put to good use."

Source: Minhaj al Abidin by al Ghazali pg. 29

Jesus said to his students:

"Many a lamp has been extinguished by the wind, and many a devout man has been destroyed by vanity."

Source: Minhaj al Abidin by al Ghazali pg. 65

Jesus said:

"God addressed the world in the following words: 'Serve him who serves me, enslave him who serves you. O world, pass quickly before my friends and do not trick them so that they are seduced by you.'"

Source: Siraj al Muluk by Ibn Abi Randaqa al Turtushi pg. 91

Jesus said:

"A ruler should not be vicious, since it is to him that mankind looks for self-restraint; nor should he be tyrannical, since it is from him that mankind demands justice."

Source: Siraj al Muluk by Ibn Abi Randaqa al Turtushi pg. 182

Jesus said:

"What is forbearance if one is impatient with ignorance? What is strength if one cannot restrain anger? What is worship if one is immodest before God almighty? When fools come to worship they come at an inopportune time and sit above their station. When a crisis occurs, wise counsel departs."

Source: Siraj al Muluk by Ibn Abi Randaqa al Turtushi pg. 577

Jesus said:

"Accept the truth from those who speak falsehood, but do not accept falsehood from those who speak the truth. Be discriminating in your speech so as not to admit into it anything which may be counterfeit."

Source: Sirat al Sayyid al Masih by Abu al Qasim ibn Asakir pg. 161 #176

Jesus used to say:

"He who prays and fasts but does not abandon sin is inscribed in the Kingdom of God as a liar."

Source: Sirat al Sayyid al Masih by Abu al Qasim ibn Asakir pg. 172 #196

Jesus said:

"No man can ever know what faith truly means unless he comes to dislike being praised for his obedience to God."

Source: Sirat al Sayyid al Masih by Abu al Qasim ibn Asakir pg. 175 #200

Jesus said:

"Let him who works good expect a good reward, and let him who works evil not be surprised when punished. He who seizes power unjustly, God will justly make him inherit humiliation; and he who unjustly seizes wealth, God will justly make him inherit poverty."

Source: Sirat al Sayyid al Masih by Abu al Qasim ibn Asakir pg. 176 #203

Jesus was asked, "Who among men is most virtuous?"

So Jesus picked up two handfuls of dust and said: "Which of these two is more virtuous? Men are born from dust, and the most honorable are the most God-fearing."

Source: Sirat al Sayyid al Masih by Abu al Qasim ibn Asakir pg. 176 #204

Jesus used to say:

"No good can come from any knowledge that does not cross the valley with you or make you improve the assembly of men."

Source: Sirat al Sayyid al Masih pg. 187 #224

Jesus said:

"Bear with patience one word from the impudent and you shall gain tenfold."

Source: Kitab Alif Ba by al Balawi 1:464

Jesus said:

"God Almighty hates the man who laughs much without cause and walks much without aim, and hates the mention of a holy book in between pleasantries and joking."

Source: Awarif al Maarif by Shihab al din Umar al Shurawardi 2:243

Jesus said:

"When someone turns a begger away empty-handed, the angels will not visit his house for seven days."

Source: al Mustatraf by al Abshihi 1:9

Jesus said:

"I treated the leper and the blind man and cured them both. I treated the fool and he made me despair. Silence is the [best] reply to the fool."

Source: al Mustatraf by al Abshihi 1:16

Jesus said:

"Woe to you, slaves of this world! What avails the blind man the broad sunlight which he cannot see? So, likewise nothing avails the scholar of great learning if he does not act according to it. How many fruits there are, but not all are useful or edible! How many scholars there are, but not all make use of their learning! Be on your guard against false scholars, who wear woolen garments and bow their heads to the ground but glare up at you from under their eyebrows like wolves. Their words are at variance with their deeds. Who reaps grapes from thorn bushes and figs from colocynth? So also the words of a false scholar yield only falsehood. For the beast of burden, if not well tethered by its owner in the wilderness, makes for its land and kind. So also the learning which is not put into practice by its possessor leaves his heart, abandons him and renders him useless. As a plant thrives only in water and soil, so too, faith can thrive only in knowledge and deed. Woe to you slaves of this world! Everything has a sign by which it is known and which testifies for or against it. Religion has three signs by which it is known: faith, knowledge and deed."

Source: Ithaf al Sada al Muttaqin by al Zabidi 1:229

Jesus was asked, "Teach us one act through which God will come to love us."

Jesus replied, "*Hate the world and God will love you.*"

Source: Kitab Dhamm al Dunya in Mawsu'at Rasa'il by ibn Abi Dunya 2:170 #415

Jesus said:

"This world is a bridge. Cross this bridge, but do not build upon it."

He was asked, "Prophet of God, would that you ordered us to build a house where we can worship God."

Jesus said, "*Go and build a house on water.*"

They asked him, "How can anything sound be built on water?"

Jesus answered, "*How can there be sound worship if it is joined with love of the world?*"

Source: Ihya by al Ghazali 4:218

Jesus said:

About water, "*This is my father.*"

About bread, "*This is my mother.*"

Meaning they nourish the body just as parents do.

Source: al Iqd al Farid by ibn Abd Rabbihi 6:290

Jesus said: "*You disciples are afraid of sin. We prophets are afraid of disbelief.*"

Source: Ihya by al Ghazali 4:169

GRADED BIBLICAL GOSPEL QUOTES ATTRIBUTED TO JESUS

Matthew 5:39-40

5:39 *"But I am saying to you,*

Not to stand against an evil man, but whoever will slap you upon your right jaw, turn also the other to him.

5:40 *And to him, who is willing to have a lawsuit against you and wants to take away your tunic, then also allow for him to take your outer garment."*

The above two verses were graded Red by the Jesus Seminar Scholars as having a 92% chance of being actually spoken by Jesus.

Luke 6:29 part A

6:29 *"Hold near to the one who beats you upon the one jaw, the other also,"*

The above verse was graded Red by the Jesus Seminar Scholars as having a 92% chance of being actually spoken by Jesus.

Luke 6:29 part B

6:29 *"and from the one who takes away your garment, do not forbid him your tunic also."*

The above verse was graded Red by the Jesus Seminar Scholars as having a 90% chance of being actually spoken by Jesus.

Luke 6:20

6:20 And he lifted up his eyes toward his disciples and said:

"You the poor are fortunate, because the kingdom of God is yours."

The above verse was graded Red by the Jesus Seminar Scholars as having a 91% chance of being actually spoken by Jesus.

Matthew 5:3

5:3 *The poor in spirit are fortunate, because theirs is the kingdom of the heavens.*

The above verse was graded Pink by the Jesus Seminar Scholars as having a 63% chance of being actually spoken by Jesus.

Matthew 5:41

5:41 *And the one who will compel you to go one mile, proceed with him two.*

The previous verse was graded Red by the Jesus Seminar Scholars as having a 90% chance of being actually spoken by Jesus.

Luke 6:27 part B

6:27 *Love your enemies*

The previous verse was graded Red by the Jesus Seminar Scholars as having a 84% chance of being actually spoken by Jesus.

Matthew 5:44 part B

5:44 *Love your enemies*

The previous verse was graded Red by the Jesus Seminar Scholars as having a 77% chance of being actually spoken by Jesus.

Luke 6:32

6:32 *And if you love those who love you, what gratitude is this for you have? For even sinners love those who love them.*

The previous verse was graded Pink by the Jesus Seminar Scholars as having a 56% chance of being actually spoken by Jesus.

Luke 6:35 part A

6:35 However, love your enemies

The previous verse was graded Pink by the Jesus Seminar Scholars as having a 56% chance of being actually spoken by Jesus.

Mark 12:17 part B

And Jesus answered and said to them,

Give to Caesar the things which are Caesar's and give to God the things which are God's.

The previous verse was graded Red by the Jesus Seminar Scholars as having a 82% chance of being actually spoken by Jesus.

Luke 20:25 part B

20:25 But he said to them,

Now-then, give to Caesar the things which are Caesar's, and to God the things which are God's.

The previous verse was graded Red by the Jesus Seminar Scholars as having a 82% chance of being actually spoken by Jesus.

Matthew 22:21 part C

22:21 They say to him, Caesar's. Then he says to them:

Therefore give to Caesar, the things which are Caesar's, and to God, the things which are God's.

The previous verse was graded Red by the Jesus Seminar Scholars as having a 82% chance of being actually spoken by Jesus.

This famous verse, loved by governments throughout the world, where Jesus is written to have said, "*give unto Caesar's that which is Caesar's*" is doubtful as to it's authenticity and many think it was intentionally inserted by the Roman government to encourage prompt tax payment. Although if we assume it is authentic and something Jesus said, then that still doesn't mean it supports taxation. There are two different ways to interpret this famous passage, the core of which is, "*So give back to Caesar what is Caesar's, and to God what is God's.*" It is of the utmost importance to recognize just who is asking the question and the context. The alleged question is posed by the Jewish Pharisees who have an evil intention. The preceding bible verses say the Pharisees told Jesus "*we know that you are a man*" and Jesus doesn't say he is anything more than a man, which if he were God or a son of God he would have been obliged to clarify. The Pharisees then ask Jesus if it is right to pay the imperial tax. Now the Pharisees already know that according to the Torah it is incorrect and illegal to pay taxes to a deified emperor, they themselves taught tax evasion in the temples during Jesus' era and didn't pay citing religious reasons. Since the Romans were also oppressing the Jews it added another reason to the list of reasons why it was wrong to pay taxes to the Roman Empire. So the Pharisees already know that it's wrong, but they just wanted Jesus to say it publicly so they could get him in trouble with the authorities(Herodians), which they brought along as an audience. If Jesus said it was right to pay taxes the Pharisees would brand him as a sell-out and Roman collaborator destroying his credibility as a religious teacher. Whether Jesus says it's right or wrong to pay taxes, the Pharisees will be able to ruin him using his own words. Thus prior to answering Jesus says " *You hypocrites, why are you trying to trap me?*" Then Jesus is famously reported to have replied, after being informed the image of Caesar is on the coin, "*So give back to Caesar what is Caesar's, and to God what is God's.*" The reason Jesus asked whose image was on the coin showed bystanders that he did not possess any roman money of his own and was unfamiliar with it. Also by having the Pharisees say the *"image of Caesar"* was on the coin it revealed that the coin itself was wrong, because it had a graven image which was against the second commandment. The coin was doubly wrong because Caesar was worshiped as a god. So the Pharisees are made to look bad for having the idolatrous coin to begin with and it shows they are materialistic, right after Jesus calls them hypocrites too. In comparison the verse shows Jesus is ascetic without idolatrous money. The verbal reply of Jesus is practically perfect. Since Jesus taught everything is created by God and everything is provided for and owned by God, his response is clear cut and implies not to pay taxes to the people killing truth and the people of truth, since Caesar doesn't really own anything and God is the owner of all. The Pharisees already knew Jesus taught this and that it was correct, but the words in which he said it wouldn't be interpreted as such if they were reported to the Romans. To the Romans they would have thought Jesus was advocating to pay taxes in Roman coin because Caesar minted the coins. As a result of the clever way Jesus said it was wrong to pay taxes, the Pharisees knew the authorities wouldn't understand it and wouldn't punish Jesus for encouraging tax evasion. This is an example of the ingenuity of Jesus in that he taught the truth in highly sensitive environment in a way that he couldn't get in trouble for it. Only someone who knew Jesus and the extent of his full teachings would understand this statement correctly. If someone didn't know Jesus and heard this statement out of context they would get a different meaning that didn't seem to be controversial and would be in favor of taxation. Although according to Jewish law it was sinful to pay this tax, had Jesus actually meant people were to pay taxes the Pharisees would have discredited him. This didn't happen because Jesus correctly taught not to pay taxes to the deified emperor, but did it in a way that only religious people would understand. Basically Jesus taught in a code, where if you knew religion and Jesus you understood him. If you didn't know religion or Jesus you wouldn't understand him correctly. This biblical verse is a microcosm of religion in general and how it is misunderstood. It displays how governments can manipulate one saying of a prophet out of context to support their policies, or manipulate a religion in order to increase the popularity of the state. Whereas in reality anyone who knew the context of what was said and took it in context with all of the teachings of Jesus would understand correctly, thereby demonstrating the importance of completely learning a religion. To take a couple of statements by themselves out of context from the whole of the religious teachings of a prophet would give one the wrong understanding and idea of that prophet and their religion. Inappropriately, many people think they can understand an entire religion based on a few verses or phrases taken out of context with the meanings provided to them, or by using their own understandings as to what the meanings are. This is caused by what I call the arrogance of ignorance, in which an individual doesn't know enough about the religion to understand what a religious saying or phrase means, but they don't know that they don't know enough to understand correctly. May God guide us and give us proper understanding and the ability to know when we are qualified to understand. I'm not saying that nothing about a religion can be understood unless a person researches the entire religion, but there are some things that simply cannot be correctly comprehended without a firm grasp upon the subject. Some things everybody can understand, while other things can only be understood by experts. Sadly, we all tend to consider ourselves experts, even when we are not. There is another way the biblical verse about giving back to Caesar what is Caesar's and to God what is God's can be interpreted. This interpretation requires knowledge of roman economics and taxation. As it pertains to the verse, what was Caesar's is widely believed and understood to have been coins with the face of Caesar on them, minted by him. Throughout the Roman Empire many alternate forms of currency were used and exchanged. However roman taxes could only be paid in roman coins, just as today American taxes can only be paid in U.S. dollars. As a side note that is the only reason why the U.S. paper/digital dollar has any value, because it will stop the U.S. government from shoving a gun in your face during tax season; there is no other reason for paper to have such a high value when it is so abundant. Anyways in this interpretation the tax question asked by the Pharisees would be concerning foreign income, which the Roman Empire taxed just as America does. For example, as an American citizen if I live and work in another country and get paid in and use that country's currency the U.S.A. will still tax me every year.

Other countries wouldn't tax you if you lived outside of their territory, but America and Eritrea are the only two countries in the world who do. However, I will not be allowed to pay off the American tax goons with foreign currency because they only accept U.S. dollars. Likewise the Roman Empire had a similar policy when it came to foreign income or income earned in Rome with foreign currency. The only ones who were paid directly in coins with Caesar on it were employees of the Roman government. Other than working for the state, the ways to obtain roman coins were limited to those who had their personal metals melted by the Roman mints or received roman coins for selling goods or services to state employees. Some business owners may have paid their employees in roman currency, but local currencies were more desirable as wages and since Roman coins came from Rome they were typically a collector's item unlikely to be paid out as wages or used much by non-Romans. Thus the question asked to Jesus was a specific tax question. To which Jesus advises what we today would call tax evasion. In that Jesus is written to have basically said: only pay Caesar if you have coins which belong to Caesar which were minted by him. Which means Jesus was saying if you don't have any roman currency then don't pay any roman taxes. Since only employees of the roman government were paid in roman coins this meant he was advocating that nobody but government employees should pay taxes to Rome and that the government has no right to take money that isn't theirs. However Jesus eloquently stated this in a way where the typical irreligious pro-taxation person wouldn't understand. By the Pharisees having Roman coins it cast suspicion on them as collaborators with the Imperial Government, with Jesus cleverly publicly telling them to give their own money back from where they got it and stop working for Rome. If Jesus were brought to court he would have an easy defense to make and it would be very hard to make the charge of teaching against paying taxes stick even though that's what he did. This is why as the bible says about the Pharisees "*When they heard this, they were amazed. So they left him and went away.*" Neither interpretation is approved by the global governments so few Christian preachers will tell it like it is. Most Christian institutions fear losing their tax-free status or being labeled as enemies of the state. Many religious organizations let this fear influence their actions. I don't mean to pick

Christian institutions out exclusively; I only mentioned them because many teachings espoused by Christian institutions contradict the teachings of the bible because of misinterpretation of the biblical texts. Personally, I tend to lean towards the first interpretation of the "paying to Caesar what is Caesar's" verse as being more correct, if the verse is legitimately attributed. Yet with an 18% chance that Jesus never said it then it is speculative regardless.

Matthew 5:42 part A

5:42 *Give to the one who asks you*

The previous verse was graded Red by the Jesus Seminar Scholars as having a 81% chance of being actually spoken by Jesus.

Luke 6:30 part A

6:30 *Give to everyone who asks you*

The previous verse was graded Red by the Jesus Seminar Scholars as having a 81% chance of being actually spoken by Jesus.

Luke 10:30-35

10:30 But Jesus, having taken it in, said,

"A certain man was going-down from Jerusalem to Jericho, and he fell among robbers, who both stripped him

and laid wounds on him. They went away, and left him, being half dead.

10:31 But a certain priest was going-down on that road according to {i.e. by} coincidence, and having seen him, he evaded him.

10:32 Now likewise, a Levite also happened to be in the place, when he came and saw him, he evaded him too.

10:33 But a certain traveling Samaritan came to him, and having seen him, had compassion.

10:34 And having gone to him, he bound up his various traumas, pouring on them oil and wine. And having mounted him upon his own animal, he led him to an inn and cared for him.

10:35 And upon the next-day, after he went out, having put out two denarii, he gave them to the innkeeper and said, Care for him, and if you spend anything over that, I will be repaying you, while I am coming back through again."

The previous verse was graded Red by the Jesus Seminar Scholars as having a 81% chance of being actually spoken by Jesus.

To understand this parable you have to understand the various denominations of Judaism. Judaism evolved to be built upon what I'd call "taqleed" or blind following of Rabbis, where they consider the words of their Rabbis to have the authority of God. Rabbinical Judaism actually teaches that it is a greater sin to oppose the teachings of the Rabbis than to oppose the teachings of their "Torah". They say this is because their "Torah" which they say is from God can be examined and any Jews who hear of such deviant teachings can realize they are wrong. Yet since Jews believe God gave Rabbis authority, similar to how Catholics view the Church Popes, Rabbinical rulings are not subject to scrutiny so one must accept them and therefore any who dispute the ruling of the Rabbis must suffer the death penalty because they are disbelieving in the Rabbinacal authority itself and there is no way a Jew who hears such teachings can find proof that the Rabbinical position is right and the dissenters opinion is wrong. That is where the Karaites differ. The Karaites are Jews who reject everything about Rabbinical Judaism and say they only follow the Torah revealed to Moses (which they think is the Tanakh) the way Moses followed it and that they don't need Rabbis to update the religion to accommodate the changing political seasons or times. Basically Karaites are Jewish Fundamentalists who claim to follow the text according to the prophet and only follow the interpretations if they agree with the text. Except they have absolutely no clue what Moses thought of the text or said about it, so basically they say their interpretations are only accepted if they think it agrees with the text. In contrast to other Jews, the Karaites trace Jewish lineage through the father instead of the mother. Rabbinical Jews say to be a Jew your mother has to be a Jew while Karaites say it's the father and not the mother that determines Jewishness based on biblical lineages always being traced through the father. Karaites also have their own unique calendar system. Karaites reject the Talmud and other Rabbinical texts and the Pharisaic methodology as do the Samaritans. Whereas unbeknownst to Christians, Samaritans are actually a different denomination of non-Rabbinical Judaism. Most Christians hear of stories about Jesus interacting with Samaritans or commenting on them and think it's a proof that Jesus was sent to all mankind, Jew and Gentile. However Samaritans are just Jews descended from 3 of the 12 tribes of Israel who rejected the taqleed doctrine of

Rabbinical authority/ infallibility. The Samaritans' book which they claim is the Torah is different than the book Rabbinical Jews claim is the Torah. Samaritans believe all the post-Moses biblical stuff is all false and their version of the Torah has about 6,000 differences with the Rabbinical Masoretic version of the Torah, as well as the Karaite version of the Torah. Thus the non-Samaritan Rabbis falsely taught that Samaritans weren't Jews. Christians later taught the same because they adopted the same doctrine of Rabbinical Authority but said it was the Church or Papal Authority and Christians adopted similar texts as Rabbinical Jews did in their Tanakh. Then because Christians found no evidence of Jesus preaching to non-Jews they found Samaritans a good ploy to exploit for the reason why Christians like Paul preached to non-Jews. Like the Karaites, the Samaritans also trace Jewish lineage through the father instead of the mother. Which may be the reason why Christians favored the Rabbinical doctrines of Judaism, because since Jesus had no physical father then technically Jesus wouldn't be Jewish according to the biblically correct way of Jewishness being traced through patrilineal genealogy. Whereas if Jesus wasn't Jewish then Christians would be in big trouble and all those alleged old testament prophecies they hijacked to claim a Jewish Messiah would be false. Although don't think the Samaritans or Karaites were upon guidance in comparison to Rabbinical Jews, both were astray; but both groups were also practicing forms of Judaism. Interestingly Samaritans also have a different version of the 10 commandments. There used to be tens of thousands of Samaritans but now there are about 900 worldwide. Samaritans consider Rabbinical Jews and Karaites as heretics, Rabbinical Jews consider Samaritans and Karaites heretics and Karaites consider the non-Karaites heretics just the same. All these Jewish groups existed long before and during the time of Jesus. In a Christian context the Rabbinical Jews are like Catholics, Karaites are like Protestants and Samaritans are like each sect of Christianity which got killed off when Catholicism was made the official religion of the Roman Empire in 380 CE. The problem with Karaites and Samaritans is the alleged authenticity of their texts and they don't have the knowledge of how Moses interpreted or implemented the text. They don't have the Torah or the "Sunnah of Moses". The Rabbinical Jews have the same authenticity issues but at least they admit they don't know how Moses interpreted the Torah, unfortunately they say they know better than he did anyways. All the Rabbinical Jews, the Karaites and Samaritans believe that Jesus was not a prophet and they don't believe in Muhammad either. Yet as with Rabbinical Jews, the Karaites and Samaritans still believe there is one religion for Jews and another for everyone else. However, many differences various Jews may have, all the learned Jews agree that Islam is the religion of Noah and that "*other religion which all non-Jews must follow to enter heaven*". The primary doctrinal difference between most forms of Judaism and Islam, aside from laws, is that Muslims believe the Jews changed the Torah because Allah says so, Muhammad said so and Jesus said so. Whereas Muslims also believe Jesus was a prophet and that his mother was a virgin when she gave birth. Whereas the Jews reject the prophethood of Jesus and Muhammad. Fundamentally this means that according to the religion of Judaism, if Jesus was a prophet then Islam is the one and only true religion. But what about Christianity? Shouldn't the Jews like Christians more than Muslims because they have just one extra prophet while Muslims have two? Well that all depends on the Jew. In Judaism there are various denominations, among them there is the Jew who practices a form of Judaism, then there are ethnic Jews and there are Zionists. Although an important thing regarding "ethnic Jews" is that your status as a ethnic Jew depends on which form of Judaism you follow. To put this in perspective it'd be like saying if you follow X branch of Christianity you have black skin and if you follow Y or Z branch of Christianity then you have white skin. So the Jews have different definitions of who is and who isn't an ethnic Jew. Ethnicity for Jews is actually a matter of religious belief, your religious denomination determines your race in Judaism. But we aren't supposed to call it racism, because it's Judaism and because of being such an old faith we are told to be polite, and some countries even ban criticism calling it antisemitism thereby protecting racist Jews and worst of all unreligious politically hungry bloodthirsty Zionists. Regarding their attitudes towards gentiles, true religious Jews like Muslims more than Christians, Zionists like Christians more than Muslims and ethnic Jews are in the middle split between both sides. Religious Jews liking Muslims more than Christians may come as a shock to Christians and the Western world at large because Christians are always talking about Judeo-Christian values. The problem with that worldview is that only Christians have propagated it, the Jews never have. Religiously Jews consider Christians to be no different than idolaters and polytheists, they even say Christians are idolaters and polytheists whom God will damn to eternal hell when they die. On the other hand Jews view Muslims as pure monotheists who like them do not make pictures or associate partners with God or invent savior man-god deities. According to Jews and Jewish law, Islam is the only other monotheistic religion in the world. Muslims don't have a reciprocal rule like this in return because in Islam the racist religion of Judaism is not and never has been valid despite them laying claim to ethnically Jewish Islamic prophets. The point is that Jews don't consider Christians to be monotheists and they don't think they worship the same God as Jews do; those who practice Judaism even say this publicly. Lamentably, most Christians have never met a genuine practicing Jew in their life but just meet ethnic Jews or fakes who do Hannukah and half-heartedly attempt to eat kosher. Which again it will shock Christians to learn that Jews don't believe in a Judeo-Christian system and say Christians don't worship who they or the Jewish prophets worshipped. The reason Christians propagated the "Judeo-Christian" notion was to make Christianity seem to have Jewish roots instead of pagan roots. Whereas because Christians kept violently eradicating Jews for thousands of years, eventually the Jewish majority stopped protesting the falsity of the Judeo-Christian notion as loudly. The Zionists exploited this to get Christian military support for Israel, while ethnic Jews frequently play along because it makes them get sympathy and respect from Christians. Thus you have Jews saying Islam is valid and Muslims saying Judaism is not valid, while the Jews say Christianity is not valid while some modern Zionist minded Christians say Judaism is valid. Religious Jews publicly declare to any who will listen to them that Jews practicing Judaism go to heaven, Christians go to hell and any non-Jew who practices Islam goes to heaven. Of course Muslims say only Muslims go to heaven but the point is that the Judeo-Christian concept is Christian propaganda. Obviously a logical person would say the Jews would be politically stupid to pander to Muslims and validify Islam while nullifying Christianity when the Muslims nullify Judaism and some Christians validify Judaism. Hence the myth of Judeo-Christian values exists, because the Jews have nothing to gain by publicizing their true religious opinions regarding Islam and Christianity and they have much to gain by allowing the myth to continue or even helping it along. Religiously Christians say the world is Judeo-Christian vs. all. Jews says the world was/is Islam-Judeo-Islam vs. all. While Muslims say it always has been and always will be Islam vs. all and Jewish ethnicity isn't important in the opinion of the Creator of all, but what matters is the creeds and deeds and that Jews just misunderstood chosen people due to many prophets being Jewish and distorted it as racism, while Christians blended Jesus with pagan polytheism of demi-gods and so Muhammad came to clarify and guide everybody from their various errors back to the pure prophetic monotheism as taught by the previous prophets.

Luke 6:21 part A

6:21 *You who hunger now are fortunate, because you will be fully-fed.*

The previous verse was graded Red by the Jesus Seminar Scholars as having a 79% chance of being actually spoken by Jesus.

Matthew 5:6

5:6 *Those who hunger and are thirsty for righteousness are fortunate, because they will be fully-fed.*

The previous verse was graded Pink by the Jesus Seminar Scholars as having a 59% chance of being actually spoken by Jesus.

Luke 6:21 part B

6:21 *You who are weeping now are fortunate, because you will be laughing.*

The previous verse was graded Red by the Jesus Seminar Scholars as having a 79% chance of being actually spoken by Jesus.

Matthew 5:4

5:4 *"Those who are mourning are fortunate, because they will be comforted."*

The previous verse was graded Pink by the Jesus Seminar Scholars as having a 73% chance of being actually spoken by Jesus.

Mark 4:30-32

4:30 And he said,

To what may be similar to the kingdom of God? Or in what parable may we put it in comparison?

4:31 *It is like a kernel of a mustard-seed, which, whenever it should be sown upon the earth, though it is least compared to all the seeds that are upon the earth,*

4:32 *yet whenever it should be sown, it shoots-up and becomes greater than all the herbs and produces great branches; so-then the birds of the heaven are able to nest under its shadow.*

The previous verse was graded Pink by the Jesus Seminar Scholars as having a 74% chance of being actually spoken by Jesus.

Luke 13:18-19

13:18 *Now he said, The kingdom of God is similar to what? And what will I make it similar to?*

13:19 *It is similar to a kernel of a mustard-seed, which a man took and cast into his own garden, and it grew and became a great tree, and the birds of the heaven nested in its branches.*

The previous verse was graded Pink by the Jesus Seminar Scholars as having a 69% chance of being actually spoken by Jesus.

Matthew 13:31-32

13:31 *He placed another parable before them, saying: The kingdom of the heavens is similar to a kernel of a mustard-seed, which a man took and sowed in his field;*

13:32 *which indeed is least compared to all of the other seeds, but whenever it is grown, it is greater than the herbs and becomes a tree, so-then the birds of the heaven come and nest in its branches.*

The previous verse was graded Pink by the Jesus Seminar Scholars as having a 67% chance of being actually spoken by Jesus.

This alleged mention of the mustard seed parable also has parallels from Quran and Hadith.

Quran 21:47

وَنَضَعُ ٱلْمَوَازِينَ ٱلْقِسْطَ لِيَوْمِ ٱلْقِيَامَةِ فَلَا تُظْلَمُ نَفْسٌ شَيْئًا ۖ وَإِن كَانَ مِثْقَالَ حَبَّةٍ مِّنْ خَرْدَلٍ أَتَيْنَا بِهَا ۗ وَكَفَىٰ بِنَا حَاسِبِينَ (٤٧)

And We place the scales of justice for the Day of Resurrection, so no soul will be treated unjustly at all. And if there is [even] the weight of a mustard seed, We will bring it forth. And sufficient are We as accountant. (47)

Quran 48:29

هُوَ ٱلَّذِىٓ أَرْسَلَ رَسُولَهُۥ بِٱلْهُدَىٰ وَدِينِ ٱلْحَقِّ لِيُظْهِرَهُۥ عَلَى ٱلدِّينِ كُلِّهِۦ ۚ وَكَفَىٰ بِٱللَّهِ شَهِيدًا (٢٨) مُّحَمَّدٌ رَّسُولُ ٱللَّهِ ۚ وَٱلَّذِينَ مَعَهُۥٓ أَشِدَّآءُ عَلَى ٱلْكُفَّارِ

رُحَمَاءُ بَيْنَهُمْ تَرَىٰهُمْ رُكَّعًا سُجَّدًا يَبْتَغُونَ فَضْلًا مِّنَ ٱللَّهِ وَرِضْوَٰنًا سِيمَاهُمْ فِى وُجُوهِهِم مِّنْ أَثَرِ ٱلسُّجُودِ ذَٰلِكَ مَثَلُهُمْ فِى ٱلتَّوْرَىٰةِ وَمَثَلُهُمْ فِى ٱلْإِنجِيلِ كَزَرْعٍ أَخْرَجَ شَطْـَٔهُۥ فَـَٔازَرَهُۥ فَٱسْتَغْلَظَ فَٱسْتَوَىٰ عَلَىٰ سُوقِهِۦ يُعْجِبُ ٱلزُّرَّاعَ لِيَغِيظَ بِهِمُ ٱلْكُفَّارَ وَعَدَ ٱللَّهُ ٱلَّذِينَ ءَامَنُوا۟ وَعَمِلُوا۟ ٱلصَّٰلِحَٰتِ مِنْهُم مَّغْفِرَةً وَأَجْرًا عَظِيمًا (٢٩)

It is He who sent His Messenger with guidance and the religion of truth to manifest it over all religion. And sufficient is Allah as Witness. (28) Muhammad is the Messenger of Allah; and those with him are powerful against the disbelievers, merciful among themselves. You see them bowing and prostrating [in prayer], seeking bounty from Allah and [His] pleasure. Their mark is on their faces from the trace of prostration. That is their description in the Torah. And their description in the Injeel is as a plant which produces its offshoots and strengthens them so they grow firm and stand upon their stalks, delighting the sowers - so that Allah may enrage by them the disbelievers. Allah has promised those who believe and do righteous deeds among them forgiveness and a great reward. (29)

It was narrated from 'Abdullah that the Messenger of Allah (ﷺ) said:

"No one will enter Paradise who has pride in his heart equal to the weight of a grain of mustard seed, and no one will enter Hell who has faith in his heart equal to the weight of a grain of mustard seed."

Source: Sunan Ibn Majah 4173 Grade: Sahih

Luke 12:22-23

12:22 *Now he said to his disciples, Because of this, I am saying to you, Do not be anxious for your life, what you might eat; nor yet what you might clothe your body with.*

12:23 *The life you have is more-than the nourishment, and the body is more-than the clothing.*

The previous verse was graded Pink by the Jesus Seminar Scholars as having a 75% chance of being actually spoken by Jesus.

Matthew 6:25

6:25 *Because of this, I am saying to you, Do not be anxious for your life, what you may eat and what you may drink; nor for what you may clothe your body with. Is not the life worth more-than the nourishment and the body worth more-than the clothing?*

The previous verse was graded Pink by the Jesus Seminar Scholars as having a 75% chance of being actually spoken by Jesus.

Luke 15:8-9

15:8 *Or what woman having ten two-denarii-coins, if she loses one two-denarii-coin, does not light a lamp and sweep the house, and seek carefully until which time she should find it?*

15:9 *And having found it, she calls together her friends and her neighbors, saying, Rejoice together with me, because I found the two-denarii-coin which I lost.*

The previous verse was graded Pink by the Jesus Seminar Scholars as having a 75% chance of being actually spoken by Jesus.

Luke 4:24

4:24 But he said, *"Assuredly I am saying to you, No prophet is acceptable in his fatherland."*

The previous verse was graded Pink by the Jesus Seminar Scholars as having a 71% chance of being actually spoken by Jesus.

John 4:44

4:44 For Jesus himself testified, *"that a prophet has no honor in his own fatherland."*

The previous verse was graded Pink by the Jesus Seminar Scholars as having a 67% chance of being actually spoken by Jesus.

Matthew 13:57

13:57 And they were being offended at him. But Jesus said to them, *"A prophet is not without honor, except in his fatherland and in his own house."*

The previous verse was graded Pink by the Jesus Seminar Scholars as having a 60% chance of being actually spoken by Jesus.

Mark 6:4

6:4 But Jesus said to them, *"A prophet is not without honor, except in his fatherland and among his own relatives and in his own house."*

The previous verse was graded Pink by the Jesus Seminar Scholars as having a 58% chance of being actually spoken by Jesus.

Luke 16:13 part A

16:13 *No domestic servant is able to serve two lords; for either he will hate the one and will love the other; for either he will hold to one and despise the other.*

The previous verse was graded Pink by the Jesus Seminar Scholars as having a 72% chance of being actually spoken by Jesus.

Matthew 6:24 part A

6:24 *"No one is able to serve two lords, for either he will hate the one and will love the other; or he will hold to one and will despise the other."*

The previous verse was graded Pink by the Jesus Seminar Scholars as having a 72% chance of being actually spoken by Jesus.

There is a Quranic parallel to this concept of serving two lords or masters.

Quran 39:29

ضَرَبَ ٱللَّهُ مَثَلًا رَّجُلًا فِيهِ شُرَكَآءُ مُتَشَٰكِسُونَ وَرَجُلًا سَلَمًا لِّرَجُلٍ هَلْ يَسْتَوِيَانِ مَثَلًا ٱلْحَمْدُ لِلَّهِ بَلْ أَكْثَرُهُمْ لَا يَعْلَمُونَ (٢٩)

Allah presents an example: a slave owned by quarreling partners and another belonging exclusively to one man - are they equal in comparison? Praise be to Allah! But most of them do not know. (29)

Quran 23:84-92

قُل لِّمَنِ ٱلْأَرْضُ وَمَن فِيهَآ إِن كُنتُمْ تَعْلَمُونَ (٨٤) سَيَقُولُونَ لِلَّهِ قُلْ أَفَلَا تَذَكَّرُونَ (٨٥) قُلْ مَن رَّبُّ ٱلسَّمَٰوَٰتِ ٱلسَّبْعِ وَرَبُّ ٱلْعَرْشِ ٱلْعَظِيمِ (٨٦) سَيَقُولُونَ لِلَّهِ قُلْ أَفَلَا تَتَّقُونَ (٨٧) قُلْ مَنْ بِيَدِهِۦ مَلَكُوتُ كُلِّ شَىْءٍ وَهُوَ يُجِيرُ وَلَا يُجَارُ عَلَيْهِ إِن كُنتُمْ تَعْلَمُونَ (٨٨) سَيَقُولُونَ لِلَّهِ قُلْ فَأَنَّىٰ تُسْحَرُونَ (٨٩) بَلْ أَتَيْنَٰهُم بِٱلْحَقِّ وَإِنَّهُمْ لَكَٰذِبُونَ (٩٠) مَا ٱتَّخَذَ ٱللَّهُ مِن وَلَدٍ وَمَا كَانَ مَعَهُۥ مِنْ إِلَٰهٍ إِذًا لَّذَهَبَ كُلُّ إِلَٰهٍۭ بِمَا خَلَقَ وَلَعَلَا بَعْضُهُمْ عَلَىٰ بَعْضٍ سُبْحَٰنَ ٱللَّهِ عَمَّا يَصِفُونَ (٩١) عَٰلِمِ ٱلْغَيْبِ وَٱلشَّهَٰدَةِ فَتَعَٰلَىٰ عَمَّا يُشْرِكُونَ (٩٢)

Say, [O Muhammad], "To whom belongs the earth and whoever is in it, if you should know?" (84) They will say, "To Allah." Say, "Then will you not remember?" (85) Say, "Who is Lord of the seven heavens and Lord of the Great Throne?" (86) They will say, "[They belong] to Allah." Say, "Then will you not fear Him?" (87) Say, "In whose hand is the realm of all things - and He protects while none can protect against Him - if you should know?" (88) They will say, "[All belongs] to Allah." Say, "Then how are you deluded?" (89) Rather, We have brought them the truth, and indeed they are liars. (90) Allah has not taken any son, nor has there ever been with Him any deity. [If there had been], then each deity would have taken what it created, and some of them would have sought to overcome others. Exalted is Allah above what they describe [concerning Him]. (91) [He is] Knower of the unseen and the witnessed, so high is He above what they associate [with Him]. (92)

Matthew 13:44

13:44 "Again, the kingdom of the heavens is similar to a treasure that has been hidden in the field; which a man found and hid, and he proceeds away and sells all his things from his joy, as many things as he has and buys that field."

The previous verse was graded Pink by the Jesus Seminar Scholars as having a 71% chance of being actually spoken by Jesus.

Matthew 13:45-46

13:45 *Again, the kingdom of the heavens is similar to a man, who is a merchant, seeking beautiful pearls;*

13:46 *who found one very precious pearl, went and has sold all his things, as many things as he had, and bought it.*

The previous verse was graded Pink by the Jesus Seminar Scholars as having a 68% chance of being actually spoken by Jesus.

Luke 15:4-6

15:4 *What man out of you, having a hundred sheep and having lost one out of them, does not leave the ninety nine in the wilderness and travel to what has been lost, until he should find it?*

15:5 *And having found it, he places it upon his own shoulders, rejoicing.*

15:6 *And after he went to his house, he calls together his friends and his neighbors, saying to them, Rejoice* together with me, because I found my sheep which has been lost.

The previous verse was graded Pink by the Jesus Seminar Scholars as having a 70% chance of being actually spoken by Jesus.

Matthew 18:12-13

18:12 "What are you thinking? If there should happen to be any man who has a hundred sheep, and one out of them might be misled, does he not seek the one which is misled, having left the ninety nine, traveling upon the mountains?

18:13 And if he happens to find it, assuredly I am saying to you, He rejoices over it more than over the ninety nine which have not been misled."

The previous verse was graded Pink by the Jesus Seminar Scholars as having a 67% chance of being actually spoken by Jesus.

There is another famous incident involving a case of 99 sheep versus 1 sheep mentioned in the Quran.

Quran 38:21-26

۞ وَهَلْ أَتَىٰكَ نَبَؤُاْ ٱلْخَصْمِ إِذْ تَسَوَّرُواْ ٱلْمِحْرَابَ (٢١) إِذْ دَخَلُواْ عَلَىٰ دَاوُۥدَ فَفَزِعَ مِنْهُمْ ۖ قَالُواْ لَا تَخَفْ ۖ خَصْمَانِ بَغَىٰ بَعْضُنَا عَلَىٰ بَعْضٍ فَٱحْكُم بَيْنَنَا بِٱلْحَقِّ وَلَا تُشْطِطْ وَٱهْدِنَآ إِلَىٰ سَوَآءِ ٱلصِّرَٰطِ (٢٢) إِنَّ هَٰذَآ أَخِى لَهُۥ تِسْعٌ

وَتِسْعُونَ نَعْجَةً وَلِيَ نَعْجَةٌ وَٰحِدَةٌ فَقَالَ أَكْفِلْنِيهَا وَعَزَّنِى فِى ٱلْخِطَابِ (٢٣) قَالَ لَقَدْ ظَلَمَكَ بِسُؤَالِ نَعْجَتِكَ إِلَىٰ نِعَاجِهِۦ ۖ وَإِنَّ كَثِيرًا مِّنَ ٱلْخُلَطَآءِ لَيَبْغِى بَعْضُهُمْ عَلَىٰ بَعْضٍ إِلَّا ٱلَّذِينَ ءَامَنُوا۟ وَعَمِلُوا۟ ٱلصَّـٰلِحَـٰتِ وَقَلِيلٌ مَّا هُمْ ۗ وَظَنَّ دَاوُۥدُ أَنَّمَا فَتَنَّـٰهُ فَٱسْتَغْفَرَ رَبَّهُۥ وَخَرَّ رَاكِعًا وَأَنَابَ ۩ (٢٤) فَغَفَرْنَا لَهُۥ ذَٰلِكَ ۖ وَإِنَّ لَهُۥ عِندَنَا لَزُلْفَىٰ وَحُسْنَ مَـَٔابٍ (٢٥) يَـٰدَاوُۥدُ إِنَّا جَعَلْنَـٰكَ خَلِيفَةً فِى ٱلْأَرْضِ فَٱحْكُم بَيْنَ ٱلنَّاسِ بِٱلْحَقِّ وَلَا تَتَّبِعِ ٱلْهَوَىٰ فَيُضِلَّكَ عَن سَبِيلِ ٱللَّهِ ۚ إِنَّ ٱلَّذِينَ يَضِلُّونَ عَن سَبِيلِ ٱللَّهِ لَهُمْ عَذَابٌ شَدِيدٌۢ بِمَا نَسُوا۟ يَوْمَ ٱلْحِسَابِ (٢٦)

And has there come to you the news of the adversaries, when they climbed over the wall of [his] prayer chamber - (21) When they entered upon David and he was alarmed by them? They said, "Fear not. [We are] two adversaries, one of whom has wronged the other, so judge between us with truth and do not exceed [it] and guide us to the sound path. (22) Indeed this, my brother, has ninety-nine ewes, and I have one ewe; so he said, 'Entrust her to me,' and he overpowered me in speech." (23) [David] said, "He has certainly wronged you in demanding your ewe [in addition] to his ewes. And indeed, many associates oppress one another, except for those who believe and do righteous deeds - and few are they." And David became certain that We had tried him, and he asked forgiveness of his Lord and fell down bowing [in prostration] and turned in repentance [to Allah]. (24) So We forgave him that; and indeed, for him is nearness to Us and a good place of return. (25) [We said], "O David, indeed We have made you a successor upon the earth, so judge *between the people in truth and do not follow [your own] desire, as it will lead you astray from the way of Allah." Indeed, those who go astray from the way of Allah will have a severe punishment for having forgotten the Day of Account. (26)*

The Tafsir commentary by Abul Al Maududdi says regarding these Quran verses about Prophet David:

"He was alarmed because the two men had appeared in the private quarters of the ruler of the land suddenly, by climbing over the wall, instead of going before him by the proper entrance.

To understand what follows one should note that the complainant did not say that the other person had taken away his only ewe and added it to his own ewes, but said that he was asking for it, and since he was a powerful person he had prevailed over him in the matter and he could not reject his demand, being a weak and poor man.

Here, one should not doubt that the Prophet David gave his decision after hearing only what one party had to say. The fact of the matter, is that when the respondent kept quiet at the complaint of the complainant and said nothing in defense it by itself amounted to a confession by him. That is why the Prophet David came to the conclusion that the facts of the case were the same as the complainant had stated.

This shows that the Prophet David had certainly committed an error, and it was an error which bore some resemblance with the case of the ewes. Therefore, when he gave a decision on it, he at once realized that he was being put to the test. But the nature of the error was not such as could be forgiven, or if forgiven, it would have deposed him from his high rank. Allah Himself says: "When he fell down prostrate and repented, he was not only forgiven but his high rank in the world and the Hereafter also remained unaffected.

This is the warning that Allah gave the Prophet David on accepting his repentance along with giving him the good news of exalting his rank. This by itself shows that the error that he had committed contained an element of the desires of the flesh; it also pertained to the abuse of power and authority; and it was an act which was unworthy of a just and fair-minded ruler.

We are confronted with three questions here:

(1) What was the error that the Prophet David committed?

(2) Why has Allah made only tacit allusions to it instead of mentioning it openly and directly?

(3) What is its relevance to the present context?

The people who have studied the Bible (the Holy Book of the Jews and Christians) are not unaware that in this

Book the Prophet David has been accused clearly of committing adultery with the wife of Uriah the Hittite and then marrying her after having Uriah intentionally slain in a battle. It has also been alleged that this same woman, who had surrendered herself to the Prophet David, while being another man's wife, was the mother of the Prophet Solomon. This story is found with all its details in chapters 11 and 12 of the Second Book of Samuel in the Old Testament. It had been included in it centuries before the revelation of the Qur'an. Any Jew or Christian who read his Holy Book anywhere in the world, or heard it read, was not only aware of this story but also believed in it as true. It spread through them, and even in the present time no book is written in the West on the history of the Israelites and the Hebrew religion, in which this charge against the Prophet David is not repeated.

When this story was so well known among the people there was no need that a detailed account of it should have been given in the Qur'an, nor is it the way of Allah to mention such things openly in His Book. That is why only tacit allusions have been made to it here as well as pointed out what the actual event was and what the people of the Book have turned it into. The actual event as one clearly understands from the aforesaid statement of the Qur'an was:

The Prophet David peace be upon him had only expressed this desire before Uriah (or whatever be the name of the man) that he should divorce his wife; as this desire had been expressed not by a common man but by an illustrious king and a great Prophet before a member of the public, the man was finding himself constrained to yield to it even in the absence of any compulsion. On this occasion, before the man could act as the Prophet David had desired, two righteous men of the nation suddenly made their appearance before David and presented before him this matter in the form of an imaginary case. At first, the Prophet David thought it was a real case, and so gave his decision after hearing it. But as soon as he uttered the words of the decision, his conscience gave the warning that the parable precisely applied to the case between him and the person, and that the act which he was describing as an injustice had issued forth from his own person. As soon as he realized this, he fell down prostrate, repented and reversed his decision. "

The question, as to how this event took the ugly shape as related in the Bible, also becomes obvious after a little consideration. It appears that the Prophet David had come to know of the unique qualities of the woman through some means and had started thinking that she should be the queen of the country instead of being the wife of an ordinary officer, Overwhelmed by the thought he expressed the desire before her husband that he should divorce her. He did not see any harm in it because it was not looked upon as anything improper among the Israelites. It was an ordinary thing among them that if a person happened to like the wife of another, he would freely request him to give her up for him. Nobody minded such a request, and often it so happened that friends would divorce their wives for each other's sake of their own accord, so that the other may marry her. However, when the Prophet David expressed this desire, he did not realize that the expression of such a desire could be without compulsion and coercion when expressed by a common Man, but it could never be so when expressed by a king. When his attention was drawn to this aspect of the matter through a parable, he gave up his desire immediately, and the thing was forgotten. But afterwards when, without any desire or planning on his part, the woman's husband fell martyr on the battlefield, and he married her, the evil genius of the Jews started concocting stories and this mischievous mentality became even more acute after a section of the Israelites turned hostile to the Prophet Solomon. Under these motives the story was invented that the Prophet David, God forbid, had seen Uriah's wife washing herself from the roof of his palace. He had her called to his house and committed adultery with her and she had conceived. Then he had sent Uriah on the battle-front to fight the children of Ammon, and had commanded Joab, the army commander, to appoint him in the forefront of the battle where he should be killed. And when he was killed, he married his widow, and from the same woman the Prophet Solomon (peace be upon him) was born. The wicked people described all these false accusations in their "Holy Book", so that they should go on reading it generation after generation and slandering the two most illustrious men of their community, who were their greatest benefactors after the Prophet Moses.

A section of the commentators of the Qur'an has almost entirely accepted these tales that have reached them through the Israelites. They have dropped only that part of these traditions in which mention has been made of the accusation of adultery against the Prophet David and the woman's having conceived. The rest of the story as found in the traditions reproduced by them is the same as it was well known among the Israelites. Another group of the commentators has altogether denied that any such act was ever committed by the Prophet David, which bore any resemblance with the case of the ewes. Instead of this, they have put forward such interpretations of this story as are wholly baseless, unauthentic and without relevance to the context of the Qur'an itself. But among the Muslim commentators themselves there are some who have accepted the truth and the facts of the story through the clear references made to it in the Qur'an. Here are, for instance, some of their views:

Both Masruq and Said bin Jubair have related this saying of Hadrat 'Abdullah bin 'abbas. "The only thing that the Prophet David did was that he expressed his desire before the woman' husband that he should give up his wife for him."

Zamakhshari writes in his commentary Al-Kashshaf. 'The way Allah has narrated the story of the Prophet David indicates that he had only expressed his desire before the man that he should leave his wife for him."

Abu Bakr al-Jassas has expressed the opinion that the woman was not the other man's wedded wife but was only his betrothed. The Prophet David had also asked for the same woman's hand in marriage. This earned him Allah's displeasure, for he had asked for her hand in spite of the fact that another Muslim had already asked for her hand, and the Prophet David had several wives already with him in his house. (Ahkam al-Qur an). Some other commentators also have expressed the same opinion, but this does not entirely conform to what the Qur'an has said. The words of the suitor as related in the Qur'an are to the effect: "I have only one ewe; he says: Give this ewe also in my charge." The Prophet David also said the same thing in his decision: "This person has certainly wronged you in demanding your ewe to be added to his ewes." This parable could apply to the case between the Prophet David and Uriah only in case the woman was the latter's wife. Had it been the case of asking for the woman's hand when another Muslim had already asked for her hand, the parable would have been like this: "I desired to have an ewe, and this man said: I crave this also for me."

Qadi Abu Bakr Ibn al-'Arabi has discussed this question in detail in his Ahkam al-Quran and concluded: "What actually happened was just that the Prophet David asked one of his men to leave his wife for him and made this demand seriously...The Qur'an does not say that the man gave up his wife on this demand and the Prophet David then married her and the Prophet Solomon was born of her womb... What displeased Allah was that he asked the woman's husband to leave her for him. This act, even if otherwise lawful, was unworthy of the office of Prophethood; that is why he earned Allah's displeasure and was admonished."

This commentary fits in well with the context in which this story has been told. A little consideration of the context shows that it has been related in the Qur'an on this occasion for two objects. The first object is to exhort the Prophet to patience, and for this purpose he has been addressed and told: Have patience on what these people say against you, and remember Our servant David." That is, 'You are being accused only of sorcery and lying, but Our servant David was even accused of adultery and having a person killed willfully, by the wicked people:

therefore, bear up against what you may have to hear from these people." The other object is to warn the disbelievers to the effect: You are committing all sorts of excesses in the world with impunity, but the God in Whose Godhead you are committing these misdeeds does not spare anyone from being called to account. Even if a favorite and beloved servant of His happens to commit but a minor error, He calls him to strict accountability. For this very object the Prophet has been asked: 'Tell them the story of Our servant David, who was a man of high character, but when he happened to commit sin, We did not even spare him but condemned him severely'. "

Prophet David it is said that he was a "possessor of the hands", it will necessarily mean that he possessed great powers. These powers may mean the physical strength which he displayed during his combat against Goliath, military and political power by which he crushed the neighboring idolatrous nations and established a strong Islamic empire, moral strength by which he ruled like a poor king and always feared Allah and observed the bounds set by Him, and the power of worship by virtue of which, besides his occupations in connection with rule and government and fighting in the cause of Allah, he fasted every alternate day and spent a third of the night in worship according to a tradition of Bukhari. Imam Bukhari in his History has related, on the authority of Hadrat Abu ad-Darda', that whenever the Prophet David was mentioned, the Prophet(Muhammad) used to say: "He was the greatest worshiper of God.""

Additionally regarding the mistake of judging the case of the 99 ewe owner versus the one ewe owner.

It was narrated that 'Ali said:

The Messenger of Allah (ﷺ) said: "*If two men come to you for judgement, do not judge in favor of the first one until you listen to what the other one says. Then you will know how to judge.*"

Source: Musnad Ahmad 1285 Grade: Hasan

Luke 15:11-32

15:11 Now he said, A certain man had two sons.

15:12 And the younger of them said to his father, Father, give to me the part of the estate that would be put toward me. And he sectioned off his livelihood to them.

15:13 And not many days after, the younger son gathered it all together and went-abroad into a far region, and he squandered his estate with riotous living there.

15:14 Now having spent all, there became a mighty famine throughout that region, and he began to have lack of things.

15:15 And traveling away, he joined himself to one of the citizens of that region, and he sent him into his fields to feed swine.

15:16 And he was desiring to fill his belly from the carob pods that the swine were eating, and no one was giving anything to him.

15:17 Now after he came to himself, he said, How-many of my father's hired servants are abounding, even of bread? But I am perishing here in famine!

15:18 When I have risen * up, I will be traveling to my father, and will say to him, Father, I sinned at heaven, and in your sight.

15:19 I am no more worthy to be called your son. Make* me like one of your hired servants.

15:20 And having stood up, he came to his father. But while he was still distant, far from him, his father saw him and had compassion, and ran and fell upon his neck and kissed him.

15:21 But the son said to him, Father, I sinned at heaven, and in your sight. I am no longer worthy to be called your son.

15:22 But the father said to his bondservants, Bring out the foremost robe and clothe him, and give him a ring for his hand and shoes for his feet;
15:23 and after you have brought the fattened calf, sacrifice it, and after we have eaten it, let us be joyous.

15:24 Because this one, my son, was dead and then lived again, and lost and then was found. And they began to be joyous.

15:25 Now his elder son was in the field and as he is coming, he drew near to the house, and he heard harmony and dancers.

15:26 And having called to him one of the young-servants, he was inquiring what these things might be.

15:27 But he said to him, Your brother is coming, and your father sacrificed the fattened calf because he has received him back healthy.

15:28 But he was angry and was not willing to enter and therefore his father went out and was pleading him.

15:29 But he answered and said to his father, Behold,

I did serve you for so-many years, and I never passed over a commandment of yours, and yet you never gave me a young-goat, in order that I might be joyous with my friends.

15:31 Now he said to him, Child, you are always with me, and all the things which are mine are yours.

15:32 But it was essential to be joyous and rejoice, because this one, your brother was dead, and then lived again, and lost and then was found.

The previous verses were graded Pink by the Jesus Seminar Scholars as having a 70% chance of being actually spoken by Jesus.

If legitimate, this story about the Prodigal Son not only paints a lesson regarding a repentant sinner being forgiven and rewarded but another lesson in terms of prophethood itself with Jesus foreshadowing Muhammad's prophethood. For if you consider the two sons of Abraham, the brothers Ishmael and Isaac, even though Ishmael was a good prophet his Arab descendants turned away from the prophetic faith into polytheism while it took longer for prophet Isaac's Israeli descendants to turn away as prophets were constantly sent to them to bring them back to guidance. Yet when the majority of Jews turned away from Jesus' message and the non-Semitic Romans and Greeks imposed the corruption of Christianity on the holy land which led to Muhammad being sent as a prophet in Arabia, the people who went thousands of years without a prophet between Ishmael and Muhammad repented and embraced monotheism. Thus the Ismailis or Arabs are the prodigal son returning to monotheism and rewarded with more rewards than the prior generations received which turns to envy. Whereas the Jews who had claimed to be clinging to monotheism and the Christians, both claiming to be working hard for God, rejected this blessing of prophethood amongst the strayed Ismailis/Arabs due to envious arrogance similar to the non-prodigal son in the story of Jesus who refused to accept his brother's repentance and reentry into the household.

Luke 12:27-28

12:27 Consider the lilies, somehow they grow. They do not labor nor do they spin; but I say to you, Even Solomon in all his glory, was not dressed like one of these.

12:28 But if God so dresses-up the grass in the field, which today is here and the next-day is cast into the oven; how-much more will he clothe you, you of small faith?

The previous verse was graded Pink by the Jesus Seminar Scholars as having a 68% chance of being actually spoken by Jesus.

Matthew 6:28 part B to 6:30

6:28 *Learn from the lilies of the field, somehow they are growing; they are not laboring, nor spinning.*

6:29 *But I am saying to you, that even Solomon in all his glory was not dressed like one of these.*

6:30 *But if God so dresses-up the grass of the field, which is here today and the next-day is cast into the oven, will he not much more clothe you? You* of small faith!*

The previous verses were graded Pink by the Jesus Seminar Scholars as having a 68% chance of being actually spoken by Jesus.

As a sidenote the bibles blasphemously slander Prophet Solomon in the Old Testament or Hebrew texts. They accuse him of idolatry and magic but the truth is Jewish racism turned against him because he married the foreigner Queen of Sheba after she accepted monotheism and he allegedly imposed a tax of 666 talents of gold on the Israelites; which the greedy thought to be excessive. Then because the Christians believed the biblical lies Solomon was charged with, the Templar Knights during the crusades excavated Jerusalem searching for Solomon's alleged magic books because they thought biblical data was other than slander. And this is another mishap that Christians fall into in that the bibles they claim are the words of God says Prophet David's son Prophet Solomon died as a magician idolater despite God in that very same book allegedly promising David that Solomon will be forever considered God's beloved firstborn son. Amazingly it is almost like all the various slanders Jews invented about their own prophets they mixed together and combined the Jews and Christians team up to slander Muhammad with the totality of all the Jewish lies said about the prophets before him. Except for the lies the bible attributes to prophets Noah and Lot. Wherein the bibles say Noah got so drunk after disembarking the Ark that he passed out naked then cursed his descendants for covering him up. Wherein the bibles say Lot the cousin of Abraham got so drunk after leaving Sodom that he had sex with both his daughters on two consecutive nights. These are clear blasphemous slanders against prophets that are in the Jewish and Christian books they label sacred revelation. Much is said in the Quran about Prophet Solomon and his lifelong goodness. Since this is a book about Jesus I will suffice with 1 Quranic quote to exonerate this other prophet whom Jesus had nothing but good things to say about, thereby opposing the slanderous Jewish texts of Hebrew, which was a language unknown to Solomon since it didn't exist in his lifetime.

Quran 2:97-103

قُلْ مَن كَانَ عَدُوًّا لِّجِبْرِيلَ فَإِنَّهُ نَزَّلَهُ عَلَىٰ قَلْبِكَ بِإِذْنِ ٱللَّهِ مُصَدِّقًا لِّمَا بَيْنَ يَدَيْهِ وَهُدًى وَبُشْرَىٰ لِلْمُؤْمِنِينَ (٩٧) مَن كَانَ عَدُوًّا لِّلَّهِ وَمَلَـٰٓئِكَتِهِۦ وَرُسُلِهِۦ وَجِبْرِيلَ وَمِيكَىٰلَ فَإِنَّ ٱللَّهَ عَدُوٌّ لِّلْكَـٰفِرِينَ (٩٨) وَلَقَدْ أَنزَلْنَآ إِلَيْكَ ءَايَـٰتٍۭ بَيِّنَـٰتٍۢ وَمَا يَكْفُرُ بِهَآ إِلَّا ٱلْفَـٰسِقُونَ (٩٩) أَوَكُلَّمَا عَـٰهَدُوا۟ عَهْدًا نَّبَذَهُۥ فَرِيقٌۭ مِّنْهُم بَلْ أَكْثَرُهُمْ لَا يُؤْمِنُونَ (١٠٠) وَلَمَّا جَآءَهُمْ رَسُولٌۭ مِّنْ عِندِ ٱللَّهِ مُصَدِّقٌۭ لِّمَا مَعَهُمْ نَبَذَ فَرِيقٌۭ مِّنَ ٱلَّذِينَ أُوتُوا۟ ٱلْكِتَـٰبَ كِتَـٰبَ ٱللَّهِ وَرَآءَ ظُهُورِهِمْ كَأَنَّهُمْ لَا يَعْلَمُونَ (١٠١) وَٱتَّبَعُوا۟ مَا تَتْلُوا۟ ٱلشَّيَـٰطِينُ عَلَىٰ مُلْكِ سُلَيْمَـٰنَ وَمَا كَفَرَ سُلَيْمَـٰنُ وَلَـٰكِنَّ ٱلشَّيَـٰطِينَ كَفَرُوا۟ يُعَلِّمُونَ ٱلنَّاسَ ٱلسِّحْرَ وَمَآ أُنزِلَ عَلَى ٱلْمَلَكَيْنِ بِبَابِلَ هَـٰرُوتَ وَمَـٰرُوتَ وَمَا يُعَلِّمَانِ مِنْ أَحَدٍ حَتَّىٰ يَقُولَآ إِنَّمَا نَحْنُ فِتْنَةٌۭ فَلَا تَكْفُرْ فَيَتَعَلَّمُونَ مِنْهُمَا مَا يُفَرِّقُونَ بِهِۦ بَيْنَ ٱلْمَرْءِ وَزَوْجِهِۦ وَمَا هُم بِضَآرِّينَ بِهِۦ مِنْ أَحَدٍ إِلَّا بِإِذْنِ ٱللَّهِ وَيَتَعَلَّمُونَ مَا يَضُرُّهُمْ وَلَا يَنفَعُهُمْ وَلَقَدْ عَلِمُوا۟ لَمَنِ ٱشْتَرَىٰهُ مَا لَهُۥ فِى ٱلْـَٔاخِرَةِ مِنْ خَلَـٰقٍۢ وَلَبِئْسَ مَا شَرَوْا۟ بِهِۦٓ أَنفُسَهُمْ لَوْ كَانُوا۟ يَعْلَمُونَ (١٠٢) وَلَوْ أَنَّهُمْ ءَامَنُوا۟ وَٱتَّقَوْا۟ لَمَثُوبَةٌۭ مِّنْ عِندِ ٱللَّهِ خَيْرٌۭ لَّوْ كَانُوا۟ يَعْلَمُونَ (١٠٣)

Say, "Whoever is an enemy to Gabriel - it is [none but] he who has brought the Qur'an down upon your heart, [O Muhammad], by permission of Allah, confirming that which was before it and as guidance and good tidings for the believers." (97) Whoever is an enemy to Allah and His angels and His messengers and Gabriel and Michael - then indeed, Allah is an enemy to the disbelievers. (98) And We have certainly revealed to you verses [which are] clear proofs, and no one would deny them except the defiantly disobedient. (99) Is it not [true] that every time they took a covenant a party of them threw it away? But, [in fact], most of them do not believe. (100) And when a messenger from Allah came to them confirming that which was with them, a party of those who had been given the Scripture threw the Scripture of Allah behind their backs as if they did not know [what it contained]. (101) And they followed [instead] what the devils had recited during the reign of Solomon. It was not Solomon who disbelieved, but the devils disbelieved, teaching people magic and that which was revealed to the two angels at Babylon, Harut and Marut. But the two angels do not teach anyone unless they say, "We are a trial, so do not disbelieve [by practicing magic]." And [yet] they learn from them that by which they cause separation between a man and his wife. But they do not harm anyone through it except by permission of Allah. And the people learn what harms them and does not *benefit them. But the Children of Israel certainly knew that whoever purchased the magic would not have in the Hereafter any share. And wretched is that for which they sold themselves, if they only knew. (102) And if they had believed and feared Allah, then the reward from Allah would have been [far] better, if they only knew. (103)*

Luke 12:24

12:24 Consider the ravens, that they do not sow nor reap for which there is no storeroom nor a barn, and God nourishes them. How-much more-value do you rather carry than the birds!

The previous verse was graded Pink by the Jesus Seminar Scholars as having a 67% chance of being actually spoken by Jesus.

Matthew 6:26

6:26 Look at the birds of the heaven, that they do not sow, nor reap, nor gather into barns, and your heavenly Father is nourishing them. Are you not rather carrying much more-value-than them?

The previous verse was graded Pink by the Jesus Seminar Scholars as having a 67% chance of being actually spoken by Jesus.

There is a Hadith from Prophet Muhammad teaching similar sentiment.

Abdullah bin Hurairah said:

I heard Abu Tameem al-Jaishani say: I heard `Umar bin al Khattab say: I heard the Messenger of Allah (ﷺ) say: *"If you really put your trust in Allah, He would provide for you as He provides for the birds. Do you not see that they go out with empty stomachs and come back with full stomachs?"*

Source: Musnad Ahmad 373 Grade: Sahih

Matthew 19:24

19:24 *But again I am saying to you, It is easier for a camel to go through a needle's eye, than for a rich man to enter into the kingdom of God.*

The previous verse was graded Pink by the Jesus Seminar Scholars as having a 67% chance of being actually spoken by Jesus.

Luke 18:25

18:25 *For it is easier for a camel to enter in through a needle's eye, than for a rich man to enter into the kingdom of God.*

The previous verse was graded Pink by the Jesus Seminar Scholars as having a 65% chance of being actually spoken by Jesus.

Mark 10:25

10:25 *It is easier for a camel to enter through a needle's eye, than for a rich man to enter into the kingdom of God.*

The previous verse was graded Pink by the Jesus Seminar Scholars as having a 64% chance of being actually spoken by Jesus.

A verse in the Quran also mentions this outlandish concept of a camel entering the eye of a needle.

Quran 7:35-40

يَـٰبَنِىٓ ءَادَمَ إِمَّا يَأْتِيَنَّكُمْ رُسُلٌ مِّنكُمْ يَقُصُّونَ عَلَيْكُمْ ءَايَـٰتِى فَمَنِ ٱتَّقَىٰ وَأَصْلَحَ فَلَا خَوْفٌ عَلَيْهِمْ وَلَا هُمْ يَحْزَنُونَ (٣٥) وَٱلَّذِينَ كَذَّبُواْ بِـَٔايَـٰتِنَا وَٱسْتَكْبَرُواْ عَنْهَآ أُوْلَـٰٓئِكَ أَصْحَـٰبُ ٱلنَّارِ هُمْ فِيهَا خَـٰلِدُونَ (٣٦) فَمَنْ أَظْلَمُ مِمَّنِ ٱفْتَرَىٰ عَلَى ٱللَّهِ كَذِبًا أَوْ كَذَّبَ بِـَٔايَـٰتِهِۦٓ أُوْلَـٰٓئِكَ يَنَالُهُمْ نَصِيبُهُم مِّنَ ٱلْكِتَـٰبِ حَتَّىٰٓ إِذَا جَآءَتْهُمْ رُسُلُنَا يَتَوَفَّوْنَهُمْ قَالُوٓاْ أَيْنَ مَا كُنتُمْ تَدْعُونَ مِن دُونِ ٱللَّهِ قَالُواْ ضَلُّواْ عَنَّا وَشَهِدُواْ عَلَىٰٓ أَنفُسِهِمْ أَنَّهُمْ كَانُواْ كَـٰفِرِينَ (٣٧) قَالَ ٱدْخُلُواْ فِىٓ أُمَمٍ قَدْ خَلَتْ مِن قَبْلِكُم مِّنَ ٱلْجِنِّ وَٱلْإِنسِ فِى ٱلنَّارِ كُلَّمَا دَخَلَتْ أُمَّةٌ لَّعَنَتْ أُخْتَهَا حَتَّىٰٓ إِذَا ٱدَّارَكُواْ فِيهَا جَمِيعًا قَالَتْ أُخْرَىٰهُمْ لِأُولَىٰهُمْ رَبَّنَا هَـٰٓؤُلَآءِ أَضَلُّونَا فَـَٔاتِهِمْ عَذَابًا ضِعْفًا مِّنَ ٱلنَّارِ قَالَ لِكُلٍّ ضِعْفٌ وَلَـٰكِن لَّا تَعْلَمُونَ (٣٨) وَقَالَتْ أُولَىٰهُمْ لِأُخْرَىٰهُمْ فَمَا كَانَ لَكُمْ عَلَيْنَا مِن فَضْلٍ فَذُوقُواْ ٱلْعَذَابَ بِمَا كُنتُمْ تَكْسِبُونَ (٣٩) إِنَّ ٱلَّذِينَ كَذَّبُواْ بِـَٔايَـٰتِنَا وَٱسْتَكْبَرُواْ عَنْهَا لَا تُفَتَّحُ لَهُمْ أَبْوَٰبُ ٱلسَّمَآءِ وَلَا يَدْخُلُونَ ٱلْجَنَّةَ حَتَّىٰ يَلِجَ ٱلْجَمَلُ فِى سَمِّ ٱلْخِيَاطِ وَكَذَٰلِكَ نَجْزِى ٱلْمُجْرِمِينَ (٤٠)

O children of Adam, if there come to you messengers from among you relating to you My verses, then whoever fears Allah and reforms - there will be no fear concerning them, nor will they grieve. (35) But the ones who deny

Our verses and are arrogant toward them - those are the companions of the Fire; they will abide therein eternally. (36) And who is more unjust than one who invents about Allah a lie or denies His verses? Those will attain their portion of the decree until when Our messengers come to them to take them in death, they will say, "Where are those you used to invoke besides Allah?" They will say, "They have departed from us," and will bear witness against themselves that they were disbelievers. (37) [Allah] will say, "Enter among nations which had passed on before you of jinn and mankind into the Fire." Every time a nation enters, it will curse its sister until, when they have all overtaken one another therein, the last of them will say about the first of them "Our Lord, these had misled us, so give them a double punishment of the Fire. He will say, "For each is double, but you do not know." (38) And the first of them will say to the last of them, "Then you had not any favor over us, so taste the punishment for what you used to earn." (39) Indeed, those who deny Our verses and are arrogant toward them - the gates of Heaven will not be opened for them, nor will they enter Paradise until a camel enters into the eye of a needle. And thus do We recompense the criminals. (40)

Luke 11:19-20

11:19 *But if I cast out demons by Beelzebub, by whom do your sons cast them out? Because of this, they will be your judges.*

11:20 *But if I cast out demons by the finger of God; consequently, the kingdom of God has arrived-unexpectedly upon you.*

The previous verses were graded Pink by the Jesus Seminar Scholars as having a 64% chance of being actually spoken by Jesus.

Matthew 12:27-28

12:27 *And if I cast out demons by Beelzebub, in whom do your sons cast them out? They will be your judges because of this.*

12:28 *But if I cast out demons with the Spirit of God; consequently, the kingdom of God has arrived-unexpectedly upon you.*

The previous verses were graded Pink by the Jesus Seminar Scholars as having a 56% chance of being actually spoken by Jesus.

What about Christian exorcisms? Not the movies, I'm referencing actual real-life demonic possession where the demon leaves after a Christian minister intervenes. I once studied to be a Catholic Exorcist and read that this stuff happens. Does that mean Christianity is true? Well Muslims, Jews, Hindus, Buddhists and Pagans all have their rites of exorcism too. It may surprise you to learn that all types of exorcism work. But they work for different reasons. Remember the goal of a demon is to get a person to worship something other than God and follow the wrong religion, if they can harass a person then that's a bonus but their number one priority is to make someone believe in a false religion. So let's say there is a pagan person who gets possessed by an evil Jinni, which would be considered a devil, science can't explain it and without a doubt it is a demonic possession. The person being a pagan goes to their pagan priest to be exorcised and have the demon cast out. After a dramatic encounter the demon finally leaves at the behest of the pagan priest. Then what? The person being freed from the demon credits this pagan religion as being what caused this demon to leave and he devotes himself wholeheartedly to this pagan faith for the rest of his life telling everyone his exciting story of being possessed and saved by the power of his pagan deity. Is this not the exact result the demon wanted? So, when a priest is standing over a person with a cross telling the demon to leave in the name of Christ, that demon has absolutely no reason to leave and the priest has no power over it no matter how much the demon may pretend to be hurt by whatever the priest says or does. Remember these demons can make statues talk and move; they can be quite theatrical when they want to be. The demon possessing this person wants the experience to be traumatic for the victim and everyone involved, especially if the people subscribe to a false religion. In that case the more publicity the demon can get the better, although they are careful to not make it seem like they are trying to get attention lest it betray their plot. The demon wants the person to follow a false religion, so when a priest puts up a cross the demon looks and thinks, "*If I leave right now and never return, this person will believe this cross saved them and the priest is truthful and that Christianity is true despite it being false. I want this person to follow a false religion and all who hear this person's story will think Christianity is true because I left. So I will leave.*" The priest then credits Christianity with the victory just as the demon desired and as with other false religions people believe in the false doctrines even more, as a result of the formerly possessed sharing their story. Islamic exorcisms are different and the Jinn are revealed for who they are. The Jinn in a Muslim exorcism are treated for what they are, free-willed creations of God who are oppressively possessing contrary to the law of God which they are supposed to obey. Sometimes the Jinni is being forced against their will to possess someone because of a magician who is oppressing them or another Jinn that is threatening them, so possession can be very complicated with multiple parties involved. Sometimes the person unintentionally harmed a invisible Jinni not knowing it and the Jinni is just taking revenge in an illegal manner. What is most remarkable about Muslim exorcisms is that the Jinn are encouraged to become Muslim. Since the Jinn have freewill, they have many religions of their own and not all follow the truth. Islam is the true religion and the only one the Creator will accept from both humans and jinn. Both humans and jinn are eligible for paradise and hell, and both were created to worship the Creator alone. Therefore the Muslim exorcist isn't content with simply getting rid of the demon, but also guiding the Jinni to worship God and become a good Muslim. Sometimes it actually happens where the Jinni becomes a Muslim, apologizes and leaves. Other times the Jinni refuses to become Muslim, but leaves because they don't want to hear Quran because it hurts them to hear the original Arabic revelation, or they fear the punishment of Allah for oppression. Sometimes the Jinni is stubborn and Allah doesn't will for it to depart at that time, so he allows it to remain and the person remains afflicted out of his wisdom. The point is that every religion can perform an exorcism that results in the demonic possession ending, so a successful exorcism alone doesn't constitute proof of that particular religion being true. Demonic possession usually happens to someone who isn't following the religion of Islam, because if Islam is practiced properly, it should protect one from jinn. But even if a practicing Muslim were afflicted by magic or jinn possession it could be in order for God to use that person's suffering as an expiation for their sins, or a way for them to get a reward they couldn't earn any other way. However sometimes demonic possession results in death. Death comes by the will of Allah when the angel of Death is sent to extract a soul, so we mustn't credit a demon with causing it, but if a demon is using exorcism to get people to believe in a false religion then why aren't exorcisms always successful? One reason for this is that an unsuccessful exorcism of a false religion sometimes has the desired demonic effect by making those who witnessed the tragic death become more devout, especially since the witnesses will likely share the story. Thus the demon's plan is successful in that respect. One difference between the Islamic exorcism and all others is that there is no elite class of exorcists. Of course some study and train to become specialists, but any Muslim could theoretically do an exorcism, even the person who is possessed. The Arabic Quran being the literal word of God verbatim has a visible effect which is very powerful and every Muslim knows some of the Arabic Quran to recite it while praying, unless they're new Muslims. Truly God is the only one who can protect us from anything and everything, including himself. In comparison if you read a bible on someone who is possessed in any language, or even someone who's not possessed it has absolutely no effect at all. Whereas even if you don't understand the Arabic Quran or even know that what you are hearing is the Quran it has an effect on everyone who hears it which is unlike anything else, particularly if they are possessed. You might be interested to see an Islamic exorcism and videos of them abound on the internet demonstrating how different and genuine Islamic exorcism is from other religions. Although personally I don't think they should be filmed because of the honor of the person afflicted. For instance if you were possessed and having unpleasant reactions/experiences you wouldn't want someone to put a video of you up on the internet so everyone can see you in such an embarrassing condition. Some other religions don't even allow exorcisms to be videotaped. When I studied to be a Catholic exorcist one of the first rules I learned was that it was forbidden to videotape an exorcism, which is why it is so ironic that Catholic exorcist hollywood movies are so popular. This is another reason why it's bad for people to base their religion on what they see in a hollywood production that has absolutely no responsibility to be factual. It is simply an entertainment business, movies are made for money and not many people will pay money to see the truth, it is much easier to sell a lie. Besides all actors and actresses are bearing false witness by acting anyways so they are lying even if its not a fiction film. Most Ahl-Kitab (people of Scripture) today are Ahl-TV (people of Television) and they spend more time watching a screen of sinfulness than studying the faith they profess. Hence people become heartless due to mindless heart numbing entertainment that creates a cycle of depression and desensitization to sin. People have become so foolish that now demons don't even need to do an actual possession to get a person to follow a false religion, all they have to do is make a movie about an exorcism and the masses flock to falsehood in fear from what they saw in the film. Although some Jinn don't take the horror approach to convert people, they take the healing approach. Jinn are capable of fixing health ailments, many of which they are capable of causing just so they can later fix them under religious auspices. There are 3 ways they can to do this. 1. They cause a disease or symptoms and then stop causing the disease/symptoms. 2. They use Jinn developed medicine to heal ailments humans have, which they may or may not have caused to begin with. 3. The Jinn use magic to heal people. Personally whenever someone tells me that people get miraculously healed at their place of worship I immediately think their religion is false because it's due to such tangible healings done by magicians that false religions get promoted and prosper. If not for the magical "healings" marketed as being miraculous typically they'd have no good logical reason to give for you to believe in their religion at all. Hence that's why Jinn employ the above 3 methods to "heal" people. Hindus, Buddhists, Jews, Muslims, Christians, Sikhs, Polytheists, everyone of every traditional faith has miraculous healing stories that are genuine where people were ill or disabled and came to X place or person and after some religious activity were "miraculously healed". So obviously we can't use such "miracle healings" as evidence to determine a true religion when every religion has genuine "miracle healings" occurring in both the past and the present. Jinn can simply pinch a nerve to cause paralysis or blindness and then leave when evil religious rituals take place in order to make people believe in any false religion. This is actually one type of magic, many magicians in the ancient as well as the modern eras heal people from medical problems explicitly by doing something for the Jinn so they in exchange medically heal the person on behalf of the magician. Just because a devil is evil doesn't mean they don't know medicine and aren't willing to heal people for evil purposes. Satan can act as a doctor too, he doesn't always want to hurt you, if physically healing you can help him achieve his goals then he will heal for the sake of evil. Yet surprisingly Christians tend to rely on such "healings" as proof of them being upon the truth more than any religious group. This is despite the bible explicitly saying there will be false preachers teaching false religions who will perform miraculous feats like healing and Jesus quotes affirming that demons can be cast out by demons. Most Christians tend to say those bible verses are about other Christians, not them and the other Christians say the same. Comically neither imagine they could both be wrong. One former neighbor of mine was a Christian Pastor, he became the Pastor because he bought the Church property. One day I went to visit him with my Christian mother who uses a walking cane. This Pastor told my mom to come to his special church where the disabled are healed completely by his prayers to Jesus and leave their canes, crutches and wheelchairs behind forever. My mom never went but in hindsight I should've asked why she had to go to his Church to get healed and couldn't get healed on the spot by him then and there if he was as powerful as he claimed. Christians tend to rely on healings because Jesus was known as a healer, so they think if they can heal it means they are right just as Jesus' healings were a proof of his truth. Yet Jesus himself according to the bible admitted that devilish people with devils can perform "miracle cures". Biblically the Jews during the time of Jesus accused him of being one such person who heals people via magic or devils and do you know what Jesus said in reply? He just said how he wasn't like that. But more importantly he never said "that's not possible because only good people upon true religions can perform miraculous healing". Jesus knew that devils can cooperate with people to cure the ill or injured "miraculously", he never refuted the concept or possibility, he just clarified that was not how he operated. However biblically Jesus did confirm that "miraculous healings" can indeed occur as a result of people who are upon a false religion doing religious activities which God hates and will punish them for. Even the anti-christ will "miraculously heal" many people. That's what makes it funny when Christians claim, genuinely or fraudulently, that "healings" take place at their religious activities because the same exact thing is done at the anti-christ's religious gatherings. So healing or exorcising doesn't mean the religious teacher isn't lying when they say they are upon truth. They truthfully may believe what they say but neither healing nor exorcism is a valid proof that any particular religion is true. Thus healings cannot be used as a proof and anyone who understands religion and has solid proof for their faith will not rely on "healings" or exorcism successes. Magicians can perform "miraculous healings" and they use the evil jinn (devils) to do so, thus when I hear of a "miracle healer" I don't take it as a "proof" but a caution sign to stay away just in case they aren't a fraud and are actually using magic or devils to heal. Rather than be skeptical of "healings" or exorcists it's smarter to be cautious for safety reasons because they could be very dangerous people working with devils, knowingly or unknowingly. Of which the one ignorantly working with devils can be even more dangerous than the intentional accomplice. However don't get too paranoid, the point is that just because a Jinn leaves after a Christian exorcism or a Christian gets healed doesn't make Christianity true in the slightest, nor does it make Jesus divine in any way. In fact the exorcisms done by Jesus as depicted in the bible are actually a proof against Christianity, because in one report when Jesus cast demons out they eagerly told people he was the "son of God" as they left and Jesus would angrily tell the demons to be silent because they were lying. The disbelieving demons were the first to ever biblically claim Jesus was a son of God. In response biblical Jesus said demons were blasphemously lying with such a claim.

Luke 20:46

20:46 Take-heed, stay away from the scribes, who wish to walk in long robes and love greetings in the marketplaces and foremost seats in the synagogues and foremost-places in the suppers;

The previous verse was graded Pink by the Jesus Seminar Scholars as having a 61% chance of being actually spoken by Jesus.

Mark 12:38-39

12:38 And he said to them in his teaching, Beware* of things from the scribes, who wish to walk in long robes and to have greetings in the marketplaces,

12:39 and the foremost seats in the synagogues and foremost-places at the suppers.

The previous verse was graded Pink by the Jesus Seminar Scholars as having a 61% chance of being actually spoken by Jesus.

Matthew 23:5-7

23:5 And they are practicing all their works in order to be seen by men. And they widen their phylacteries and magnify the hems of their garments,

23:6 *and they love the foremost-place in the suppers and the foremost seats in the synagogues,*

23:7 *and the greetings in the marketplaces and to be called by men, Rabbi, rabbi.*

The previous verse was graded Pink by the Jesus Seminar Scholars as having a 53% chance of being actually spoken by Jesus.

Luke 11:43

11:43 *Woe to you Pharisees! Because you love the foremost seat in the synagogues and the greetings in the marketplaces.*

The previous verse was graded Pink by the Jesus Seminar Scholars as having a 53% chance of being actually spoken by Jesus.

Matthew 6:3

6:3 *But when you are doing charity, do not let your left hand know what your right hand is doing,*

The previous verse was graded Pink by the Jesus Seminar Scholars as having a 60% chance of being actually spoken by Jesus.

There is a Hadith from Prophet Muhammad matching this alleged statement of Jesus and elaborating on the reward for compliance with it.

Narrated Abu Huraira:

The Prophet (ﷺ) said, "*Seven (people) will be shaded by Allah by His Shade on the Day of Resurrection when there will be no shade except His Shade.*

(They will be), a just ruler,

a young man who has been brought up in the worship of Allah,

a man who remembers Allah in seclusion and his eyes are then flooded with tears,

a man whose heart is attached to mosques (offers his compulsory congregational prayers in the mosque),

two men who love each other for Allah's Sake,

a man who is called by a charming lady of noble birth to commit illegal sexual intercourse with her, and he says, 'I am afraid of Allah,'

and (finally), a man who gives in charity so secretly that his left hand does not know what his right hand has given."

Source: Sahih al-Bukhari 6806

Luke 12:16-20

12:16 Now he spoke a parable to them, saying:

The farmland of a certain rich man was fertile;

12:17 *and he was reasoning in himself, saying, What should I do , because I have nowhere, in which, I will gather together my fruits?*

12:18 *And he said, I will be doing this: I will be taking down my barns and build greater ones. And I will be gathering together there, all my fruits of labor and my good things.*

12:19 *And I will be saying to my soul, Soul, you have many good things laying up for many years; rest yourself, eat, drink, and be joyous.*

12:20 *But God said to him, Fool, your soul is asked back from you in this night, and the things which you prepared, to whom will they be going?*

The previous verses were graded Pink by the Jesus Seminar Scholars as having a 59% chance of being actually spoken by Jesus.

Matthew 7:3-5

7:3 *And why are you looking at the speck, the one in your brother's eye, but do not consider the beam in your own eye?*

7:4 *Or how will you say to your brother, Allow me, that I may cast out the speck from your eye, and behold, the beam in your own eye?*

7:5 *You hypocrite, first cast out the beam out of your own eye, and then you will see precisely to cast out the speck from your brother's eye.*

The previous verses were graded Pink by the Jesus Seminar Scholars as having a 56% chance of being actually spoken by Jesus.

Luke 6:41-42

6:41 *But why are you looking at the speck which is in your brother's eye, but do not consider the beam which is in your own eye?*

6:42 *Or how are you able to say to your brother, Brother, Allow me, that I may cast out the speck which is in your eye, while you yourself do not see the beam which is in your own eye? You hypocrite, cast out the beam first out of your own eye, and then you will see precisely to cast out the speck which is in your brother's eye.*

The previous verses were graded Pink by the Jesus Seminar Scholars as having a 54% chance of being actually spoken by Jesus.

Matthew 20:1-15

20:1 *For the kingdom of the heavens is similar to a man who is a householder, who went out at the same time every morning to hire workers into his vineyard.*

20:2 *And having agreed together with the workers at a denarius a day {a standard day's pay}, he sent them into his vineyard.*

20:3 *And he went out around the third hour {i.e. 9:00 AM} and saw others standing idle in the marketplace;*

20:4 *and he said to those men, You also, proceed* into the vineyard and I will be giving you whatever is just. And they went.*

20:5 *Again, they went out around the sixth {i.e. Noon} and the ninth hour; {i.e. 3:00 PM} and he did* likewise.*

20:6 *Now around the eleventh hour, {i.e. 5:00 PM} he went out and found others standing idle, and he says to them, Why are you* standing here idle the whole day?*

20:7 They say to him, Because no one hired us. So he says to them, You also, proceed into the vineyard and you will be receiving whatever is just.

20:8 Now after it became evening, the lord of the vineyard says to his commissioner, Call the workers and after you have begun from the last until the first, give to them their wages.

20:9 And after those hired around the eleventh hour {i.e. 5:00 PM} came, they each received a denarius apiece.

20:10 Now after the first came, they supposed that they will be receiving more, but they themselves also received a denarius apiece.

20:11 But having received it, they were murmuring against the householder,

20:12 saying, These last ones did* only one hour of work, and you made* them equal to us, who bore the burden of the day and the burning heat.

20:13 But he answered and said to one of them, Comrade, I am not wronging you. Did you not agree together with me for a denarius?

20:14 Take up the thing which is yours and proceed

away. It is my will to give to this last one, as I also did to you.

20:15 *Or is it not legal for me to do what I will in the things which are mine? Or should your eye be evil, because I am good?*

The previous verses were graded Red by the Jesus Seminar Scholars as having a 77% chance of being actually spoken by Jesus.

Matthew 20:16

20:16 *So the last will be first, and the first last; for* many are invited but few are chosen.*

The previous verse was graded Pink by the Jesus Seminar Scholars as having a 58% chance of being actually spoken by Jesus.

Mark 10:31

10:31 *But many who are first will be last, and the last will be first.*

The previous verse was graded Pink by the Jesus Seminar Scholars as having a 50% chance of being actually spoken by Jesus.

Matthew 19:30

19:30 *But many will be last who are first, and first who are last.*

The previous verse was graded Pink by the Jesus Seminar Scholars as having a 50% chance of being actually spoken by Jesus.

Luke 13:30

13:30 *And behold, there are last who will be first and there are first who will be last.*

The previous verse was graded Pink by the Jesus Seminar Scholars as having a 47% chance of being actually spoken by Jesus.

This alleged statement of the first being last and the last being first has baffled Christians for centuries but there are Hadith from Prophet Muhammad that explains and matches what Jesus allegedly taught.

It was narrated that Abu Hurairah said:

"The Messenger of Allah (ﷺ) said: 'Allah led those who came before us astray from Friday. Saturday was for the Jews and Sunday was for the Christians. And they will lag behind us until the Day of Resurrection. We are the last of the people of this world but we will be the first to be judged among all of creation.'"

Source: Sunan Ibn Majah 1083 Grade: Sahih

Narrated Abu Musa: *The Prophet (ﷺ) said,*

"The example of Muslims, Jews and Christians is like the example of a man who employed laborers to work for him from morning till night. They worked till midday and they said, 'We are not in need of your reward.' So the man employed another batch and said to them, 'Complete the rest of the day and yours will be the wages I had fixed (for the first batch). They worked until the time of the `Asr prayer and said, 'Whatever we have done is for you.' He employed another batch. They worked for the rest of the day till sunset, and they received the wages of the two former batches."

Source: Sahih al-Bukhari 558

Luke 18:10 to 18:14 part A

18:10 *Two men went-up into the temple to pray; the first one a Pharisee and the other a tax collector.*

18:11 *The Pharisee stood with {i.e. by} himself, was praying these things with himself, God, I give-thanks to you, that I am not like the rest of men: ravening, unrighteous ones, adulterers or just-like this tax collector.*

18:12 *I fast twice in the week; I tithe of all things, as many things as I procure.*

18:13 *And the tax collector, standing from afar, was not even willing to lift up his eyes to heaven, but was beating at his chest, saying, God, be lenient to me, the sinner.*

18:14 *I say to you, This one went-down to his house, having been made righteous rather than that man.*

The previous verses were graded Pink by the Jesus Seminar Scholars as having a 77% chance of being actually spoken by Jesus.

Advice to Christians from Allah in the Quran, the Prophet Muhammad and Muslim Scholars

Quran 2:135-136

وَقَالُواْ كُونُواْ هُودًا أَوْ نَصَٰرَىٰ تَهْتَدُواْ ۗ قُلْ بَلْ مِلَّةَ إِبْرَٰهِۦمَ حَنِيفًا ۖ وَمَا كَانَ مِنَ ٱلْمُشْرِكِينَ (١٣٥) قُولُوٓاْ ءَامَنَّا بِٱللَّهِ وَمَآ أُنزِلَ إِلَيْنَا وَمَآ أُنزِلَ إِلَىٰٓ إِبْرَٰهِۦمَ وَإِسْمَٰعِيلَ وَإِسْحَٰقَ وَيَعْقُوبَ وَٱلْأَسْبَاطِ وَمَآ أُوتِيَ مُوسَىٰ وَعِيسَىٰ وَمَآ أُوتِيَ ٱلنَّبِيُّونَ مِن رَّبِّهِمْ لَا نُفَرِّقُ بَيْنَ أَحَدٍ مِّنْهُمْ وَنَحْنُ لَهُۥ مُسْلِمُونَ (١٣٦)

They say, "Be Jews or Christians [so] you will be guided." Say, "Rather, [we follow] the religion of Abraham, inclining toward truth, and he was not of the polytheists." (135) Say, [O believers], "We have believed in Allah and what has been revealed to us and what has been revealed to Abraham and Ishmael and Isaac and Jacob and the Descendants and what was given to Moses and Jesus and what was given to the prophets from their Lord. We make no distinction between any of them, and we are Muslims [in submission] to Him." (136)

Quran 2:140-141

أَمْ تَقُولُونَ إِنَّ إِبْرَاهِيمَ وَإِسْمَاعِيلَ وَإِسْحَاقَ وَيَعْقُوبَ وَالْأَسْبَاطَ كَانُوا هُودًا أَوْ نَصَارَىٰ ۗ قُلْ أَأَنتُمْ أَعْلَمُ أَمِ اللَّهُ ۗ وَمَنْ أَظْلَمُ مِمَّن كَتَمَ شَهَادَةً عِندَهُ مِنَ اللَّهِ ۗ وَمَا اللَّهُ بِغَافِلٍ عَمَّا تَعْمَلُونَ ﴿١٤٠﴾ تِلْكَ أُمَّةٌ قَدْ خَلَتْ ۖ لَهَا مَا كَسَبَتْ وَلَكُم مَّا كَسَبْتُمْ ۖ وَلَا تُسْأَلُونَ عَمَّا كَانُوا يَعْمَلُونَ ﴿١٤١﴾

Or do you say that Abraham and Ishmael and Isaac and Jacob and the Descendants were Jews or Christians? Say, "Are you more knowing or is Allah?" And who is more unjust than one who conceals a testimony he has from Allah? And Allah is not unaware of what you do. (140) That is a nation which has passed on. It will have [the consequence of] what it earned, and you will have what you have earned. And you will not be asked about what they used to do. (141)

Quran 2:146-147

الَّذِينَ آتَيْنَاهُمُ الْكِتَابَ يَعْرِفُونَهُ كَمَا يَعْرِفُونَ أَبْنَاءَهُمْ ۖ وَإِنَّ فَرِيقًا مِّنْهُمْ لَيَكْتُمُونَ الْحَقَّ وَهُمْ يَعْلَمُونَ ﴿١٤٦﴾ الْحَقُّ مِن رَّبِّكَ ۖ فَلَا تَكُونَنَّ مِنَ الْمُمْتَرِينَ ﴿١٤٧﴾

Those to whom We gave the Scripture know him(the coming of Prophet Muhammad) as they know their own sons. But indeed, a party of them conceal the truth while they know [it]. (146) The truth is from your Lord, so never be among the doubters. (147)

Quran 2:252-257

تِلْكَ آيَاتُ اللَّهِ نَتْلُوهَا عَلَيْكَ بِالْحَقِّ ۚ وَإِنَّكَ لَمِنَ الْمُرْسَلِينَ ﴿٢٥٢﴾ تِلْكَ الرُّسُلُ فَضَّلْنَا بَعْضَهُمْ عَلَىٰ بَعْضٍ ۘ مِّنْهُم مَّن كَلَّمَ اللَّهُ ۖ وَرَفَعَ بَعْضَهُمْ دَرَجَاتٍ ۚ

وَءَاتَيْنَا عِيسَى ٱبْنَ مَرْيَمَ ٱلْبَيِّنَـٰتِ وَأَيَّدْنَـٰهُ بِرُوحِ ٱلْقُدُسِ ۗ وَلَوْ شَآءَ ٱللَّهُ مَا ٱقْتَتَلَ ٱلَّذِينَ مِنۢ بَعْدِهِم مِّنۢ بَعْدِ مَا جَآءَتْهُمُ ٱلْبَيِّنَـٰتُ وَلَـٰكِنِ ٱخْتَلَفُوا۟ فَمِنْهُم مَّنْ ءَامَنَ وَمِنْهُم مَّن كَفَرَ ۚ وَلَوْ شَآءَ ٱللَّهُ مَا ٱقْتَتَلُوا۟ وَلَـٰكِنَّ ٱللَّهَ يَفْعَلُ مَا يُرِيدُ (٢٥٣) يَـٰٓأَيُّهَا ٱلَّذِينَ ءَامَنُوٓا۟ أَنفِقُوا۟ مِمَّا رَزَقْنَـٰكُم مِّن قَبْلِ أَن يَأْتِىَ يَوْمٌ لَّا بَيْعٌ فِيهِ وَلَا خُلَّةٌ وَلَا شَفَـٰعَةٌ ۗ وَٱلْكَـٰفِرُونَ هُمُ ٱلظَّـٰلِمُونَ (٢٥٤) ٱللَّهُ لَآ إِلَـٰهَ إِلَّا هُوَ ٱلْحَىُّ ٱلْقَيُّومُ ۚ لَا تَأْخُذُهُۥ سِنَةٌ وَلَا نَوْمٌ ۚ لَّهُۥ مَا فِى ٱلسَّمَـٰوَٰتِ وَمَا فِى ٱلْأَرْضِ ۗ مَن ذَا ٱلَّذِى يَشْفَعُ عِندَهُۥٓ إِلَّا بِإِذْنِهِۦ ۚ يَعْلَمُ مَا بَيْنَ أَيْدِيهِمْ وَمَا خَلْفَهُمْ ۖ وَلَا يُحِيطُونَ بِشَىْءٍ مِّنْ عِلْمِهِۦٓ إِلَّا بِمَا شَآءَ ۚ وَسِعَ كُرْسِيُّهُ ٱلسَّمَـٰوَٰتِ وَٱلْأَرْضَ ۖ وَلَا يَـُٔودُهُۥ حِفْظُهُمَا ۚ وَهُوَ ٱلْعَلِىُّ ٱلْعَظِيمُ (٢٥٥) لَآ إِكْرَاهَ فِى ٱلدِّينِ ۖ قَد تَّبَيَّنَ ٱلرُّشْدُ مِنَ ٱلْغَىِّ ۚ فَمَن يَكْفُرْ بِٱلطَّـٰغُوتِ وَيُؤْمِنۢ بِٱللَّهِ فَقَدِ ٱسْتَمْسَكَ بِٱلْعُرْوَةِ ٱلْوُثْقَىٰ لَا ٱنفِصَامَ لَهَا ۗ وَٱللَّهُ سَمِيعٌ عَلِيمٌ (٢٥٦) ٱللَّهُ وَلِىُّ ٱلَّذِينَ ءَامَنُوا۟ يُخْرِجُهُم مِّنَ ٱلظُّلُمَـٰتِ إِلَى ٱلنُّورِ ۖ وَٱلَّذِينَ كَفَرُوٓا۟ أَوْلِيَآؤُهُمُ ٱلطَّـٰغُوتُ يُخْرِجُونَهُم مِّنَ ٱلنُّورِ إِلَى ٱلظُّلُمَـٰتِ ۗ أُو۟لَـٰٓئِكَ أَصْحَـٰبُ ٱلنَّارِ ۖ هُمْ فِيهَا خَـٰلِدُونَ (٢٥٧)

These are the verses of Allah which We recite to you, [O Muhammad], in truth. And indeed, you are from among the messengers. (252) Those messengers - some of them We caused to exceed others. Among them were those to whom Allah spoke, and He raised some of them in degree. And We gave Jesus, the Son of Mary, clear proofs, and We supported him with the Pure Spirit. If Allah had willed, those [generations] succeeding them would not have fought each other after the clear proofs had come to them. But they differed, and some of them believed and some of them disbelieved. And if Allah had willed, they would not have fought each other, but Allah does what He intends. (253) O you who have believed, spend from that which We have provided for you before there comes a

Day in which there is no exchange and no friendship and no intercession. And the disbelievers - they are the wrongdoers. (254) Allah - there is no deity except Him, the Ever-Living, the Sustainer of [all] existence. Neither drowsiness overtakes Him nor sleep. To Him belongs whatever is in the heavens and whatever is on the earth. Who is it that can intercede with Him except by His permission? He knows what is [presently] before them and what will be after them, and they encompass not a thing of His knowledge except for what He wills. His Kursi extends over the heavens and the earth, and their preservation tires Him not. And He is the Most High, the Most Great. (255) There shall be no compulsion in [acceptance of] the religion. The right course has become clear from the wrong. So whoever disbelieves in Taghut(false deities/leaders) and believes in Allah has grasped the most trustworthy handhold with no break in it. And Allah is Hearing and Knowing. (256) Allah is the ally of those who believe. He brings them out from darknesses into the light. And those who disbelieve - their allies are Taghut. They take them out of the light into darknesses. Those are the companions of the Fire; they will abide eternally therein. (257)

Quran 2:284-286

لِلَّهِ مَا فِى ٱلسَّمَٰوَٰتِ وَمَا فِى ٱلْأَرْضِ ۗ وَإِن تُبْدُوا۟ مَا فِىٓ أَنفُسِكُمْ أَوْ تُخْفُوهُ يُحَاسِبْكُم بِهِ ٱللَّهُ ۖ فَيَغْفِرُ لِمَن يَشَآءُ وَيُعَذِّبُ مَن يَشَآءُ ۗ وَٱللَّهُ عَلَىٰ كُلِّ شَىْءٍ قَدِيرٌ

(٢٨٤) ءَامَنَ ٱلرَّسُولُ بِمَآ أُنزِلَ إِلَيْهِ مِن رَّبِّهِۦ وَٱلْمُؤْمِنُونَ ۚ كُلٌّ ءَامَنَ بِٱللَّهِ وَمَلَٰٓئِكَتِهِۦ وَكُتُبِهِۦ وَرُسُلِهِۦ لَا نُفَرِّقُ بَيْنَ أَحَدٍ مِّن رُّسُلِهِۦ ۚ وَقَالُوا۟ سَمِعْنَا وَأَطَعْنَا ۖ غُفْرَانَكَ رَبَّنَا وَإِلَيْكَ ٱلْمَصِيرُ (٢٨٥) لَا يُكَلِّفُ ٱللَّهُ نَفْسًا إِلَّا وُسْعَهَا ۚ لَهَا مَا كَسَبَتْ وَعَلَيْهَا مَا ٱكْتَسَبَتْ ۗ رَبَّنَا لَا تُؤَاخِذْنَآ إِن نَّسِينَآ أَوْ أَخْطَأْنَا ۚ رَبَّنَا وَلَا تَحْمِلْ عَلَيْنَآ إِصْرًا كَمَا حَمَلْتَهُۥ عَلَى ٱلَّذِينَ مِن قَبْلِنَا ۚ رَبَّنَا وَلَا تُحَمِّلْنَا مَا لَا طَاقَةَ لَنَا بِهِۦ ۖ وَٱعْفُ عَنَّا وَٱغْفِرْ لَنَا وَٱرْحَمْنَآ ۚ أَنتَ مَوْلَىٰنَا فَٱنصُرْنَا عَلَى ٱلْقَوْمِ ٱلْكَٰفِرِينَ (٢٨٦)

To Allah belongs whatever is in the heavens and whatever is in the earth. Whether you show what is within yourselves or conceal it, Allah will bring you to account for it. Then He will forgive whom He wills and punish whom He wills, and Allah is over all things competent. (284) The Messenger has believed in what was revealed to him from his Lord, and [so have] the believers. All of them have believed in Allah and His angels and His books and His messengers, [saying], "We make no distinction between any of His messengers." And they say, "We hear and we obey. [We seek] Your forgiveness, our Lord, and to You is the [final] destination." (285) Allah does not charge a soul except [with that within] its capacity. It will have [the consequence of] what [good] it has gained, and it will bear [the consequence of] what [evil] it has earned. "Our Lord, do not impose blame upon us if we have forgotten or erred. Our Lord, and lay not upon us a burden like that which You laid upon those before us. Our Lord, and burden us not with that which we have no ability to bear.

And pardon us; and forgive us; and have mercy upon us. You are our protector, so give us victory over the disbelieving people." (286)

Quran 3:18-20

شَهِدَ ٱللَّهُ أَنَّهُۥ لَآ إِلَٰهَ إِلَّا هُوَ وَٱلْمَلَٰٓئِكَةُ وَأُو۟لُوا۟ ٱلْعِلْمِ قَآئِمًۢا بِٱلْقِسْطِ ۚ لَآ إِلَٰهَ إِلَّا هُوَ ٱلْعَزِيزُ ٱلْحَكِيمُ (١٨) إِنَّ ٱلدِّينَ عِندَ ٱللَّهِ ٱلْإِسْلَٰمُ ۗ وَمَا ٱخْتَلَفَ ٱلَّذِينَ أُوتُوا۟ ٱلْكِتَٰبَ إِلَّا مِنۢ بَعْدِ مَا جَآءَهُمُ ٱلْعِلْمُ بَغْيًۢا بَيْنَهُمْ ۗ وَمَن يَكْفُرْ بِـَٔايَٰتِ ٱللَّهِ فَإِنَّ ٱللَّهَ سَرِيعُ ٱلْحِسَابِ (١٩) فَإِنْ حَآجُّوكَ فَقُلْ أَسْلَمْتُ وَجْهِىَ لِلَّهِ وَمَنِ ٱتَّبَعَنِ ۗ وَقُل لِّلَّذِينَ أُوتُوا۟ ٱلْكِتَٰبَ وَٱلْأُمِّيِّـۧنَ ءَأَسْلَمْتُمْ ۚ فَإِنْ أَسْلَمُوا۟ فَقَدِ ٱهْتَدَوا۟ ۖ وَّإِن تَوَلَّوْا۟ فَإِنَّمَا عَلَيْكَ ٱلْبَلَٰغُ ۗ وَٱللَّهُ بَصِيرٌۢ بِٱلْعِبَادِ (٢٠)

Allah witnesses that there is no deity except Him, and [so do] the angels and those of knowledge - [that He is] maintaining [creation] in justice. There is no deity except Him, the Exalted in Might, the Wise. (18) Indeed, the religion in the sight of Allah is Islam. And those who were given the Scripture did not differ except after knowledge had come to them - out of jealous animosity between themselves. And whoever disbelieves in the verses of Allah, then indeed, Allah is swift in [taking] account. (19) So if they argue with you(Muhammad), say, "I have submitted myself to Allah [in Islam], and [so have] those who follow me." And say to those who were given the Scripture and [to] the unlearned, "Have you submitted yourselves?" And if they submit [in Islam], they are rightly guided; but if they turn away - then upon you is only the [duty of] notification. And Allah is Seeing of [His] servants. (20)

Quran 3:31-32

قُلْ إِن كُنتُمْ تُحِبُّونَ ٱللَّهَ فَٱتَّبِعُونِى يُحْبِبْكُمُ ٱللَّهُ وَيَغْفِرْ لَكُمْ ذُنُوبَكُمْ ۗ وَٱللَّهُ غَفُورٌ رَّحِيمٌ (٣١) قُلْ أَطِيعُواْ ٱللَّهَ وَٱلرَّسُولَ ۖ فَإِن تَوَلَّوْاْ فَإِنَّ ٱللَّهَ لَا يُحِبُّ ٱلْكَٰفِرِينَ (٣٢)

Say, [O Muhammad], "If you should love Allah, then follow me, [so] Allah will love you and forgive you your sins. And Allah is Forgiving and Merciful." (31) Say, "Obey Allah and the Messenger." But if they turn away - then indeed, Allah does not like the disbelievers. (32)

Quran 3:98-99

قُلْ يَٰٓأَهْلَ ٱلْكِتَٰبِ لِمَ تَكْفُرُونَ بِـَٔايَٰتِ ٱللَّهِ وَٱللَّهُ شَهِيدٌ عَلَىٰ مَا تَعْمَلُونَ (٩٨) قُلْ يَٰٓأَهْلَ ٱلْكِتَٰبِ لِمَ تَصُدُّونَ عَن سَبِيلِ ٱللَّهِ مَنْ ءَامَنَ تَبْغُونَهَا عِوَجًا وَأَنتُمْ شُهَدَآءُ ۗ وَمَا ٱللَّهُ بِغَٰفِلٍ عَمَّا تَعْمَلُونَ (٩٩)

Say, "O People of the Scripture, why do you disbelieve in the verses of Allah while Allah is Witness over what you do?" (98) Say, "O People of the Scripture, why do you avert from the way of Allah those who believe, seeking to make it [seem] deviant, while you are witnesses [to the truth]? And Allah is not unaware of what you do." (99)

Quran 4:47-51

يَٰٓأَيُّهَا ٱلَّذِينَ أُوتُواْ ٱلْكِتَٰبَ ءَامِنُواْ بِمَا نَزَّلْنَا مُصَدِّقًا لِّمَا مَعَكُم مِّن قَبْلِ أَن نَّطْمِسَ وُجُوهًا فَنَرُدَّهَا عَلَىٰٓ أَدْبَارِهَآ أَوْ نَلْعَنَهُمْ كَمَا لَعَنَّآ أَصْحَٰبَ ٱلسَّبْتِ ۚ

وَكَانَ أَمْرُ ٱللَّهِ مَفْعُولًا (٤٧) إِنَّ ٱللَّهَ لَا يَغْفِرُ أَن يُشْرَكَ بِهِۦ وَيَغْفِرُ مَا دُونَ ذَٰلِكَ لِمَن يَشَآءُ وَمَن يُشْرِكْ بِٱللَّهِ فَقَدِ ٱفْتَرَىٰٓ إِثْمًا عَظِيمًا (٤٨) أَلَمْ تَرَ إِلَى ٱلَّذِينَ يُزَكُّونَ أَنفُسَهُم بَلِ ٱللَّهُ يُزَكِّى مَن يَشَآءُ وَلَا يُظْلَمُونَ فَتِيلًا (٤٩) ٱنظُرْ كَيْفَ يَفْتَرُونَ عَلَى ٱللَّهِ ٱلْكَذِبَ وَكَفَىٰ بِهِۦٓ إِثْمًا مُّبِينًا (٥٠) أَلَمْ تَرَ إِلَى ٱلَّذِينَ أُوتُوا۟ نَصِيبًا مِّنَ ٱلْكِتَـٰبِ يُؤْمِنُونَ بِٱلْجِبْتِ وَٱلطَّـٰغُوتِ وَيَقُولُونَ لِلَّذِينَ كَفَرُوا۟ هَـٰٓؤُلَآءِ أَهْدَىٰ مِنَ ٱلَّذِينَ ءَامَنُوا۟ سَبِيلًا (٥١)

O you who were given the Scripture, believe in what We have sent down [to Muhammad], confirming that which is with you, before We obliterate faces and turn them toward their backs or curse them as We cursed the sabbath-breakers. And ever is the decree of Allah accomplished. (47) Indeed, Allah does not forgive association(in worship or partnership) with Him, but He forgives what is less than that for whom He wills. And he who associates others with Allah has certainly fabricated a tremendous sin. (48) Have you not seen those who claim themselves to be pure? Rather, Allah purifies whom He wills, and injustice is not done to them, [even] as much as a thread [inside a date seed]. (49) Look how they invent about Allah untruth, and sufficient is that as a manifest sin. (50) Have you not seen those who were given a portion of the Scripture, who believe in superstition and false objects of worship and say about the disbelievers, "These are better guided than the believers(Muslims) as to the way"? (51)

Quran 4:136

يَٰٓأَيُّهَا ٱلَّذِينَ ءَامَنُوٓاْ ءَامِنُواْ بِٱللَّهِ وَرَسُولِهِۦ وَٱلۡكِتَٰبِ ٱلَّذِى نَزَّلَ عَلَىٰ رَسُولِهِۦ وَٱلۡكِتَٰبِ ٱلَّذِىٓ أَنزَلَ مِن قَبۡلُۚ وَمَن يَكۡفُرۡ بِٱللَّهِ وَمَلَٰٓئِكَتِهِۦ وَكُتُبِهِۦ وَرُسُلِهِۦ وَٱلۡيَوۡمِ ٱلۡأٓخِرِ فَقَدۡ ضَلَّ ضَلَٰلَۢا بَعِيدًا (١٣٦)

O you who have believed, believe in Allah and His Messenger and the Book that He sent down upon His Messenger and the Scripture which He sent down before. And whoever disbelieves in Allah, His angels, His books, His messengers, and the Last Day has certainly gone far astray. (136)

Quran 4:150-175

إِنَّ ٱلَّذِينَ يَكۡفُرُونَ بِٱللَّهِ وَرُسُلِهِۦ وَيُرِيدُونَ أَن يُفَرِّقُواْ بَيۡنَ ٱللَّهِ وَرُسُلِهِۦ وَيَقُولُونَ نُؤۡمِنُ بِبَعۡضٍ وَنَكۡفُرُ بِبَعۡضٍ وَيُرِيدُونَ أَن يَتَّخِذُواْ بَيۡنَ ذَٰلِكَ سَبِيلًا (١٥٠) أُوْلَٰٓئِكَ هُمُ ٱلۡكَٰفِرُونَ حَقًّاۚ وَأَعۡتَدۡنَا لِلۡكَٰفِرِينَ عَذَابًا مُّهِينًا (١٥١) وَٱلَّذِينَ ءَامَنُواْ بِٱللَّهِ وَرُسُلِهِۦ وَلَمۡ يُفَرِّقُواْ بَيۡنَ أَحَدٍ مِّنۡهُمۡ أُوْلَٰٓئِكَ سَوۡفَ يُؤۡتِيهِمۡ أُجُورَهُمۡۚ وَكَانَ ٱللَّهُ غَفُورًا رَّحِيمًا (١٥٢) يَسۡـَٔلُكَ أَهۡلُ ٱلۡكِتَٰبِ أَن تُنَزِّلَ عَلَيۡهِمۡ كِتَٰبًا مِّنَ ٱلسَّمَآءِۚ فَقَدۡ سَأَلُواْ مُوسَىٰٓ أَكۡبَرَ مِن ذَٰلِكَ فَقَالُوٓاْ أَرِنَا ٱللَّهَ جَهۡرَةً فَأَخَذَتۡهُمُ ٱلصَّٰعِقَةُ بِظُلۡمِهِمۡۚ ثُمَّ ٱتَّخَذُواْ ٱلۡعِجۡلَ مِنۢ بَعۡدِ مَا جَآءَتۡهُمُ ٱلۡبَيِّنَٰتُ فَعَفَوۡنَا عَن ذَٰلِكَۚ وَءَاتَيۡنَا مُوسَىٰ سُلۡطَٰنًا مُّبِينًا (١٥٣) وَرَفَعۡنَا فَوۡقَهُمُ ٱلطُّورَ بِمِيثَٰقِهِمۡ وَقُلۡنَا لَهُمُ ٱدۡخُلُواْ ٱلۡبَابَ سُجَّدًا وَقُلۡنَا لَهُمۡ لَا تَعۡدُواْ فِى ٱلسَّبۡتِ وَأَخَذۡنَا مِنۡهُم مِّيثَٰقًا غَلِيظًا (١٥٤) فَبِمَا نَقۡضِهِم مِّيثَٰقَهُمۡ وَكُفۡرِهِم بِـَٔايَٰتِ ٱللَّهِ وَقَتۡلِهِمُ ٱلۡأَنۢبِيَآءَ بِغَيۡرِ حَقٍّ وَقَوۡلِهِمۡ قُلُوبُنَا غُلۡفٌۢۚ بَلۡ طَبَعَ ٱللَّهُ عَلَيۡهَا بِكُفۡرِهِمۡ فَلَا يُؤۡمِنُونَ إِلَّا قَلِيلًا (١٥٥) وَبِكُفۡرِهِمۡ وَقَوۡلِهِمۡ عَلَىٰ مَرۡيَمَ بُهۡتَٰنًا عَظِيمًا (١٥٦) وَقَوۡلِهِمۡ إِنَّا قَتَلۡنَا ٱلۡمَسِيحَ عِيسَى ٱبۡنَ مَرۡيَمَ رَسُولَ ٱللَّهِ وَمَا قَتَلُوهُ وَمَا صَلَبُوهُ وَلَٰكِن شُبِّهَ لَهُمۡۚ وَإِنَّ ٱلَّذِينَ ٱخۡتَلَفُواْ فِيهِ لَفِى شَكٍّ مِّنۡهُۚ مَا لَهُم بِهِۦ مِنۡ عِلۡمٍ إِلَّا ٱتِّبَاعَ ٱلظَّنِّۚ وَمَا قَتَلُوهُ يَقِينَۢا (١٥٧) بَل رَّفَعَهُ ٱللَّهُ إِلَيۡهِۚ وَكَانَ ٱللَّهُ عَزِيزًا حَكِيمًا (١٥٨) وَإِن مِّنۡ أَهۡلِ ٱلۡكِتَٰبِ إِلَّا لَيُؤۡمِنَنَّ بِهِۦ قَبۡلَ مَوۡتِهِۦۖ وَيَوۡمَ ٱلۡقِيَٰمَةِ يَكُونُ عَلَيۡهِمۡ شَهِيدًا (١٥٩) فَبِظُلۡمٍ مِّنَ ٱلَّذِينَ هَادُواْ حَرَّمۡنَا عَلَيۡهِمۡ طَيِّبَٰتٍ أُحِلَّتۡ لَهُمۡ وَبِصَدِّهِمۡ عَن

سَبِيلِ ٱللَّهِ كَثِيرًا (١٦٠) وَأَخْذِهِمُ ٱلرِّبَوٰا۟ وَقَدْ نُهُوا۟ عَنْهُ وَأَكْلِهِمْ أَمْوَالَ ٱلنَّاسِ بِٱلْبَٰطِلِ ۚ وَأَعْتَدْنَا لِلْكَٰفِرِينَ مِنْهُمْ عَذَابًا أَلِيمًا (١٦١) لَّٰكِنِ ٱلرَّٰسِخُونَ فِى ٱلْعِلْمِ مِنْهُمْ وَٱلْمُؤْمِنُونَ يُؤْمِنُونَ بِمَآ أُنزِلَ إِلَيْكَ وَمَآ أُنزِلَ مِن قَبْلِكَ ۚ وَٱلْمُقِيمِينَ ٱلصَّلَوٰةَ ۚ وَٱلْمُؤْتُونَ ٱلزَّكَوٰةَ وَٱلْمُؤْمِنُونَ بِٱللَّهِ وَٱلْيَوْمِ ٱلْءَاخِرِ أُو۟لَٰٓئِكَ سَنُؤْتِيهِمْ أَجْرًا عَظِيمًا (١٦٢) ۞ إِنَّآ أَوْحَيْنَآ إِلَيْكَ كَمَآ أَوْحَيْنَآ إِلَىٰ نُوحٍ وَٱلنَّبِيِّۦنَ مِنۢ بَعْدِهِۦ ۚ وَأَوْحَيْنَآ إِلَىٰٓ إِبْرَٰهِيمَ وَإِسْمَٰعِيلَ وَإِسْحَٰقَ وَيَعْقُوبَ وَٱلْأَسْبَاطِ وَعِيسَىٰ وَأَيُّوبَ وَيُونُسَ وَهَٰرُونَ وَسُلَيْمَٰنَ ۚ وَءَاتَيْنَا دَاوُۥدَ زَبُورًا (١٦٣) وَرُسُلًا قَدْ قَصَصْنَٰهُمْ عَلَيْكَ مِن قَبْلُ وَرُسُلًا لَّمْ نَقْصُصْهُمْ عَلَيْكَ ۚ وَكَلَّمَ ٱللَّهُ مُوسَىٰ تَكْلِيمًا (١٦٤) رُّسُلًا مُّبَشِّرِينَ وَمُنذِرِينَ لِئَلَّا يَكُونَ لِلنَّاسِ عَلَى ٱللَّهِ حُجَّةٌۢ بَعْدَ ٱلرُّسُلِ ۚ وَكَانَ ٱللَّهُ عَزِيزًا حَكِيمًا (١٦٥) لَّٰكِنِ ٱللَّهُ يَشْهَدُ بِمَآ أَنزَلَ إِلَيْكَ ۖ أَنزَلَهُۥ بِعِلْمِهِۦ ۖ وَٱلْمَلَٰٓئِكَةُ يَشْهَدُونَ ۚ وَكَفَىٰ بِٱللَّهِ شَهِيدًا (١٦٦) إِنَّ ٱلَّذِينَ كَفَرُوا۟ وَصَدُّوا۟ عَن سَبِيلِ ٱللَّهِ قَدْ ضَلُّوا۟ ضَلَٰلًۢا بَعِيدًا (١٦٧) إِنَّ ٱلَّذِينَ كَفَرُوا۟ وَظَلَمُوا۟ لَمْ يَكُنِ ٱللَّهُ لِيَغْفِرَ لَهُمْ وَلَا لِيَهْدِيَهُمْ طَرِيقًا (١٦٨) إِلَّا طَرِيقَ جَهَنَّمَ خَٰلِدِينَ فِيهَآ أَبَدًا ۚ وَكَانَ ذَٰلِكَ عَلَى ٱللَّهِ يَسِيرًا (١٦٩) يَٰٓأَيُّهَا ٱلنَّاسُ قَدْ جَآءَكُمُ ٱلرَّسُولُ بِٱلْحَقِّ مِن رَّبِّكُمْ فَـَٔامِنُوا۟ خَيْرًا لَّكُمْ ۚ وَإِن تَكْفُرُوا۟ فَإِنَّ لِلَّهِ مَا فِى ٱلسَّمَٰوَٰتِ وَٱلْأَرْضِ ۚ وَكَانَ ٱللَّهُ عَلِيمًا حَكِيمًا (١٧٠) يَٰٓأَهْلَ ٱلْكِتَٰبِ لَا تَغْلُوا۟ فِى دِينِكُمْ وَلَا تَقُولُوا۟ عَلَى ٱللَّهِ إِلَّا ٱلْحَقَّ ۚ إِنَّمَا ٱلْمَسِيحُ عِيسَى ٱبْنُ مَرْيَمَ رَسُولُ ٱللَّهِ وَكَلِمَتُهُۥٓ أَلْقَىٰهَآ إِلَىٰ مَرْيَمَ وَرُوحٌ مِّنْهُ ۖ فَـَٔامِنُوا۟ بِٱللَّهِ وَرُسُلِهِۦ ۖ وَلَا تَقُولُوا۟ ثَلَٰثَةٌ ۚ ٱنتَهُوا۟ خَيْرًا لَّكُمْ ۚ إِنَّمَا ٱللَّهُ إِلَٰهٌ وَٰحِدٌ ۖ سُبْحَٰنَهُۥٓ أَن يَكُونَ لَهُۥ وَلَدٌ ۘ لَّهُۥ مَا فِى ٱلسَّمَٰوَٰتِ وَمَا فِى ٱلْأَرْضِ ۗ وَكَفَىٰ بِٱللَّهِ وَكِيلًا (١٧١) لَّن يَسْتَنكِفَ ٱلْمَسِيحُ أَن يَكُونَ عَبْدًا لِّلَّهِ وَلَا ٱلْمَلَٰٓئِكَةُ ٱلْمُقَرَّبُونَ ۚ وَمَن يَسْتَنكِفْ عَنْ عِبَادَتِهِۦ وَيَسْتَكْبِرْ فَسَيَحْشُرُهُمْ إِلَيْهِ جَمِيعًا (١٧٢) فَأَمَّا ٱلَّذِينَ ءَامَنُوا۟ وَعَمِلُوا۟ ٱلصَّٰلِحَٰتِ فَيُوَفِّيهِمْ أُجُورَهُمْ وَيَزِيدُهُم مِّن فَضْلِهِۦ ۖ وَأَمَّا ٱلَّذِينَ ٱسْتَنكَفُوا۟ وَٱسْتَكْبَرُوا۟ فَيُعَذِّبُهُمْ عَذَابًا أَلِيمًا وَلَا يَجِدُونَ لَهُم مِّن دُونِ ٱللَّهِ وَلِيًّا وَلَا نَصِيرًا (١٧٣) يَٰٓأَيُّهَا ٱلنَّاسُ قَدْ جَآءَكُم بُرْهَٰنٌ مِّن رَّبِّكُمْ وَأَنزَلْنَآ إِلَيْكُمْ نُورًا مُّبِينًا (١٧٤) فَأَمَّا ٱلَّذِينَ ءَامَنُوا۟ بِٱللَّهِ وَٱعْتَصَمُوا۟ بِهِۦ فَسَيُدْخِلُهُمْ فِى رَحْمَةٍ مِّنْهُ وَفَضْلٍ وَيَهْدِيهِمْ إِلَيْهِ صِرَٰطًا مُّسْتَقِيمًا (١٧٥)

Indeed, those who disbelieve in Allah and His messengers and wish to discriminate between Allah and His messengers and say, "We believe in some and disbelieve in others," and wish to adopt a way in between - (150) Those are the disbelievers, truly. And We have prepared for the disbelievers a humiliating punishment. (151) But they who believe in Allah and His messengers and do not discriminate between any of them - to those He is going to give their rewards. And ever is Allah Forgiving and Merciful. (152) The People of the Scripture ask you to bring down to them a book from the heaven. But they had asked of Moses [even] greater than that and said, "Show us Allah outright," so the thunderbolt struck them for their wrongdoing. Then they took the calf [for worship] after clear evidences had come to them, and We pardoned that. And We gave Moses a clear authority. (153) And We raised over them the mount for [refusal of] their covenant; and We said to them, "Enter the gate bowing humbly", and We said to them, "Do not transgress on the sabbath", and We took from them a solemn covenant. (154) And [We cursed them] for their breaking of the covenant and their disbelief in the signs of Allah and their killing of the prophets without right and their saying, "Our hearts are wrapped". Rather, Allah has sealed them because of their disbelief, so they believe not, except for a few. (155) And [We cursed them] for their disbelief and their saying against Mary a great slander, (156) And [for] their saying, "Indeed, we have killed the Messiah, Jesus, the son of Mary, the messenger of Allah." And they did not kill him, nor did they crucify him; but [another] was made to resemble him to them. And indeed, those who differ over it are in doubt about it. They have no knowledge of it except the following of assumption. And they did not kill him, for certain. (157) Rather, Allah raised him to Himself. And ever is Allah Exalted in Might and Wise. (158) And there is none from the People of the Scripture but that he will surely believe in Jesus before his death. And on the Day of Resurrection he will be against them a witness. (159) For wrongdoing on the part of the Jews, We made unlawful for them [certain] good foods which had been lawful to them, and for their averting from the way of Allah many [people], (160) And [for] their taking of usury while they had been forbidden from it, and their consuming of the people's wealth unjustly. And we have prepared for the disbelievers among them a painful punishment. (161) But those firm in knowledge among them and the believers believe in what has been revealed to you, [O Muhammad], and what was revealed before you. And the establishers of prayer [especially] and the givers of zakah(charity) and the believers in Allah and the Last Day - those We will give a great reward. (162) Indeed, We have revealed to you, [O Muhammad], as We revealed to Noah and the *prophets after him. And we revealed to Abraham, Ishmael, Isaac, Jacob, the Descendants, Jesus, Job, Jonah, Aaron, and Solomon, and to David We gave the book. (163) And [We sent] messengers about whom We have related [their stories] to you before and messengers about whom We have not related to you. And Allah spoke to Moses with [direct] speech. (164) [We sent] messengers as bringers of good tidings and warners so that mankind will have no argument against Allah after the messengers. And ever is Allah Exalted in Might and Wise. (165) But Allah bears witness to that which He has revealed to you. He has sent it down with His knowledge, and the angels bear witness [as well]. And sufficient is Allah as Witness. (166) Indeed, those who disbelieve and avert [people] from the way of Allah have certainly gone far astray. (167) Indeed, those who disbelieve and commit wrong [or injustice] - never will Allah forgive them, nor will He guide them to a path. (168) Except the path of Hell; they will abide therein forever. And that, for Allah, is [always] easy. (169) O Mankind, the Messenger has come to you with the truth from your Lord, so believe; it is better for you. But if you disbelieve - then indeed, to Allah belongs whatever is in the heavens and earth. And ever is Allah Knowing and Wise. (170) O People of the Scripture, do not commit excess in your religion or say about Allah except the truth. The Messiah, Jesus, the son of Mary, was but a messenger of Allah and His word* which He directed to Mary and a soul [created at a command] from Him. So believe in Allah and His messengers. And do not say, "Three"; desist - it is better for you. Indeed, Allah is but one God. Exalted is He above having a son. To Him belongs whatever is in the heavens and whatever is on the earth. And sufficient is Allah as Disposer of affairs. (171) Never would the Messiah disdain to be a servant of Allah, nor would the angels near [to Him]. And whoever disdains His worship and is arrogant - He will gather them to Himself all together. (172) And as for those who believed and did righteous deeds, He will give them in full their rewards and grant them extra from His bounty. But as for those who disdained and were arrogant, He will punish them with a painful punishment, and they will not find for themselves besides Allah any protector or helper. (173) O mankind, there has come to you a conclusive proof from your Lord, and We have sent down to you a clear light. (174) So those who believe in Allah and hold fast to Him - He will admit them to mercy from Himself and bounty and guide them to Himself on a straight path. (175)

Quran 5:12-19

۞ وَلَقَدْ أَخَذَ ٱللَّهُ مِيثَٰقَ بَنِىٓ إِسْرَٰٓءِيلَ وَبَعَثْنَا مِنْهُمُ ٱثْنَىْ عَشَرَ نَقِيبًا ۖ وَقَالَ ٱللَّهُ إِنِّى مَعَكُمْ ۖ لَئِنْ أَقَمْتُمُ ٱلصَّلَوٰةَ وَءَاتَيْتُمُ ٱلزَّكَوٰةَ وَءَامَنتُم بِرُسُلِى وَعَزَّرْتُمُوهُمْ وَأَقْرَضْتُمُ ٱللَّهَ قَرْضًا حَسَنًا لَّأُكَفِّرَنَّ عَنكُمْ سَيِّـَٔاتِكُمْ وَلَأُدْخِلَنَّكُمْ جَنَّٰتٍ تَجْرِى مِن تَحْتِهَا ٱلْأَنْهَٰرُ ۚ فَمَن كَفَرَ بَعْدَ ذَٰلِكَ مِنكُمْ فَقَدْ ضَلَّ سَوَآءَ ٱلسَّبِيلِ (١٢) فَبِمَا نَقْضِهِم مِّيثَٰقَهُمْ لَعَنَّٰهُمْ وَجَعَلْنَا قُلُوبَهُمْ قَٰسِيَةً ۖ يُحَرِّفُونَ ٱلْكَلِمَ عَن

مَوَاضِعِهِۦ ۛ وَنَسُواْ حَظًّا مِّمَّا ذُكِّرُواْ بِهِۦ ۚ وَلَا تَزَالُ تَطَّلِعُ عَلَىٰ خَآئِنَةٍ مِّنْهُمْ إِلَّا قَلِيلًا مِّنْهُمْ ۖ فَٱعْفُ عَنْهُمْ وَٱصْفَحْ ۚ إِنَّ ٱللَّهَ يُحِبُّ ٱلْمُحْسِنِينَ (١٣) وَمِنَ ٱلَّذِينَ قَالُوٓاْ إِنَّا نَصَٰرَىٰٓ أَخَذْنَا مِيثَٰقَهُمْ فَنَسُواْ حَظًّا مِّمَّا ذُكِّرُواْ بِهِۦ فَأَغْرَيْنَا بَيْنَهُمُ ٱلْعَدَاوَةَ وَٱلْبَغْضَآءَ إِلَىٰ يَوْمِ ٱلْقِيَٰمَةِ ۚ وَسَوْفَ يُنَبِّئُهُمُ ٱللَّهُ بِمَا كَانُواْ يَصْنَعُونَ (١٤) يَٰٓأَهْلَ ٱلْكِتَٰبِ قَدْ جَآءَكُمْ رَسُولُنَا يُبَيِّنُ لَكُمْ كَثِيرًا مِّمَّا كُنتُمْ تُخْفُونَ مِنَ ٱلْكِتَٰبِ وَيَعْفُواْ عَن كَثِيرٍ ۚ قَدْ جَآءَكُم مِّنَ ٱللَّهِ نُورٌ وَكِتَٰبٌ مُّبِينٌ (١٥) يَهْدِى بِهِ ٱللَّهُ مَنِ ٱتَّبَعَ رِضْوَٰنَهُۥ سُبُلَ ٱلسَّلَٰمِ وَيُخْرِجُهُم مِّنَ ٱلظُّلُمَٰتِ إِلَى ٱلنُّورِ بِإِذْنِهِۦ وَيَهْدِيهِمْ إِلَىٰ صِرَٰطٍ مُّسْتَقِيمٍ (١٦) لَّقَدْ كَفَرَ ٱلَّذِينَ قَالُوٓاْ إِنَّ ٱللَّهَ هُوَ ٱلْمَسِيحُ ٱبْنُ مَرْيَمَ ۚ قُلْ فَمَن يَمْلِكُ مِنَ ٱللَّهِ شَيْـًٔا إِنْ أَرَادَ أَن يُهْلِكَ ٱلْمَسِيحَ ٱبْنَ مَرْيَمَ وَأُمَّهُۥ وَمَن فِى ٱلْأَرْضِ جَمِيعًا ۗ وَلِلَّهِ مُلْكُ ٱلسَّمَٰوَٰتِ وَٱلْأَرْضِ وَمَا بَيْنَهُمَا ۚ يَخْلُقُ مَا يَشَآءُ ۚ وَٱللَّهُ عَلَىٰ كُلِّ شَىْءٍ قَدِيرٌ (١٧) وَقَالَتِ ٱلْيَهُودُ وَٱلنَّصَٰرَىٰ نَحْنُ أَبْنَٰٓؤُاْ ٱللَّهِ وَأَحِبَّٰٓؤُهُۥ ۚ قُلْ فَلِمَ يُعَذِّبُكُم بِذُنُوبِكُم ۖ بَلْ أَنتُم بَشَرٌ مِّمَّنْ خَلَقَ ۚ يَغْفِرُ لِمَن يَشَآءُ وَيُعَذِّبُ مَن يَشَآءُ ۚ وَلِلَّهِ مُلْكُ ٱلسَّمَٰوَٰتِ وَٱلْأَرْضِ وَمَا بَيْنَهُمَا ۖ وَإِلَيْهِ ٱلْمَصِيرُ (١٨) يَٰٓأَهْلَ ٱلْكِتَٰبِ قَدْ جَآءَكُمْ رَسُولُنَا يُبَيِّنُ لَكُمْ عَلَىٰ فَتْرَةٍ مِّنَ ٱلرُّسُلِ أَن تَقُولُواْ مَا جَآءَنَا مِنۢ بَشِيرٍ وَلَا نَذِيرٍ ۖ فَقَدْ جَآءَكُم بَشِيرٌ وَنَذِيرٌ ۗ وَٱللَّهُ عَلَىٰ كُلِّ شَىْءٍ قَدِيرٌ (١٩)

And Allah had already taken a covenant from the Children of Israel, and We delegated from among them twelve leaders. And Allah said, "I am with you. If you establish prayer and give zakah(charity) and believe in My messengers and support them and loan Allah a goodly loan, I will surely remove from you your misdeeds and admit you to gardens beneath which rivers flow. But whoever of you disbelieves after that has certainly strayed from the soundness of the way." (12) So for their breaking of the covenant We cursed them and made their hearts hard. They distort words from their [proper] usages and have forgotten a portion of that of which they were reminded. And you will still observe deceit among them, except a few of them. But pardon them and overlook [their misdeeds]. Indeed, Allah loves the doers of good. (13) And from those who say, "We are Christians" We took their covenant; but they forgot a portion of that of which they were reminded. So We caused among them animosity and hatred until the Day of Resurrection. And Allah is going to inform them about what they used to do. (14) O People of the Scripture, there has come to you Our Messenger making clear to you much of what you used to conceal of the Scripture and overlooking much. There has come to you from Allah a light and a clear Book. (15) By which Allah guides those who pursue His pleasure to the ways of peace and brings them out from darknesses into the light, by His permission, and guides them to a straight path. (16) They have certainly disbelieved who say that Allah is Christ, the son of Mary. Say, "Then who could prevent Allah at all if He had intended to destroy Christ, the son of Mary, or his mother or everyone on the earth?" And to Allah belongs the dominion of the heavens and the earth and whatever is between them. He creates what He wills, and Allah is over all things competent. (17) But the Jews and the Christians say, "We are the children of Allah and His beloved." Say, "Then why does He punish you for your sins?" Rather, you are human beings from among those He has created. He forgives whom He wills, and He punishes whom He wills. And to Allah belongs the dominion of the heavens and the earth and whatever is between them, and to Him is the [final] destination. (18) O People of the Scripture, there has come to you Our Messenger to make clear to you [the religion] after a period [of suspension] of messengers, lest you say, "There came not to us any bringer of good tidings or a warner." But there has come to you a bringer of good tidings and a warner. And Allah is over all things competent. (19)

Quran 4:44-49

إِنَّآ أَنزَلْنَا ٱلتَّوْرَىٰةَ فِيهَا هُدًى وَنُورٌ يَحْكُمُ بِهَا ٱلنَّبِيُّونَ ٱلَّذِينَ أَسْلَمُواْ لِلَّذِينَ هَادُواْ وَٱلرَّبَّـٰنِيُّونَ وَٱلْأَحْبَارُ بِمَا ٱسْتُحْفِظُواْ مِن كِتَـٰبِ ٱللَّهِ وَكَانُواْ عَلَيْهِ شُهَدَآءَ فَلَا تَخْشَوُاْ ٱلنَّاسَ وَٱخْشَوْنِ وَلَا تَشْتَرُواْ بِـَٔايَـٰتِى ثَمَنًا قَلِيلًا وَمَن لَّمْ يَحْكُم بِمَآ أَنزَلَ ٱللَّهُ فَأُوْلَـٰٓئِكَ هُمُ ٱلْكَـٰفِرُونَ (٤٤) وَكَتَبْنَا عَلَيْهِمْ فِيهَآ أَنَّ ٱلنَّفْسَ بِٱلنَّفْسِ وَٱلْعَيْنَ بِٱلْعَيْنِ وَٱلْأَنفَ بِٱلْأَنفِ وَٱلْأُذُنَ بِٱلْأُذُنِ وَٱلسِّنَّ بِٱلسِّنِّ وَٱلْجُرُوحَ قِصَاصٌ فَمَن تَصَدَّقَ بِهِۦ فَهُوَ كَفَّارَةٌ لَّهُۥ وَمَن لَّمْ يَحْكُم بِمَآ أَنزَلَ ٱللَّهُ فَأُوْلَـٰٓئِكَ هُمُ ٱلظَّـٰلِمُونَ (٤٥) وَقَفَّيْنَا عَلَىٰٓ ءَاثَـٰرِهِم بِعِيسَى ٱبْنِ مَرْيَمَ مُصَدِّقًا لِّمَا بَيْنَ يَدَيْهِ مِنَ ٱلتَّوْرَىٰةِ وَءَاتَيْنَـٰهُ ٱلْإِنجِيلَ فِيهِ هُدًى وَنُورٌ وَمُصَدِّقًا لِّمَا بَيْنَ يَدَيْهِ مِنَ ٱلتَّوْرَىٰةِ وَهُدًى وَمَوْعِظَةً لِّلْمُتَّقِينَ (٤٦) وَلْيَحْكُمْ أَهْلُ ٱلْإِنجِيلِ بِمَآ أَنزَلَ ٱللَّهُ فِيهِ وَمَن لَّمْ يَحْكُم بِمَآ أَنزَلَ ٱللَّهُ فَأُوْلَـٰٓئِكَ هُمُ ٱلْفَـٰسِقُونَ (٤٧) وَأَنزَلْنَآ إِلَيْكَ ٱلْكِتَـٰبَ بِٱلْحَقِّ مُصَدِّقًا لِّمَا بَيْنَ يَدَيْهِ مِنَ ٱلْكِتَـٰبِ وَمُهَيْمِنًا عَلَيْهِ فَٱحْكُم بَيْنَهُم بِمَآ أَنزَلَ ٱللَّهُ وَلَا تَتَّبِعْ أَهْوَآءَهُمْ عَمَّا جَآءَكَ مِنَ ٱلْحَقِّ لِكُلٍّ جَعَلْنَا مِنكُمْ شِرْعَةً وَمِنْهَاجًا وَلَوْ شَآءَ ٱللَّهُ لَجَعَلَكُمْ أُمَّةً وَٰحِدَةً وَلَـٰكِن لِّيَبْلُوَكُمْ فِى مَآ ءَاتَىٰكُمْ فَٱسْتَبِقُواْ ٱلْخَيْرَٰتِ إِلَى ٱللَّهِ مَرْجِعُكُمْ جَمِيعًا فَيُنَبِّئُكُم بِمَا كُنتُمْ فِيهِ تَخْتَلِفُونَ (٤٨) وَأَنِ ٱحْكُم بَيْنَهُم بِمَآ أَنزَلَ ٱللَّهُ وَلَا تَتَّبِعْ أَهْوَآءَهُمْ وَٱحْذَرْهُمْ أَن يَفْتِنُوكَ عَنۢ بَعْضِ مَآ أَنزَلَ ٱللَّهُ إِلَيْكَ فَإِن تَوَلَّوْاْ فَٱعْلَمْ أَنَّمَا يُرِيدُ ٱللَّهُ أَن يُصِيبَهُم بِبَعْضِ ذُنُوبِهِمْ وَإِنَّ كَثِيرًا مِّنَ ٱلنَّاسِ لَفَـٰسِقُونَ (٤٩)

Indeed, We sent down the Torah, in which was guidance and light. The prophets who submitted [to Allah] judged by it for the Jews, as did the rabbis and scholars by that with which they were entrusted of the Scripture of Allah, and they were witnesses thereto. So do not fear the people but fear Me, and do not exchange My verses for a small price. And whoever does not judge by what Allah has revealed - then it is those who are the disbelievers.
(44) And We ordained for them therein a life for a life, an eye for an eye, a nose for a nose, an ear for an ear, a tooth for a tooth, and for wounds is legal retribution. But whoever gives [up his right as] charity, it is an expiation for him. And whoever does not judge by what Allah has revealed - then it is those who are the wrongdoers.
(45) And We sent, following in their footsteps, Jesus, the son of Mary, confirming that which came before him in the Torah; and We gave him the Injeel, in which was guidance and light and confirming that which preceded it of the Torah as guidance and instruction for the righteous. (46) And let the People of the Injeel judge by what Allah has revealed therein. And whoever does not judge by what Allah has revealed - then it is those who are the defiantly disobedient. (47) And We have revealed to you, [O Muhammad], the Book in truth, confirming that which preceded it of the Scripture and as a criterion over it. So judge between them by what Allah has revealed and do not follow their inclinations away from

what has come to you of the truth. To each of you We prescribed a law and a method. Had Allah willed, He would have made you one nation [united in religion], but [He intended] to test you in what He has given you; so race to [all that is] good. To Allah is your return all together, and He will [then] inform you concerning that over which you used to differ. (48) And judge, [O Muhammad], between them by what Allah has revealed and do not follow their inclinations and beware of them, lest they tempt you away from some of what Allah has revealed to you. And if they turn away - then know that Allah only intends to afflict them with some of their [own] sins. And indeed, many among the people are defiantly disobedient. (49)

Quran 5:59-77

قُلْ يَٰٓأَهْلَ ٱلْكِتَٰبِ هَلْ تَنقِمُونَ مِنَّآ إِلَّآ أَنْ ءَامَنَّا بِٱللَّهِ وَمَآ أُنزِلَ إِلَيْنَا وَمَآ أُنزِلَ مِن قَبْلُ وَأَنَّ أَكْثَرَكُمْ فَٰسِقُونَ (٥٩) قُلْ هَلْ أُنَبِّئُكُم بِشَرٍّ مِّن ذَٰلِكَ مَثُوبَةً عِندَ ٱللَّهِ مَن لَّعَنَهُ ٱللَّهُ وَغَضِبَ عَلَيْهِ وَجَعَلَ مِنْهُمُ ٱلْقِرَدَةَ وَٱلْخَنَازِيرَ وَعَبَدَ ٱلطَّٰغُوتَ أُو۟لَٰٓئِكَ شَرٌّ مَّكَانًا وَأَضَلُّ عَن سَوَآءِ ٱلسَّبِيلِ (٦٠) وَإِذَا جَآءُوكُمْ قَالُوٓا۟ ءَامَنَّا وَقَد دَّخَلُوا۟ بِٱلْكُفْرِ وَهُمْ قَدْ خَرَجُوا۟ بِهِۦ وَٱللَّهُ أَعْلَمُ بِمَا كَانُوا۟ يَكْتُمُونَ (٦١) وَتَرَىٰ كَثِيرًا مِّنْهُمْ يُسَٰرِعُونَ فِى ٱلْإِثْمِ وَٱلْعُدْوَٰنِ وَأَكْلِهِمُ ٱلسُّحْتَ لَبِئْسَ مَا كَانُوا۟ يَعْمَلُونَ (٦٢) لَوْلَا يَنْهَىٰهُمُ ٱلرَّبَّٰنِيُّونَ وَٱلْأَحْبَارُ عَن قَوْلِهِمُ ٱلْإِثْمَ وَأَكْلِهِمُ ٱلسُّحْتَ لَبِئْسَ مَا كَانُوا۟ يَصْنَعُونَ (٦٣) وَقَالَتِ ٱلْيَهُودُ يَدُ ٱللَّهِ مَغْلُولَةٌ غُلَّتْ أَيْدِيهِمْ وَلُعِنُوا۟ بِمَا قَالُوا۟ بَلْ يَدَاهُ مَبْسُوطَتَانِ يُنفِقُ كَيْفَ يَشَآءُ وَلَيَزِيدَنَّ كَثِيرًا مِّنْهُم مَّآ أُنزِلَ إِلَيْكَ مِن رَّبِّكَ طُغْيَٰنًا وَكُفْرًا وَأَلْقَيْنَا بَيْنَهُمُ ٱلْعَدَٰوَةَ وَٱلْبَغْضَآءَ إِلَىٰ يَوْمِ ٱلْقِيَٰمَةِ كُلَّمَآ أَوْقَدُوا۟ نَارًا لِّلْحَرْبِ أَطْفَأَهَا ٱللَّهُ وَيَسْعَوْنَ فِى ٱلْأَرْضِ فَسَادًا وَٱللَّهُ لَا يُحِبُّ ٱلْمُفْسِدِينَ (٦٤) وَلَوْ أَنَّ أَهْلَ ٱلْكِتَٰبِ ءَامَنُوا۟

وَأَتَّقَوْاْ لَكَفَّرْنَا عَنْهُمْ سَيِّـَٔاتِهِمْ وَلَأَدْخَلْنَـٰهُمْ جَنَّـٰتِ ٱلنَّعِيمِ (٦٥) وَلَوْ أَنَّهُمْ أَقَامُواْ ٱلتَّوْرَىٰةَ وَٱلْإِنجِيلَ وَمَآ أُنزِلَ إِلَيْهِم مِّن رَّبِّهِمْ لَأَكَلُواْ مِن فَوْقِهِمْ وَمِن تَحْتِ أَرْجُلِهِمْ ۚ مِّنْهُمْ أُمَّةٌ مُّقْتَصِدَةٌ ۖ وَكَثِيرٌ مِّنْهُمْ سَآءَ مَا يَعْمَلُونَ (٦٦) يَـٰٓأَيُّهَا ٱلرَّسُولُ بَلِّغْ مَآ أُنزِلَ إِلَيْكَ مِن رَّبِّكَ ۖ وَإِن لَّمْ تَفْعَلْ فَمَا بَلَّغْتَ رِسَالَتَهُۥ ۚ وَٱللَّهُ يَعْصِمُكَ مِنَ ٱلنَّاسِ ۗ إِنَّ ٱللَّهَ لَا يَهْدِى ٱلْقَوْمَ ٱلْكَـٰفِرِينَ (٦٧) قُلْ يَـٰٓأَهْلَ ٱلْكِتَـٰبِ لَسْتُمْ عَلَىٰ شَىْءٍ حَتَّىٰ تُقِيمُواْ ٱلتَّوْرَىٰةَ وَٱلْإِنجِيلَ وَمَآ أُنزِلَ إِلَيْكُم مِّن رَّبِّكُمْ ۗ وَلَيَزِيدَنَّ كَثِيرًا مِّنْهُم مَّآ أُنزِلَ إِلَيْكَ مِن رَّبِّكَ طُغْيَـٰنًا وَكُفْرًا ۖ فَلَا تَأْسَ عَلَى ٱلْقَوْمِ ٱلْكَـٰفِرِينَ (٦٨) إِنَّ ٱلَّذِينَ ءَامَنُواْ وَٱلَّذِينَ هَادُواْ وَٱلصَّـٰبِـُٔونَ وَٱلنَّصَـٰرَىٰ مَنْ ءَامَنَ بِٱللَّهِ وَٱلْيَوْمِ ٱلْـَٔاخِرِ وَعَمِلَ صَـٰلِحًا فَلَا خَوْفٌ عَلَيْهِمْ وَلَا هُمْ يَحْزَنُونَ (٦٩) لَقَدْ أَخَذْنَا مِيثَـٰقَ بَنِىٓ إِسْرَٰٓءِيلَ وَأَرْسَلْنَآ إِلَيْهِمْ رُسُلًا ۖ كُلَّمَا جَآءَهُمْ رَسُولٌۢ بِمَا لَا تَهْوَىٰٓ أَنفُسُهُمْ فَرِيقًا كَذَّبُواْ وَفَرِيقًا يَقْتُلُونَ (٧٠) وَحَسِبُوٓاْ أَلَّا تَكُونَ فِتْنَةٌ فَعَمُواْ وَصَمُّواْ ثُمَّ تَابَ ٱللَّهُ عَلَيْهِمْ ثُمَّ عَمُواْ وَصَمُّواْ كَثِيرٌ مِّنْهُمْ ۚ وَٱللَّهُ بَصِيرٌۢ بِمَا يَعْمَلُونَ (٧١) لَقَدْ كَفَرَ ٱلَّذِينَ قَالُوٓاْ إِنَّ ٱللَّهَ هُوَ ٱلْمَسِيحُ ٱبْنُ مَرْيَمَ ۖ وَقَالَ ٱلْمَسِيحُ يَـٰبَنِىٓ إِسْرَٰٓءِيلَ ٱعْبُدُواْ ٱللَّهَ رَبِّى وَرَبَّكُمْ ۖ إِنَّهُۥ مَن يُشْرِكْ بِٱللَّهِ فَقَدْ حَرَّمَ ٱللَّهُ عَلَيْهِ ٱلْجَنَّةَ وَمَأْوَىٰهُ ٱلنَّارُ ۖ وَمَا لِلظَّـٰلِمِينَ مِنْ أَنصَارٍ (٧٢) لَقَدْ كَفَرَ ٱلَّذِينَ قَالُوٓاْ إِنَّ ٱللَّهَ ثَالِثُ ثَلَـٰثَةٍ ۘ وَمَا مِنْ إِلَـٰهٍ إِلَّآ إِلَـٰهٌ وَٰحِدٌ ۚ وَإِن لَّمْ يَنتَهُواْ عَمَّا يَقُولُونَ لَيَمَسَّنَّ ٱلَّذِينَ كَفَرُواْ مِنْهُمْ عَذَابٌ أَلِيمٌ (٧٣) أَفَلَا يَتُوبُونَ إِلَى ٱللَّهِ وَيَسْتَغْفِرُونَهُۥ ۚ وَٱللَّهُ غَفُورٌ رَّحِيمٌ (٧٤) مَّا ٱلْمَسِيحُ ٱبْنُ مَرْيَمَ إِلَّا رَسُولٌ قَدْ خَلَتْ مِن قَبْلِهِ ٱلرُّسُلُ وَأُمُّهُۥ صِدِّيقَةٌ ۖ كَانَا يَأْكُلَانِ ٱلطَّعَامَ ۗ ٱنظُرْ كَيْفَ نُبَيِّنُ لَهُمُ ٱلْـَٔايَـٰتِ ثُمَّ ٱنظُرْ أَنَّىٰ يُؤْفَكُونَ (٧٥) قُلْ أَتَعْبُدُونَ مِن دُونِ ٱللَّهِ مَا لَا يَمْلِكُ لَكُمْ ضَرًّا وَلَا نَفْعًا ۚ وَٱللَّهُ هُوَ ٱلسَّمِيعُ ٱلْعَلِيمُ (٧٦) قُلْ يَـٰٓأَهْلَ ٱلْكِتَـٰبِ لَا تَغْلُواْ فِى دِينِكُمْ غَيْرَ ٱلْحَقِّ وَلَا تَتَّبِعُوٓاْ أَهْوَآءَ قَوْمٍ قَدْ ضَلُّواْ مِن قَبْلُ وَأَضَلُّواْ كَثِيرًا وَضَلُّواْ عَن سَوَآءِ ٱلسَّبِيلِ (٧٧)

Say, "O People of the Scripture, do you resent us except [for the fact] that we have believed in Allah and what was revealed to us and what was revealed before and because most of you are defiantly disobedient?" (59) Say, "Shall I inform you of [what is] worse than that as penalty from

Allah? [It is that of] those whom Allah has cursed and with whom He became angry and made of them apes and pigs and slaves of Taghut. Those are worse in position and further astray from the sound way." (60) And when they come to you, they say, "We believe." But they have entered with disbelief [in their hearts], and they have certainly left with it. And Allah is most knowing of what they were concealing. (61) And you see many of them hastening into sin and aggression and the devouring of [what is] unlawful. How wretched is what they have been doing. (62) Why do the rabbis and religious scholars not forbid them from saying what is sinful and devouring what is unlawful? How wretched is what they have been practicing. (63) And the Jews say, "The hand of Allah is chained." Chained are their hands, and cursed are they for what they say. Rather, both His hands are extended; He spends however He wills. And that which has been revealed to you from your Lord will surely increase many of them in transgression and disbelief. And We have cast among them animosity and hatred until the Day of Resurrection. Every time they kindled the fire of war [against you], Allah extinguished it. And they strive throughout the land [causing] corruption, and Allah does not like corrupters. (64) And if only the People of the Scripture had believed and feared Allah, We would have removed from them their misdeeds and admitted them to Gardens of Pleasure. (65) And if only they upheld [the law of] the Torah, the Injeel, and what has been revealed to them from their Lord, they would have consumed [provision] from above them and from beneath their feet. Among them are a moderate community, but many of them - evil is that which they do. (66) O Messenger, announce that which has been revealed to you from your Lord, and if you do not, then you have not conveyed His message. And Allah will protect you from the people. Indeed, Allah does not guide the disbelieving people. (67) Say, "O People of the Scripture, you are [standing] on nothing until you uphold [the law of] the Torah, the Injeel, and what has been revealed to you from your Lord." And that which has been revealed to you from your Lord will surely increase many of them in transgression and disbelief. So do not grieve over the disbelieving people. (68) Indeed, those who have believed [in Prophet Muhammad] and those [before Him] who were Jews or Sabeans or Christians - those [among them] who believed in Allah and the Last Day and did righteousness - no fear will there be concerning them, nor will they grieve. (69) We had already taken the covenant of the Children of Israel and had sent to them messengers. Whenever there came to them a messenger with what their souls did not desire, a party [of messengers] they denied, and another party they killed. (70) And they thought there would be no [resulting] punishment, so they became blind and deaf. Then Allah turned to them in *forgiveness; then [again] many of them became blind and deaf. And Allah is Seeing of what they do. (71) They have certainly disbelieved who say, "Allah is the Messiah, the son of Mary" while the Messiah has said, "O Children of Israel, worship Allah, my Lord and your Lord." Indeed, he who associates others with Allah - Allah has forbidden him Paradise, and his refuge is the Fire. And there are not for the wrongdoers any helpers. (72) They have certainly disbelieved who say, "Allah is the third of three." And there is no god except one God. And if they do not desist from what they are saying, there will surely afflict the disbelievers among them a painful punishment. (73) So will they not repent to Allah and seek His forgiveness? And Allah is Forgiving and Merciful. (74) The Messiah, son of Mary, was not but a messenger; [other] messengers have passed on before him. And his mother was a supporter of truth. They both used to eat food. Look how We make clear to them the signs; then look how they are deluded. (75) Say, "Do you worship besides Allah that which holds for you no [power of] harm or benefit while it is Allah who is the Hearing, the Knowing?" (76) Say, "O People of the Scripture, do not exceed limits in your religion beyond the truth and do not follow the inclinations of a people who had gone astray before and misled many and have strayed from the soundness of the way." (77)*

Quran 6:19-28

قُلْ أَيُّ شَىْءٍ أَكْبَرُ شَهَٰدَةً ۖ قُلِ ٱللَّهُ ۖ شَهِيدٌۢ بَيْنِى وَبَيْنَكُمْ ۚ وَأُوحِىَ إِلَىَّ هَٰذَا ٱلْقُرْءَانُ لِأُنذِرَكُم بِهِۦ وَمَنۢ بَلَغَ ۚ أَئِنَّكُمْ لَتَشْهَدُونَ أَنَّ مَعَ ٱللَّهِ ءَالِهَةً أُخْرَىٰ ۚ قُل لَّآ أَشْهَدُ ۚ قُلْ إِنَّمَا هُوَ إِلَٰهٌ وَٰحِدٌ وَإِنَّنِى بَرِىٓءٌ مِّمَّا تُشْرِكُونَ (١٩) ٱلَّذِينَ ءَاتَيْنَٰهُمُ ٱلْكِتَٰبَ يَعْرِفُونَهُۥ كَمَا يَعْرِفُونَ أَبْنَآءَهُمُ ۘ ٱلَّذِينَ خَسِرُوٓاْ أَنفُسَهُمْ فَهُمْ لَا يُؤْمِنُونَ (٢٠) وَمَنْ أَظْلَمُ مِمَّنِ ٱفْتَرَىٰ عَلَى ٱللَّهِ كَذِبًا أَوْ كَذَّبَ بِـَٔايَٰتِهِۦٓ ۗ إِنَّهُۥ لَا يُفْلِحُ ٱلظَّٰلِمُونَ (٢١) وَيَوْمَ نَحْشُرُهُمْ جَمِيعًا ثُمَّ نَقُولُ لِلَّذِينَ أَشْرَكُوٓاْ أَيْنَ شُرَكَآؤُكُمُ ٱلَّذِينَ كُنتُمْ تَزْعُمُونَ (٢٢) ثُمَّ لَمْ تَكُن فِتْنَتُهُمْ إِلَّآ أَن قَالُواْ وَٱللَّهِ رَبِّنَا مَا كُنَّا مُشْرِكِينَ (٢٣) ٱنظُرْ كَيْفَ كَذَبُواْ عَلَىٰٓ أَنفُسِهِمْ ۚ وَضَلَّ عَنْهُم مَّا كَانُواْ يَفْتَرُونَ (٢٤) وَمِنْهُم مَّن يَسْتَمِعُ إِلَيْكَ ۖ وَجَعَلْنَا عَلَىٰ قُلُوبِهِمْ أَكِنَّةً أَن يَفْقَهُوهُ وَفِىٓ ءَاذَانِهِمْ وَقْرًا ۚ وَإِن يَرَوْاْ كُلَّ ءَايَةٍ لَّا يُؤْمِنُواْ بِهَا ۚ حَتَّىٰٓ إِذَا جَآءُوكَ يُجَٰدِلُونَكَ يَقُولُ ٱلَّذِينَ كَفَرُوٓاْ إِنْ هَٰذَآ إِلَّآ أَسَٰطِيرُ ٱلْأَوَّلِينَ (٢٥) وَهُمْ يَنْهَوْنَ عَنْهُ وَيَنْـَٔوْنَ عَنْهُ ۖ وَإِن يُهْلِكُونَ إِلَّآ أَنفُسَهُمْ وَمَا يَشْعُرُونَ (٢٦) وَلَوْ تَرَىٰٓ إِذْ وُقِفُواْ عَلَى ٱلنَّارِ فَقَالُواْ يَٰلَيْتَنَا نُرَدُّ وَلَا نُكَذِّبَ بِـَٔايَٰتِ رَبِّنَا وَنَكُونَ مِنَ ٱلْمُؤْمِنِينَ (٢٧) بَلْ بَدَا لَهُم مَّا كَانُواْ يُخْفُونَ مِن قَبْلُ ۖ وَلَوْ رُدُّواْ لَعَادُواْ لِمَا نُهُواْ عَنْهُ وَإِنَّهُمْ لَكَٰذِبُونَ (٢٨)

Say, "What thing is greatest in testimony?" Say, "Allah is witness between me and you. And this Qur'an was revealed to me that I may warn you thereby and whomever it reaches. Do you [truly] testify that with Allah there are other deities?" Say, "I will not testify [with you]." Say, "Indeed, He is but one God, and indeed, I am free of what you associate [with Him]." (19) Those to whom We have given the Scripture recognize it as they recognize their [own] sons. Those who will lose themselves [in the Hereafter] do not believe. (20) And who is more unjust than one who invents about Allah a lie or denies His verses? Indeed, the wrongdoers will not succeed. (21) And [mention, O Muhammad], the Day We will gather them all together; then We will say to those who associated others with Allah, "Where are your 'partners' that you used to claim [with Him]?" (22) Then there will be no [excuse upon] examination except they will say, "By Allah, our Lord, we were not those who associated." (23) See how they will lie about themselves. And lost from them will be what they used to invent. (24) And among them are those who listen to you, but We have placed over their hearts coverings, lest they understand it, and in their ears deafness. And if they should see every sign, they will not believe in it. Even when they come to you arguing with you, those who disbelieve say, "This is not but legends of the former peoples." (25) And they prevent [others] from him and are [themselves] remote from him. And they do not destroy except themselves, but they perceive [it] not. (26) If you could but see when they are made to stand before the Fire and will say, "Oh, would that we could be returned [to life on earth] and not deny the signs of our Lord and be among the believers." (27) But what they concealed before has [now] appeared to them. And even if they were returned, they would return to that which they were forbidden; and indeed, they are liars. (28)

Quran 13:43

وَيَقُولُ ٱلَّذِينَ كَفَرُوا۟ لَسْتَ مُرْسَلًا ۚ قُلْ كَفَىٰ بِٱللَّهِ شَهِيدًۢا بَيْنِى وَبَيْنَكُمْ وَمَنْ عِندَهُۥ عِلْمُ ٱلْكِتَٰبِ (٤٣)

And those who have disbelieved say, "You are not a messenger." Say, [O Muhammad], "Sufficient is Allah as Witness between me and you, and [the witness of] whoever has knowledge of the Scripture." (43)

Quran 29:46-49

۞ وَلَا تُجَٰدِلُوٓا۟ أَهْلَ ٱلْكِتَٰبِ إِلَّا بِٱلَّتِى هِىَ أَحْسَنُ إِلَّا ٱلَّذِينَ ظَلَمُوا۟ مِنْهُمْ ۖ وَقُولُوٓا۟ ءَامَنَّا بِٱلَّذِىٓ أُنزِلَ إِلَيْنَا وَأُنزِلَ إِلَيْكُمْ وَإِلَٰهُنَا وَإِلَٰهُكُمْ وَٰحِدٌ وَنَحْنُ لَهُۥ مُسْلِمُونَ (٤٦) وَكَذَٰلِكَ أَنزَلْنَآ إِلَيْكَ ٱلْكِتَٰبَ ۚ فَٱلَّذِينَ ءَاتَيْنَٰهُمُ ٱلْكِتَٰبَ يُؤْمِنُونَ بِهِۦ ۖ وَمِنْ هَٰٓؤُلَآءِ مَن يُؤْمِنُ بِهِۦ ۚ وَمَا يَجْحَدُ بِـَٔايَٰتِنَآ إِلَّا ٱلْكَٰفِرُونَ (٤٧) وَمَا كُنتَ تَتْلُوا۟ مِن قَبْلِهِۦ مِن كِتَٰبٍ وَلَا تَخُطُّهُۥ بِيَمِينِكَ ۖ إِذًا لَّٱرْتَابَ ٱلْمُبْطِلُونَ (٤٨) بَلْ هُوَ ءَايَٰتٌۢ بَيِّنَٰتٌ فِى صُدُورِ ٱلَّذِينَ أُوتُوا۟ ٱلْعِلْمَ ۚ وَمَا يَجْحَدُ بِـَٔايَٰتِنَآ إِلَّا ٱلظَّٰلِمُونَ (٤٩)

And do not argue with the People of the Scripture except in a way that is best, except for those who commit injustice among them, and say, "We believe in that which has been revealed to us and revealed to you. And our God and your God is one; and we are Muslims [in submission] to Him." (46) And thus We have sent down to you the Qur'an. And those to whom We [previously] gave the Scripture believe in it. And among these [people of Makkah] are those who believe in it. And none reject Our verses except the disbelievers. (47) And you did not recite before it any scripture, nor did you inscribe one with your right hand. Otherwise the falsifiers would have had [cause for] doubt. (48) Rather, the Qur'an is distinct verses [preserved] within the breasts of those who have been given knowledge. And none reject Our verses except the wrongdoers. (49)

Quran 4:4-12

قُلْ أَرَءَيْتُم مَّا تَدْعُونَ مِن دُونِ ٱللَّهِ أَرُونِى مَاذَا خَلَقُوا۟ مِنَ ٱلْأَرْضِ أَمْ لَهُمْ شِرْكٌ فِى ٱلسَّمَـٰوَٰتِ ٱئْتُونِى بِكِتَـٰبٍ مِّن قَبْلِ هَـٰذَآ أَوْ أَثَـٰرَةٍ مِّنْ عِلْمٍ إِن كُنتُمْ صَـٰدِقِينَ (٤) وَمَنْ أَضَلُّ مِمَّن يَدْعُوا۟ مِن دُونِ ٱللَّهِ مَن لَّا يَسْتَجِيبُ لَهُۥٓ إِلَىٰ يَوْمِ ٱلْقِيَـٰمَةِ وَهُمْ عَن دُعَآئِهِمْ غَـٰفِلُونَ (٥) وَإِذَا حُشِرَ ٱلنَّاسُ كَانُوا۟ لَهُمْ أَعْدَآءً وَكَانُوا۟ بِعِبَادَتِهِمْ كَـٰفِرِينَ (٦) وَإِذَا تُتْلَىٰ عَلَيْهِمْ ءَايَـٰتُنَا بَيِّنَـٰتٍ قَالَ ٱلَّذِينَ كَفَرُوا۟ لِلْحَقِّ لَمَّا جَآءَهُمْ هَـٰذَا سِحْرٌ مُّبِينٌ (٧) أَمْ يَقُولُونَ ٱفْتَرَىٰهُ قُلْ إِنِ ٱفْتَرَيْتُهُۥ فَلَا تَمْلِكُونَ لِى مِنَ ٱللَّهِ شَيْـًٔا هُوَ أَعْلَمُ بِمَا تُفِيضُونَ فِيهِ كَفَىٰ بِهِۦ شَهِيدًۢا بَيْنِى وَبَيْنَكُمْ وَهُوَ ٱلْغَفُورُ ٱلرَّحِيمُ (٨) قُلْ مَا كُنتُ بِدْعًا مِّنَ ٱلرُّسُلِ وَمَآ أَدْرِى مَا يُفْعَلُ بِى وَلَا بِكُمْ إِنْ أَتَّبِعُ إِلَّا مَا يُوحَىٰٓ إِلَىَّ وَمَآ أَنَا۠ إِلَّا نَذِيرٌ مُّبِينٌ (٩) قُلْ أَرَءَيْتُمْ إِن كَانَ مِنْ عِندِ ٱللَّهِ وَكَفَرْتُم بِهِۦ وَشَهِدَ شَاهِدٌ مِّنۢ بَنِىٓ إِسْرَٰٓءِيلَ عَلَىٰ مِثْلِهِۦ فَـَٔامَنَ وَٱسْتَكْبَرْتُمْ إِنَّ ٱللَّهَ لَا يَهْدِى ٱلْقَوْمَ ٱلظَّـٰلِمِينَ (١٠) وَقَالَ ٱلَّذِينَ كَفَرُوا۟ لِلَّذِينَ ءَامَنُوا۟ لَوْ كَانَ خَيْرًا مَّا سَبَقُونَآ إِلَيْهِ وَإِذْ لَمْ يَهْتَدُوا۟ بِهِۦ فَسَيَقُولُونَ هَـٰذَآ إِفْكٌ قَدِيمٌ (١١) وَمِن قَبْلِهِۦ كِتَـٰبُ مُوسَىٰٓ إِمَامًا وَرَحْمَةً وَهَـٰذَا كِتَـٰبٌ مُّصَدِّقٌ لِّسَانًا عَرَبِيًّا لِّيُنذِرَ ٱلَّذِينَ ظَلَمُوا۟ وَبُشْرَىٰ لِلْمُحْسِنِينَ (١٢)

Say, [O Muhammad], "Have you considered that which you invoke besides Allah? Show me what they have created of the earth; or did they have partnership in [creation of] the heavens? Bring me a scripture [revealed] before this or a [remaining] trace of knowledge, if you should be truthful." (4) And who is more astray than he who invokes besides Allah those who will not respond to him until the Day of Resurrection, and they, of their *invocation, are unaware. (5) And when the people are gathered [that Day], they [who were invoked] will be enemies to them, and they will be deniers of their worship. (6) And when Our verses are recited to them as clear evidences, those who disbelieve say of the truth when it has come to them, "This is obvious magic." (7) Or do they say, "He has invented it?" Say, "If I have invented it, you will not possess for me [the power of protection] from Allah at all. He is most knowing of that in which you are involved. Sufficient is He as Witness between me and you, and He is the Forgiving the Merciful." (8) Say, "I am not something original among the messengers, nor do I know what will be done with me or with you. I only follow that which is revealed to me, and I am not but a clear warner." (9) Say, "Have you considered: if the Qur'an was from Allah, and you disbelieved in it while a witness from the Children of Israel has testified to something similar and believed while you were arrogant?" Indeed, Allah does not guide the wrongdoing people. (10) And those who disbelieve say of those who believe, "If it had [truly] been good, they would not have preceded us to it." And when they are not guided by it, they will say, "This is an ancient falsehood." (11) And before it was the scripture of Moses to lead and as a mercy. And this is a confirming Book in an Arabic tongue to warn those who have wronged and as good tidings to the doers of good. (12)*

Quran 57:26-29

وَلَقَدْ أَرْسَلْنَا نُوحًا وَإِبْرَٰهِيمَ وَجَعَلْنَا فِى ذُرِّيَّتِهِمَا ٱلنُّبُوَّةَ وَٱلْكِتَٰبَ فَمِنْهُم مُّهْتَدٍ وَكَثِيرٌ مِّنْهُمْ فَٰسِقُونَ (٢٦) ثُمَّ قَفَّيْنَا عَلَىٰٓ ءَاثَٰرِهِم بِرُسُلِنَا وَقَفَّيْنَا بِعِيسَى ٱبْنِ مَرْيَمَ وَءَاتَيْنَٰهُ ٱلْإِنجِيلَ وَجَعَلْنَا فِى قُلُوبِ ٱلَّذِينَ ٱتَّبَعُوهُ رَأْفَةً وَرَحْمَةً وَرَهْبَانِيَّةً ٱبْتَدَعُوهَا مَا كَتَبْنَٰهَا عَلَيْهِمْ إِلَّا ٱبْتِغَآءَ رِضْوَٰنِ ٱللَّهِ فَمَا رَعَوْهَا حَقَّ رِعَايَتِهَا فَـَٔاتَيْنَا ٱلَّذِينَ ءَامَنُوا۟ مِنْهُمْ أَجْرَهُمْ وَكَثِيرٌ مِّنْهُمْ فَٰسِقُونَ (٢٧) يَٰٓأَيُّهَا ٱلَّذِينَ ءَامَنُوا۟ ٱتَّقُوا۟ ٱللَّهَ وَءَامِنُوا۟ بِرَسُولِهِۦ يُؤْتِكُمْ كِفْلَيْنِ مِن رَّحْمَتِهِۦ وَيَجْعَل لَّكُمْ نُورًا تَمْشُونَ بِهِۦ وَيَغْفِرْ لَكُمْ وَٱللَّهُ غَفُورٌ رَّحِيمٌ (٢٨) لِّئَلَّا يَعْلَمَ أَهْلُ ٱلْكِتَٰبِ أَلَّا يَقْدِرُونَ عَلَىٰ شَىْءٍ مِّن فَضْلِ ٱللَّهِ وَأَنَّ ٱلْفَضْلَ بِيَدِ ٱللَّهِ يُؤْتِيهِ مَن يَشَآءُ وَٱللَّهُ ذُو ٱلْفَضْلِ ٱلْعَظِيمِ (٢٩)

And We have already sent Noah and Abraham and placed in their descendants prophethood and scripture; and among them is he who is guided, but many of them are defiantly disobedient. (26) Then We sent following their footsteps Our messengers and followed [them] with Jesus, the son of Mary, and gave him the Injeel. And We placed in the hearts of those who followed him compassion and mercy, and monasticism, which they innovated; We did not prescribe it for them except [that they did so] seeking the approval of Allah. But they did not observe it with due observance. So We gave the ones who believed among them their reward, but many of them are defiantly disobedient. (27) O you who have believed, fear Allah and believe in His Messenger; He will [then] give you a double portion of His mercy and make for you a light by which you will walk and forgive you; and Allah is Forgiving and Merciful. (28) [This is] so that the People of the Scripture may know that they are not able [to obtain] anything from the bounty of Allah and that [all] bounty is in the hand of Allah; He gives it to whom He wills. And Allah is the possessor of great bounty. (29)

Quran chapter 98

لَمْ يَكُنِ ٱلَّذِينَ كَفَرُوا۟ مِنْ أَهْلِ ٱلْكِتَـٰبِ وَٱلْمُشْرِكِينَ مُنفَكِّينَ حَتَّىٰ تَأْتِيَهُمُ ٱلْبَيِّنَةُ (١) رَسُولٌ مِّنَ ٱللَّهِ يَتْلُوا۟ صُحُفًا مُّطَهَّرَةً (٢) فِيهَا كُتُبٌ قَيِّمَةٌ (٣) وَمَا تَفَرَّقَ ٱلَّذِينَ أُوتُوا۟ ٱلْكِتَـٰبَ إِلَّا مِنۢ بَعْدِ مَا جَآءَتْهُمُ ٱلْبَيِّنَةُ (٤) وَمَآ أُمِرُوٓا۟ إِلَّا لِيَعْبُدُوا۟ ٱللَّهَ مُخْلِصِينَ لَهُ ٱلدِّينَ حُنَفَآءَ وَيُقِيمُوا۟ ٱلصَّلَوٰةَ وَيُؤْتُوا۟ ٱلزَّكَوٰةَ وَذَٰلِكَ دِينُ ٱلْقَيِّمَةِ (٥) إِنَّ ٱلَّذِينَ كَفَرُوا۟ مِنْ أَهْلِ ٱلْكِتَـٰبِ وَٱلْمُشْرِكِينَ فِى نَارِ جَهَنَّمَ خَـٰلِدِينَ فِيهَآ أُو۟لَـٰٓئِكَ هُمْ شَرُّ ٱلْبَرِيَّةِ (٦) إِنَّ ٱلَّذِينَ ءَامَنُوا۟ وَعَمِلُوا۟ ٱلصَّـٰلِحَـٰتِ أُو۟لَـٰٓئِكَ هُمْ خَيْرُ ٱلْبَرِيَّةِ (٧) جَزَآؤُهُمْ عِندَ رَبِّهِمْ جَنَّـٰتُ عَدْنٍ تَجْرِى مِن تَحْتِهَا ٱلْأَنْهَـٰرُ خَـٰلِدِينَ فِيهَآ أَبَدًا ۖ رَّضِىَ ٱللَّهُ عَنْهُمْ وَرَضُوا۟ عَنْهُ ۚ ذَٰلِكَ لِمَنْ خَشِىَ رَبَّهُۥ (٨)

Those who disbelieved among the People of the Scripture and the polytheists were not to be parted [from misbelief] until there came to them clear evidence - (1) A Messenger from Allah, reciting purified scriptures (2) Within which are correct writings. (3) Nor did those who were given the Scripture become divided until after there had come to them clear evidence. (4) And they were not commanded except to worship Allah, [being] sincere to Him in religion, inclining to truth, and to establish prayer and to give zakah(charity). And that is the correct religion. (5) Indeed, they who disbelieved among the People of the Scripture and the polytheists will be in the fire of Hell, abiding eternally therein. Those are the worst of creatures. (6) Indeed, they who have believed and done righteous deeds - those are the best of creatures. (7) Their reward with Allah will be gardens of perpetual residence beneath which rivers flow, wherein they will abide forever, Allah being pleased with them and they with Him. That is for whoever has feared his Lord. (8)

Quran 3:58-71

ذَٰلِكَ نَتْلُوهُ عَلَيْكَ مِنَ ٱلْءَايَٰتِ وَٱلذِّكْرِ ٱلْحَكِيمِ (٥٨) إِنَّ مَثَلَ عِيسَىٰ عِندَ ٱللَّهِ كَمَثَلِ ءَادَمَ ۖ خَلَقَهُۥ مِن تُرَابٍ ثُمَّ قَالَ لَهُۥ كُن فَيَكُونُ (٥٩) ٱلْحَقُّ مِن رَّبِّكَ فَلَا تَكُن مِّنَ ٱلْمُمْتَرِينَ (٦٠) فَمَنْ حَآجَّكَ فِيهِ مِنۢ بَعْدِ مَا جَآءَكَ مِنَ ٱلْعِلْمِ فَقُلْ تَعَالَوْاْ نَدْعُ أَبْنَآءَنَا وَأَبْنَآءَكُمْ وَنِسَآءَنَا وَنِسَآءَكُمْ وَأَنفُسَنَا وَأَنفُسَكُمْ ثُمَّ نَبْتَهِلْ فَنَجْعَل لَّعْنَتَ ٱللَّهِ عَلَى ٱلْكَٰذِبِينَ (٦١) إِنَّ هَٰذَا لَهُوَ ٱلْقَصَصُ ٱلْحَقُّ ۚ وَمَا مِنْ إِلَٰهٍ إِلَّا ٱللَّهُ ۚ وَإِنَّ ٱللَّهَ لَهُوَ ٱلْعَزِيزُ ٱلْحَكِيمُ (٦٢) فَإِن تَوَلَّوْاْ فَإِنَّ ٱللَّهَ عَلِيمٌۢ بِٱلْمُفْسِدِينَ (٦٣) قُلْ يَٰٓأَهْلَ ٱلْكِتَٰبِ تَعَالَوْاْ إِلَىٰ كَلِمَةٍ سَوَآءٍۭ بَيْنَنَا وَبَيْنَكُمْ أَلَّا نَعْبُدَ إِلَّا ٱللَّهَ وَلَا نُشْرِكَ بِهِۦ شَيْـًٔا وَلَا يَتَّخِذَ بَعْضُنَا بَعْضًا أَرْبَابًۭا مِّن دُونِ ٱللَّهِ ۚ فَإِن تَوَلَّوْاْ فَقُولُواْ ٱشْهَدُواْ بِأَنَّا مُسْلِمُونَ (٦٤) يَٰٓأَهْلَ ٱلْكِتَٰبِ لِمَ تُحَآجُّونَ فِىٓ إِبْرَٰهِيمَ وَمَآ أُنزِلَتِ ٱلتَّوْرَىٰةُ وَٱلْإِنجِيلُ إِلَّا مِنۢ بَعْدِهِۦٓ ۚ أَفَلَا تَعْقِلُونَ (٦٥) هَٰٓأَنتُمْ هَٰٓؤُلَآءِ حَٰجَجْتُمْ فِيمَا لَكُم بِهِۦ عِلْمٌ فَلِمَ تُحَآجُّونَ فِيمَا لَيْسَ لَكُم بِهِۦ عِلْمٌ ۚ وَٱللَّهُ يَعْلَمُ وَأَنتُمْ لَا تَعْلَمُونَ (٦٦) مَا كَانَ إِبْرَٰهِيمُ يَهُودِيًّۭا وَلَا نَصْرَانِيًّۭا وَلَٰكِن كَانَ حَنِيفًۭا مُّسْلِمًۭا وَمَا كَانَ مِنَ ٱلْمُشْرِكِينَ (٦٧) إِنَّ أَوْلَى ٱلنَّاسِ بِإِبْرَٰهِيمَ لَلَّذِينَ ٱتَّبَعُوهُ وَهَٰذَا ٱلنَّبِىُّ وَٱلَّذِينَ ءَامَنُواْ ۗ وَٱللَّهُ وَلِىُّ ٱلْمُؤْمِنِينَ (٦٨) وَدَّت طَّآئِفَةٌۭ مِّنْ أَهْلِ ٱلْكِتَٰبِ لَوْ يُضِلُّونَكُمْ وَمَا يُضِلُّونَ إِلَّآ أَنفُسَهُمْ وَمَا يَشْعُرُونَ (٦٩) يَٰٓأَهْلَ ٱلْكِتَٰبِ لِمَ تَكْفُرُونَ بِـَٔايَٰتِ ٱللَّهِ وَأَنتُمْ تَشْهَدُونَ (٧٠) يَٰٓأَهْلَ ٱلْكِتَٰبِ لِمَ تَلْبِسُونَ ٱلْحَقَّ بِٱلْبَٰطِلِ وَتَكْتُمُونَ ٱلْحَقَّ وَأَنتُمْ تَعْلَمُونَ (٧١)

This is what We recite to you, [O Muhammad], of [Our] verses and the precise [and wise] message. (58) Indeed, the example of Jesus to Allah is like that of Adam. He created Him from dust; then He said to him, "Be," and he was. (59) The truth is from your Lord, so do not be among the doubters. (60) Then whoever argues with you about it after [this] knowledge has come to you - say, "Come, let us call our sons and your sons, our women and your women, ourselves and yourselves, then supplicate earnestly [together] and invoke the curse of Allah upon the liars [among us]." (61) Indeed, this is the true narration. And there is no deity except Allah. And indeed, Allah is the Exalted in Might, the Wise. (62) But if they turn away, then indeed - Allah is Knowing of the corrupters. (63) Say, "O People of the Scripture, come to a word that is equitable between us and you - that we will not worship except Allah and not associate anything with Him and not take one another as lords instead of Allah." But if they turn away, then say, "Bear witness that we are Muslims [submitting to Him]." (64) O People of the Scripture, why do you argue about Abraham while the Torah and the Injeel were not revealed until after him? Then will you not reason? (65) Here you are - those who have argued about that of which you have [some] knowledge, but why do you argue about that of which you have no knowledge? And Allah knows, while you know not. (66) Abraham was neither a Jew nor a Christian, but he was one inclining toward truth, a Muslim [submitting to Allah]. And he was not of the polytheists. (67) Indeed, the most worthy of Abraham among the people are those who followed him [in submission to Allah] and this prophet, and those who believe [in his message]. And Allah is the ally of the believers. (68) A faction of the people of the Scripture wish they could mislead you. But they do not mislead except themselves, and they perceive [it] not. (69) O People of the Scripture, why do you disbelieve in the verses of Allah while you witness [to their truth]? (70) O People of the Scripture, why do you confuse the truth with falsehood and conceal the truth while you know [it]? (71)

Quran 3:77-85

إِنَّ ٱلَّذِينَ يَشْتَرُونَ بِعَهْدِ ٱللَّهِ وَأَيْمَٰنِهِمْ ثَمَنًا قَلِيلًا أُوْلَٰٓئِكَ لَا خَلَٰقَ لَهُمْ فِى ٱلْءَاخِرَةِ وَلَا يُكَلِّمُهُمُ ٱللَّهُ وَلَا يَنظُرُ إِلَيْهِمْ يَوْمَ ٱلْقِيَٰمَةِ وَلَا يُزَكِّيهِمْ وَلَهُمْ عَذَابٌ أَلِيمٌ (٧٧) وَإِنَّ مِنْهُمْ لَفَرِيقًا يَلْوُۥنَ أَلْسِنَتَهُم بِٱلْكِتَٰبِ لِتَحْسَبُوهُ مِنَ ٱلْكِتَٰبِ وَمَا هُوَ مِنَ ٱلْكِتَٰبِ وَيَقُولُونَ هُوَ مِنْ عِندِ ٱللَّهِ وَمَا هُوَ مِنْ عِندِ ٱللَّهِ وَيَقُولُونَ عَلَى ٱللَّهِ ٱلْكَذِبَ وَهُمْ يَعْلَمُونَ (٧٨) مَا كَانَ لِبَشَرٍ أَن يُؤْتِيَهُ ٱللَّهُ ٱلْكِتَٰبَ وَٱلْحُكْمَ وَٱلنُّبُوَّةَ ثُمَّ يَقُولَ لِلنَّاسِ كُونُواْ عِبَادًا لِّى مِن دُونِ ٱللَّهِ وَلَٰكِن كُونُواْ رَبَّٰنِيِّۦنَ بِمَا كُنتُمْ تُعَلِّمُونَ ٱلْكِتَٰبَ وَبِمَا كُنتُمْ تَدْرُسُونَ (٧٩) وَلَا يَأْمُرَكُمْ أَن تَتَّخِذُواْ ٱلْمَلَٰٓئِكَةَ وَٱلنَّبِيِّۦنَ أَرْبَابًا أَيَأْمُرُكُم بِٱلْكُفْرِ بَعْدَ إِذْ أَنتُم مُّسْلِمُونَ (٨٠) وَإِذْ أَخَذَ ٱللَّهُ مِيثَٰقَ ٱلنَّبِيِّۦنَ لَمَا ءَاتَيْتُكُم مِّن كِتَٰبٍ وَحِكْمَةٍ ثُمَّ جَآءَكُمْ رَسُولٌ مُّصَدِّقٌ لِّمَا مَعَكُمْ لَتُؤْمِنُنَّ بِهِۦ وَلَتَنصُرُنَّهُۥ قَالَ ءَأَقْرَرْتُمْ وَأَخَذْتُمْ عَلَىٰ ذَٰلِكُمْ إِصْرِى قَالُوٓاْ أَقْرَرْنَا قَالَ فَٱشْهَدُواْ وَأَنَا۠ مَعَكُم مِّنَ ٱلشَّٰهِدِينَ (٨١) فَمَن تَوَلَّىٰ بَعْدَ ذَٰلِكَ فَأُوْلَٰٓئِكَ هُمُ ٱلْفَٰسِقُونَ (٨٢) أَفَغَيْرَ دِينِ ٱللَّهِ يَبْغُونَ وَلَهُۥٓ أَسْلَمَ مَن فِى ٱلسَّمَٰوَٰتِ وَٱلْأَرْضِ طَوْعًا وَكَرْهًا وَإِلَيْهِ يُرْجَعُونَ (٨٣) قُلْ ءَامَنَّا بِٱللَّهِ وَمَآ أُنزِلَ عَلَيْنَا وَمَآ أُنزِلَ عَلَىٰٓ إِبْرَٰهِيمَ وَإِسْمَٰعِيلَ وَإِسْحَٰقَ وَيَعْقُوبَ

وَٱلْأَسْبَاطِ وَمَا أُوتِىَ مُوسَىٰ وَعِيسَىٰ وَٱلنَّبِيُّونَ مِن رَّبِّهِمْ لَا نُفَرِّقُ بَيْنَ أَحَدٍ مِّنْهُمْ وَنَحْنُ لَهُۥ مُسْلِمُونَ (٨٤) وَمَن يَبْتَغِ غَيْرَ ٱلْإِسْلَٰمِ دِينًا فَلَن يُقْبَلَ مِنْهُ وَهُوَ فِى ٱلْأَخِرَةِ مِنَ ٱلْخَٰسِرِينَ (٨٥)

Indeed, those who exchange the covenant of Allah and their [own] oaths for a small price will have no share in the Hereafter, and Allah will not speak to them or look at them on the Day of Resurrection, nor will He purify them; and they will have a painful punishment. (77) And indeed, there is among them a party who alter the Scripture with their tongues so you may think it is from the Scripture, but it is not from the Scripture. And they say, "This is from Allah," but it is not from Allah. And they speak untruth about Allah while they know. (78) It is not for a human [prophet] that Allah should give him the Scripture and authority and prophethood and then he would say to the people, "Be servants to me rather than Allah," but [instead, he would say], "Be pious scholars of the Lord because of what you have taught of the Scripture and because of what you have studied." (79) Nor could he order you to take the angels and prophets as lords. Would he order you to disbelief after you had been Muslims? (80) And [recall, O People of the Scripture], when Allah took the covenant of the prophets, [saying], "Whatever I give you of the Scripture and wisdom and then there comes to you a messenger confirming what is with you, you [must] believe in him and support him." [Allah] said, "Have you acknowledged and taken upon that My

commitment?" They said, "We have acknowledged it."
He said, "Then bear witness, and I am with you among
the witnesses." (81) And whoever turned away after that
- they were the defiantly disobedient. (82) So is it other
than the religion of Allah they desire, while to Him have
submitted [all] those within the heavens and earth,
willingly or by compulsion, and to Him they will be
returned? (83) Say, "We have believed in Allah and in
what was revealed to us and what was revealed to
Abraham, Ishmael, Isaac, Jacob, and the Descendants,
and in what was given to Moses and Jesus and to the
prophets from their Lord. We make no distinction
between any of them, and we are Muslims [submitting]
to Him." (84) And whoever desires other than Islam as
religion - never will it be accepted from him, and he, in
the Hereafter, will be among the losers. (85)

Quran 5:82-86

۞ لَتَجِدَنَّ أَشَدَّ ٱلنَّاسِ عَدَٰوَةً لِّلَّذِينَ ءَامَنُوا۟ ٱلْيَهُودَ وَٱلَّذِينَ أَشْرَكُوا۟ۖ وَلَتَجِدَنَّ أَقْرَبَهُم مَّوَدَّةً لِّلَّذِينَ ءَامَنُوا۟ ٱلَّذِينَ قَالُوٓا۟ إِنَّا نَصَٰرَىٰۚ ذَٰلِكَ بِأَنَّ مِنْهُمْ قِسِّيسِينَ وَرُهْبَانًا وَأَنَّهُمْ لَا يَسْتَكْبِرُونَ (٨٢) وَإِذَا سَمِعُوا۟ مَآ أُنزِلَ إِلَى ٱلرَّسُولِ تَرَىٰٓ أَعْيُنَهُمْ تَفِيضُ مِنَ ٱلدَّمْعِ مِمَّا عَرَفُوا۟ مِنَ ٱلْحَقِّۖ يَقُولُونَ رَبَّنَآ ءَامَنَّا فَٱكْتُبْنَا مَعَ ٱلشَّٰهِدِينَ (٨٣) وَمَا لَنَا لَا نُؤْمِنُ بِٱللَّهِ وَمَا جَآءَنَا مِنَ ٱلْحَقِّ وَنَطْمَعُ أَن يُدْخِلَنَا رَبُّنَا مَعَ ٱلْقَوْمِ ٱلصَّٰلِحِينَ (٨٤) فَأَثَٰبَهُمُ ٱللَّهُ بِمَا قَالُوا۟ جَنَّٰتٍ تَجْرِى مِن تَحْتِهَا ٱلْأَنْهَٰرُ خَٰلِدِينَ فِيهَاۚ وَذَٰلِكَ جَزَآءُ ٱلْمُحْسِنِينَ (٨٥) وَٱلَّذِينَ كَفَرُوا۟ وَكَذَّبُوا۟ بِـَٔايَٰتِنَآ أُو۟لَٰٓئِكَ أَصْحَٰبُ ٱلْجَحِيمِ (٨٦)

You will surely find the most intense of the people in animosity toward the believers [to be] the Jews and those who associate others with Allah; and you will find the nearest of them in affection to the believers those who say, "We are Christians." That is because among them are priests and monks and because they are not arrogant. (82) And when they hear what has been revealed to the Messenger(Muhammad), you see their eyes overflowing with tears because of what they have recognized of the truth. They say, "Our Lord, we have believed, so register us among the witnesses. (83) And why should we not believe in Allah and what has come to us of the truth? And we aspire that our Lord will admit us [to Paradise] with the righteous people." (84) So Allah rewarded them for what they said with gardens [in Paradise] beneath which rivers flow, wherein they abide eternally. And that is the reward of doers of good. (85) But those who disbelieved and denied Our signs - they are the companions of Hellfire. (86)

Quran chapter 112

قُلْ هُوَ ٱللَّهُ أَحَدٌ (١) ٱللَّهُ ٱلصَّمَدُ (٢) لَمْ يَلِدْ وَلَمْ يُولَدْ (٣) وَلَمْ يَكُن لَّهُۥ كُفُوًا أَحَدٌۢ (٤)

Say, "He is Allah, [who is] One, (1) Allah, the Eternal Refuge. (2) He neither begets nor is born, (3) Nor is there to Him any equivalent." (4)

Abu Huraira reported Allah's Messenger (ﷺ) as saying:

"I am most akin to Jesus Christ among the whole of mankind, and all the Prophets are of different mothers but belong to one religion and no Prophet was raised between me and Jesus."

Source: Sahih Muslim 2365b

Abu Huraira reported Allah's Messenger (ﷺ) as saying:

The mother of every person gives him birth according to his true nature. It is subsequently his parents who make him a Jew or a Christian or a Magian. Had his parents been Muslim he would have also remained a Muslim. Every person to whom his mother gives birth (has two aspects of his life); when his mother gives birth Satan strikes him but it was not the case with Mary and her son (Jesus Christ).

Source: Sahih Muslim 2659a

Abu Hurairah reported:

The Prophet (ﷺ) said, "None spoke in the cradle but only three (persons), Isa (Jesus) son of Maryam (Mary), the second one was the companion of Juraij who was a pious person. Juraij took a secluded monastery for worship and confined himself in it. His mother came to him as he was busy in prayer and she called: 'Juraij.' He said: 'My Lord, my mother (is calling me while I am engaged in) my prayer.' He continued with the prayer. She returned and she came on the next day and he was (still) busy in prayer. She called: 'Juraij.' And he said: 'My Lord, my mother (is calling me while I am engaged) in prayer, and he continued with the prayer,' and she returned. Then on the next day she again came while he was busy in prayer and called: 'Juraij.' And he said: 'My Lord, my mother (is calling me while I am engaged) in my prayer.' And he continued with the prayer. She said: 'My Lord, don't let him die until he has seen the faces of the prostitutes.' The story of Juraij and that of his meditation and prayer spread amongst Banu Israel. There was a prostitute who had been a beauty personified. She said (to the people): 'If you like, I can lure him to evil.' She presented herself to him but he paid no heed (to her). She came to a shepherd who lived near the temple and she offered herself to him. He (the shepherd) had sexual intercourse with her and so she became pregnant. When she gave birth to a baby she said: 'This is from Juraij.' So they came and asked Juraij to get down and demolished the temple and began to beat him. He asked them what the matter was. They said: 'You have committed fornication with this prostitute and she has given birth to a baby from you.' He said: 'Where is the baby?' They brought him (the baby) and then he said: 'Just leave me so that I should perform prayer.' He *performed prayer and when he finished, he lifted the baby in his stomach and asked him: 'O boy, who is your father?' The baby answered: 'He is such and such a shepherd.' So, the people turned towards Juraij, kissed him and touched him (for seeking blessing) and said: 'We are prepared to construct your temple with gold.' He said, 'No just, rebuild it with mud as it had been,' and so they did".* (The Prophet (ﷺ) continued:) "Then there was a baby who was sucking at his mother's breast when a person dressed in fine garment came on a priceless riding animal's back. His mother said: 'O Allah, make my child like this one.' He (the babe) left sucking and looked at him, and said: 'O Allah, don't make me like him.' He then returned to the breast and resumed sucking." He (Abu Hurairah said: As though I can see Messenger of Allah (ﷺ) as he is illustrating the scene of his sucking milk with his forefinger in his mouth and sucking that. He (Abu Hurairah) further reported Messenger of Allah (ﷺ) as saying, "There happened to pass by them a slave girl who was being beaten and they were saying: 'You have committed fornication and theft.' She was saying: 'Allah is enough for me and He is my Good Protector, and his mother said: 'O Allah, don't make my child like her.' He left sucking looked at her and said: 'O Allah! Make me like her.' It was followed by a conversation between the mother and the child. She said: 'A good looking man happened to pass by and I said: O Allah, make my child like him, and you said: O Allah, don't make me like him, and there passed a girl while they were beating her and saying: You committed fornication and theft, and I said: O Allah, don't make my child like her, and you said: O Allah, make me like her.' The child said: 'That man was a tyrant, and I said: O Allah don't make me like him; and they were saying about the girl: You committed fornication, whereas in fact she had not committed that and they were saying: You have committed theft, whereas she had not committed theft, so I said: O Allah, make me like her".

Source: Riyad as-Salihin 259 Grade: Sahih

An-Nawwas bin Sam`an reported:

One morning the Messenger of Allah (ﷺ) made a mention of Dajjal(Antichrist), and he described him to be insignificant and at the same time described him so significant that we thought he was on the date-palm trees (i.e., nearby). When we went to him (the Prophet (ﷺ)) in the evening, he perceived the sign of fear on our faces. He said, "What is the matter with you?'' We said: "O Messenger of Allah, you talked about Dajjal(Antichrist) this morning raising your voice and lowering it until we thought he was hiding in the palm-trees grove: He said: "Something other than Dajjal(Antichrist) make worry about you. If he appears while I am with you, I will defend you against him. But if he appears after I die, then *everyone of you is his own defender. Allah is the One Who remains after me to guide every Muslim. Dajjal(Antichrist) will be a young man with very curly hair with one eye protruding (with which he cannot see). I compare (his appearance) to that of Al-`Uzza bin Qatan. He who amongst you survives to see him, should recite over him the opening Ayat of Surat Al-Kahf (i.e., Surat 18: Verses 1-8). He will appear on the way between Syria and Iraq and will spread mischief right and left. O slaves of Allah! Remain adhered to the truth.''* We asked: "O Messenger of Allah! How long will he stay on the earth?'' He said, "For forty days. One day will be like a year, one day like a month, one day like a week and the rest of the days will be like your days.'' We said: "O Messenger of Allah! Will one day's Salat (prayer) suffice for the Salat of that day which will be equal to one year?'' Thereupon he said, "No, but you must make an estimate of time and then offer Salat.'' We said: "O Messenger of Allah! How quickly will he walk upon the earth?'' Thereupon he said, "Like cloud driven by the wind (i.e., very quickly). He will come to the people and call them to his obedience and they will affirm their faith in him and respond to him. He will then give command to the sky and it will send its rain upon the earth and he will then send his command to the earth and it will grow vegetation. Then in the evening their pasturing animals will come to them with their humps very high and their udders full of milk and their flanks stretched. He will then come to another people and invite them, but they will reject him and he will leave them, in barren lands and without any goods and chattels! He would then walk through the waste land and say to it: `Bring forth your treasures', and the treasures will come out and follow him like swarms of bees. He will then call a person brimming with youth and strike him with the sword and cut him into two pieces and make these pieces lie at a distance, which is generally between the archer and his target. He will then call that young man and he will come forward, laughing, with his face gleaming out of joy; and it will be at this very time that Allah will send `Isa (Jesus), son of Maryam (Mary) who will descend at the white minaret in the eastern side of Damascus, wearing two garments lightly dyed and placing his hands on the wings of two angels. When he will lower his head, there would fall drops of water from his head, and when he will raise it up, drops like pearls would scatter from it. Every disbeliever who will find his (i.e., `Jesus') smell will die and his smell will reach as far as he will be able to see. He will then search for Dajjal(Antichrist) until he will catch hold of him at the gate of Ludd (village near Jerusalem), and will kill him. Then the people, whom Allah will have protected, will come to `Isa(Jesus) son of Maryam, and he will wipe their faces and will inform them of their ranks in Paradise, and it will be under such conditions that Allah will reveal to `Isa(Jesus) these words: `I have brought forth from amongst my slaves such people against whom none will be able to fight, so take these people safely to the mountain.' And then Allah will send Ya'juj and Ma'juj (Gog and Magog people) and they will swoop down from every slope. The first of them will pass the Lake Tabariyah (near the Dead Sea in Palestine) and drink all its water. And when the last of them will pass, he will say: `There was once water there.' Prophet `Isa (Jesus) and his companions will then be so much hard-pressed that the head of an ox will be dearer to them than one hundred dinar, and `Isa(Jesus) along with his companions, will make supplication to Allah, Who will send insects which will attack their (Ya'juj and Ma'juj people) neck until they all will perish like a single person. Prophet, Isa(Jesus) and his companions will then come down and they will not find in the earth as much space as a single span which would not be filled with their corpses and their stench. Prophet `Isa(Jesus) and his companions will then again beseech Allah, Who will send birds whose necks will be like those of Bactrian camels, and they will carry them and throw them where Allah will desire. Then Allah will send down rain which will spare no house in the city or in the countryside. It would wash away the earth until it appears like a mirror. Then the earth will be told to bring forth its fruit and restore its blessings; and as a result of this, there will grow such a big pomegranate that a group of people will eat from it and seek shelter under its skin. Milk will be so blessed that the milk of one she-camel will suffice for a large company and the cow will give so much milk, that it will suffice for a whole tribe. The sheep will give so much milk that the whole family will be able to drink out of that, and at that time Allah will send a pleasant wind which will soothe people even under their armpits, and will take the life of every Muslim and true believer, and only the wicked will survive. They will commit adultery in public like asses and the Resurrection Day will be held."

Source: Riyad As-Saliheen 1808 Grade: Sahih

Jabir bin 'Abdullah reported:

I heard the Messenger of Allah (ﷺ) say: A section of my people will not cease fighting for the Truth and will prevail till the Day of Resurrection. He said: Jesus son of Mary would then descend and their (Muslims') commander would invite him to come and lead them in prayer, but he (Jesus) would say: No, some amongst you are commanders over some (amongst you). This is the honour from Allah for this Ummah.

Source: Sahih Muslim 156

It was narrated that Thawban, the freed slave of the Messenger of Allah (ﷺ), said:

"The Messenger of Allah (ﷺ) said: 'There are two groups of my Ummah whom Allah will free from the Fire: The group that invades India, and the group that will be with 'Isa(Jesus) bin Maryam, peace be upon him.'"

Source: Sunan an-Nasa'i 3175 Grade: Hasan

Hanzala al-Aslami reported:

I heard Abu Huraira (Allah be pleased with him) as narrating from Allah's Messenger (ﷺ) who said: By Him in Whose Hand is my life. Ibn Maryam (Jesus Christ) would certainly pronounce Talbiya for Hajj or for Umra or for both (simultaneously as a Qiran) In the valley of Rauha.

Source: Sahih Muslim 1252a

Narrated Abu Hurayrah:

The Prophet (ﷺ) said: There is no prophet between me and him, that is, Jesus (ﷺ). He will descent (to the earth). When you see him, recognize him: a man of medium height, reddish fair, wearing two light yellow garments, looking as if drops were falling down from his head though it will not be wet. He will fight the people for the cause of Islam. He will break the cross, kill swine, and abolish jizyah. Allah will perish all religions except Islam. He will destroy the Antichrist and will live on the earth for forty years and then he will die. The Muslims will pray over him.

Source: Sunan Abi Dawud 4324 Grade: Sahih

Narrated 'Ubada:

The Prophet (ﷺ) said:

"If anyone testifies that None has the right to be worshipped but Allah Alone Who has no partners, and that Muhammad is His Slave and His Messenger, and that Jesus is Allah's Slave and His Messenger and His Word which He bestowed on Mary and a Spirit created by Him, and that Paradise is true, and Hell is true, Allah will admit him into Paradise with the deeds which he had done even if those deeds were few." (Junada, the sub-narrator said, " 'Ubada added, 'Such a person can enter Paradise through any of its eight gates he likes.")

Source: Sahih al-Bukhari 3435

Narrated Abu Burda's father:

Allah's Messenger (ﷺ) said "Three persons will have a double reward:

1. A Person from the people of the scriptures who believed in his prophet (Jesus or Moses) and then believed in the Prophet (ﷺ) Muhammad (i.e. has embraced Islam).

2. A slave who discharges his duties to Allah and his master.

3. A master of a woman-slave who teaches her good manners and educates her in the best possible way (the religion) and manumits her and then marries her."

Source: Sahih al-Bukhari 97

Narrated Abu Sa`id Al-Khudri:

During the lifetime of the Prophet (ﷺ) some people said: O Allah's Messenger (ﷺ)! Shall we see our Lord on the Day of Resurrection?" The Prophet (ﷺ) said, "Yes; do you have any difficulty in seeing the sun at midday when it is bright and there is no cloud in the sky?" They replied, "No." He said, "Do you have any difficulty in seeing the moon on a full moon night when it is bright and there is no cloud in the sky?" They replied, "No." The Prophet (ﷺ) said, "(Similarly) you will have no difficulty in seeing Allah on the Day of Resurrection as you have no difficulty in seeing either of them. On the Day of Resurrection, a call-maker will announce, "Let every nation follow that which they used to worship." Then none of those who used to worship anything other than Allah like idols and other deities but will fall in Hell (Fire), till there will remain none but those who used to worship Allah, both those who were obedient (i.e. good) and those who were disobedient (i.e. bad) and the remaining party of the people of the Scripture. Then the Jews will be called upon and it will be said to them, 'Who do you use to worship?' They will say, 'We used to worship Ezra, the son of Allah.' It will be said to them, 'You are liars, for Allah has never taken anyone as a wife or a son. What do you want now?' They will say, 'O our Lord! We are thirsty, so give us something to drink.' They will be directed and addressed thus, 'Will you drink,' whereupon they will be gathered unto Hell (Fire) which will look like a mirage whose different sides will be destroying each other. Then they will fall into the Fire. Afterwards the Christians will be called upon and it will be said to them, 'Who do you use to worship?' They will say, 'We used to worship Jesus, the son of Allah.' It will be said to them, 'You are liars, for Allah has never taken anyone as a wife or a son,' Then it will be said to them, 'What do you want?' They will say what the former people have said. Then, when there remain (in the gathering) none but those who used to worship Allah (Alone, the real Lord of the Worlds) whether they were obedient or disobedient. Then (Allah) the Lord of the worlds will come to them in a shape nearest to the picture they had in their minds about Him. It will be said, 'What are you waiting for?' Every nation have followed what they used to worship.' They will reply, 'We left the people in the world when we were in great need of them and we did not take them as friends. Now we are waiting for our Lord Whom we used to worship.' Allah will say, 'I am your Lord.' They will say twice or thrice, 'We do not worship any besides Allah.' "

Source: Sahih al-Bukhari 4581

Narrated Anas:

The Prophet said, "The believers will be kept (waiting) on the Day of Resurrection so long that they will become worried and say, "Let us ask somebody to intercede far us with our Lord so that He may relieve us from our place.

Then they will go to Adam and say, 'You are Adam, the father of the people. Allah created you with His Own Hand and made you reside in His Paradise and ordered His angels to prostrate before you, and taught you the names of all things will you intercede for us with your Lord so that He may relieve us from this place of ours? Adam will say, 'I am not fit for this undertaking.' He will mention his mistakes he had committed, i.e., his eating off the tree though he had been forbidden to do so. He will add, 'Go to Noah, the first prophet sent by Allah to the people of the Earth.' The people will go to Noah who will say, 'I am not fit for this undertaking' He will mention his mistake which he had done, i.e., his asking his Lord without knowledge.' He will say (to them), 'Go to Abraham, Khalil Ar-Rahman.' They will go to Abraham who will say, 'I am not fit for this undertaking. He would mention three words by which he told a lie, and say (to them). 'Go to Moses, a slave whom Allah gave the Torah and spoke to, directly and brought near Him, for conversation.'

They will go to Moses who will say, 'I am not fit for this undertaking. He will mention his mistake he made, i.e., killing a person, and will say (to them), 'Go to Jesus, Allah's slave and His Apostle, and a soul created by Him and His Word.' (Be: And it was.) They will go to Jesus who will say, 'I am not fit for this undertaking but you'd better go to Muhammad the slave whose past and future sins have been forgiven by Allah.' So they will come to me, and I will ask my Lord's permission to enter His House and then I will be permitted. When I see Him I will fall down in prostration before Him, and He will leave me (in prostration) as long as He will, and then He will say, 'O Muhammad, lift up your head and speak, for you will be listened to, and intercede, for your intercession will be accepted, and ask (for anything) for it will be granted:' Then I will raise my head and glorify my Lord with certain praises which He has taught me. Allah will put a limit for me (to intercede for a certain type of people) I will take them out and make them enter Paradise." (Qatada said: I heard Anas saying that), the Prophet said, "I will go out and take them out of Hell (Fire) and let them enter Paradise, and then I will return and ask my Lord for permission to enter His House and I will be permitted.

When I will see Him I will fall down in prostration before Him and He will leave me in prostration as long as He will let me (in that state), and then He will say, 'O

Muhammad, raise your head and speak, for you will be listened to, and intercede, for your intercession will be accepted, and ask, your request will be granted.' " The Prophet added, "So I will raise my head and glorify and praise Him as He has taught me. Then I will intercede and He will put a limit for me (to intercede for a certain type of people). I will take them out and let them enter Paradise." (Qatada added: I heard Anas saying that) the Prophet said, 'I will go out and take them out of Hell (Fire) and let them enter Paradise, and I will return for the third time and will ask my Lord for permission to enter His house, and I will be allowed to enter.

When I see Him, I will fall down in prostration before Him, and will remain in prostration as long as He will, and then He will say, 'Raise your head, O Muhammad, and speak, for you will be listened to, and intercede, for your intercession will be accepted, and ask, for your request will be granted.' So I will raise my head and praise Allah as He has taught me and then I will intercede and He will put a limit for me (to intercede for a certain type of people). I will take them out and let them enter Paradise." (Qatada said: I heard Anas saying that) the Prophet said, "So I will go out and take them out of Hell (Fire) and let them enter Paradise, till none will remain in the Fire except those whom Quran will imprison (i.e., those who are destined for eternal life in the fire)." The narrator then recited the Verse:-- "It may be that your Lord will raise you to a Station of Praise and Glory.' (17.79) The narrator added: This is the Station of Praise and Glory which Allah has promised to your Prophet.

Source: Sahih al-Bukhari 7440

Narrated Abu Sa'eed Al-Khudri:

that the Messenger of Allah (ﷺ) said: "I am the chief of the children of Adam on the Day of Judgement and I am not boasting, and in my hand is the banner of praise and I am not boasting, and there has been no Prophet since Adam or other than him, except that he is under my banner. And I am the first for whom the earth will split open, and I am not boasting." He said: "The people will be frightened by three frights. So they will come to Adam saying: 'You are our father Adam, so intercede for us with your Lord.' So he says: 'I committed a sin for which I was expelled to the earth, so go to Nuh.' So they will come to Nuh and he will say: 'I supplicated against the people of the earth, so they were destroyed. So go to Ibrahim.' So they will go to Ibrahim, and he says: 'I lied three times.'" Then the Messenger of Allah (ﷺ) said: "He did not lie except defending Allah's religion." "So go to Musa.' So they will come to Musa, and he will say: 'I took a life. So go to 'Eisa(Jesus). So they go to 'Eisa(Jesus) and he says: 'I was worshiped besides Allah. So go to Muhammad (ﷺ).'" He said: "So they will come to me, and I will go to them." (One of the narrators) Ibn Ju'dan said: "Anas said: 'It is as if I am looking at the Messenger of Allah (ﷺ), and he is saying: "So I will take hold of a ring of a gate of Paradise to rattle it, and it will be said: 'Who is there?' It will be said: 'Muhammad.' They will open it for me, and welcome me saying, 'Welcome.' I will fall prostrate and Allah will inspire me with statements of gratitude and praise and it will be said to me: 'Raise your head, ask and you shall be given, intercede, and your intercession shall be accepted, speak, and your saying shall be heard.' And that is Al-Maqam Al-Mahmud about which Allah said: It may be that your Lord will raise you to Maqaman-Mahmud (17:79)." Sufyan said: "None of it is from Anas except this sentence: 'I will take hold of a ring of a gate of Paradise to rattle it.'"

Source: Jami` at-Tirmidhi 3148 Grade: Hasan

Abu Huraira reported God's messenger as saying:

"Every prophet has a supplication which receives an answer, but whereas every prophet made his supplication in this world, I have kept mine till the day of resurrection to be used in intercession for my people, and if God will, it will reach those of my people who have died without associating anything with God."

Sources: Mishkat al-Masabih 2223, Sahih Bukhari and Sahih Muslim

Ibn Buraidah narrated from his father that the Messenger of Allah said:

"The people of Paradise are a hundred and twenty rows, eighty of them are from this nation, and forty are from the rest of the nations."

Source: Jami` at-Tirmidhi 2546 Grade: Hasan

Narrated Anas:

I heard the Prophet (ﷺ) saying, "On the Day of Resurrection I will intercede and say, "O my Lord! Admit into Paradise (even) those who have faith equal to a mustard seed in their hearts." Such people will enter Paradise, and then I will say, 'O (Allah) admit into Paradise (even) those who have the least amount of faith in their hearts." Anas then said: As if I were just now looking at the fingers of Allah's Prophet.

Source: Sahih al-Bukhari 7509

Narrated Abu Sa'id Al-Khudri:

We said, "O Allah's Messenger (ﷺ)! Shall we see our Lord on the Day of Resurrection?" He said, "Do you have any difficulty in seeing the sun and the moon when the sky is clear?" We said, "No." He said, "So you will have no difficulty in seeing your Lord on that Day as you

have no difficulty in seeing the sun and the moon (in a clear sky)." The Prophet then said, "Somebody will then announce, 'Let every nation follow what they used to worship.' So the companions of the cross will go with their cross, and the idolators (will go) with their idols, and the companions of every god (false deities) (will go) with their god, till there remain those who used to worship Allah, both the obedient ones and the mischievous ones, and some of the people of the Scripture. Then Hell will be presented to them as if it were a mirage. Then it will be said to the Jews, "What did you use to worship?' They will reply, 'We used to worship Ezra, the son of Allah.' It will be said to them, 'You are liars, for Allah has neither a wife nor a son. What do you want (now)?' They will reply, 'We want You to provide us with water.' Then it will be said to them 'Drink,' and they will fall down in Hell (instead). Then it will be said to the Christians, 'What did you use to worship?'

They will reply, 'We used to worship Messiah, the son of Allah.' It will be said, 'You are liars, for Allah has neither a wife nor a son. What: do you want (now)?' They will say, 'We want You to provide us with water.' It will be said to them, 'Drink,' and they will fall down in Hell (instead). When there remain only those who used to worship Allah (Alone), both the obedient ones and the mischievous ones, it will be said to them, 'What keeps you here when all the people have gone?' They will say, 'We parted with them (in the world) when we were in greater need of them than we are today, we heard the call of one proclaiming, 'Let every nation follow what they used to worship,' and now we are waiting for our Lord.' Then the Almighty will come to them in a shape other than the one which they saw the first time, and He will say, 'I am your Lord,' and they will say, 'You are not our Lord.' And none will speak: to Him then but the Prophets, and then it will be said to them, 'Do you know any sign by which you can recognize Him?' They will say. 'The Shin,' and so Allah will then uncover His Shin whereupon every believer will prostrate before Him and there will remain those who used to prostrate before Him just for showing off and for gaining good reputation. These people will try to prostrate but their backs will be rigid like one piece of a wood (and they will not be able to prostrate). Then the bridge will be laid across Hell." We, the companions of the Prophet (ﷺ) said, "O Allah's Messenger (ﷺ)! What is the bridge?'

He said, "It is a slippery (bridge) on which there are clamps and (Hooks like) a thorny seed that is wide at one side and narrow at the other and has thorns with bent ends. Such a thorny seed is found in Najd and is called As-Sa'dan. Some of the believers will cross the bridge as quickly as the wink of an eye, some others as quick as lightning, a strong wind, fast horses or she-camels. So some will be safe without any harm; some will be safe *after receiving some scratches, and some will fall down into Hell (Fire). The last person will cross by being dragged (over the bridge)."* The Prophet (ﷺ) said, *"You (Muslims) cannot be more pressing in claiming from me a right that has been clearly proved to be yours than the believers in interceding with Almighty for their (Muslim) brothers on that Day, when they see themselves safe.*

They will say, 'O Allah! (Save) our brothers (for they) used to pray with us, fast with us and also do good deeds with us.' Allah will say, 'Go and take out (of Hell) anyone in whose heart you find faith equal to the weight of one (gold) Dinar.' Allah will forbid the Fire to burn the faces of those sinners. They will go to them and find some of them in Hell (Fire) up to their feet, and some up to the middle of their legs. So they will take out those whom they will recognize and then they will return, and Allah will say (to them), 'Go and take out (of Hell) anyone in whose heart you find faith equal to the weight of one half Dinar.' They will take out whomever they will recognize and return, and then Allah will say, 'Go and take out (of Hell) anyone in whose heart you find faith equal to the weight of an atom (or a smallest ant), and so they will take out all those whom they will recognize." Abu Sa'id said: *If you do not believe me then read the Verse:--'Surely! Allah wrongs not even of the weight of* an atom (or a smallest ant) but if there is any good (done) He doubles it.' (4.40)

The Prophet added, "Then the prophets and Angels and the believers will intercede, and (last of all) the Almighty (Allah) will say, 'Now remains My Intercession. He will then hold a handful of the Fire from which He will take out some people whose bodies have been burnt, and they will be thrown into a river at the entrance of Paradise, called the water of life.

They will grow on its banks, as a seed carried by the torrent grows. You have noticed how it grows beside a rock or beside a tree, and how the side facing the sun is usually green while the side facing the shade is white. Those people will come out (of the River of Life) like pearls, and they will have (golden) necklaces, and then they will enter Paradise whereupon the people of Paradise will say, 'These are the people emancipated by the Beneficent. He has admitted them into Paradise without them having done any good deeds and without sending forth any good (for themselves).' Then it will be said to them, 'For you is what you have seen and its equivalent as well.'"

Source: Sahih al-Bukhari 7439

It was narrated from Abu Hurairah that the Prophet (ﷺ) said:

"The Fire will consume all of the son of Adam except the mark of prostration. Allah has forbidden the Fire to consume the mark of prostration."

Source: Sunan Ibn Majah 4326 Grade: Sahih

Narrated Anas:

The Prophet (ﷺ) said, "Some people will be scorched by Hell (Fire) as a punishment for sins they have committed, and then Allah will admit them into Paradise by the grant of His Mercy. These people will be called, 'Al-Jahannamiyyin' (the people of Hell).

Source: Sahih al-Bukhari 7450

In Ibn Kathir's Tafsir commentary of Quran 15:2 (*How much would those who disbelieved wish that they had been Muslims*) Ibn Jarir reported that Ibn `Abbas and Anas bin Malik explained that this Ayah refers to the Day when Allah will detain the sinful Muslims in Hell along with the idolators. He said: "The idolators will say to them, `What you used to worship on earth has not helped you.' Then by virtue of His mercy, Allah will be angry for their sake, and He will remove them from it.

Narrated Salman al Farsi:

"The interval between Jesus and Muhammad was six hundred years."

Source: Sahih al-Bukhari 3948

In his Tafsir, Ibn Kathir wrote about the Muslim belief regarding Jesus' departure from Earth:

"Ibn Abi Hatim recorded that Ibn `Abbas said: "Just before Allah raised `Jesus to the heavens, `Jesus went to his companions, who were twelve inside the house. When he arrived, his hair was dripping water and he said, `There are those among you who will disbelieve in me twelve times after he had believed in me.' He then asked, `Who volunteers that his image appear as mine, and be killed in my place. He will be with me (in Paradise)' One of the youngest ones among them volunteered and `Jesus asked him to sit down. `Jesus again asked for a volunteer, and the young man kept volunteering and `Jesus asking him to sit down. Then the young man volunteered again and `Jesus said, `You will be that man,' and the resemblance of `Jesus was cast over that man while `Jesus ascended to heaven from a hole in the house. When the Jews came looking for `Jesus, they found that young man and crucified him. Some of `Jesus' followers disbelieved in him twelve times after they had believed in him. They then divided into three groups. One group, Al-Ya`qubiyyah (Jacobites), said, `Allah remained with us as long as He willed and then ascended to heaven.' Another group, An-Nasturiyyah (Nestorians), said, `The son of Allah was with us as long as he willed and Allah took

him to heaven.' Another group, Muslims, said, `The servant and Messenger of Allah remained with us as long as Allah willed, and Allah then took him to Him.' The two disbelieving groups cooperated against the Muslim group and they killed them. Ever since that happened, Islam was then veiled until Allah sent Muhammad." This statement has an authentic chain of narration leading to Ibn `Abbas, and An-Nasa'i narrated it through Abu Kurayb who reported it from Abu Mu`awiyah."

The scholar al-Baydawi said in his tafsir:

There is a story that a group of Jews insulted Jesus and his mother, whereupon he appealed to God against them. When God transformed those [who had insulted them] into monkeys and swine, the Jews took counsel to kill Jesus. Then God told Jesus that He would raise him up to heaven, and so Jesus said to his disciples: "Who among you will agree to take a form similar to mine and die [in my place] and be crucified and then go [straight] to paradise?" A man among them offered himself, so God changed him into a form resembling Jesus' and he was killed and crucified.

Others say that a man pretended [to be a believer] in Jesus' presence but then went off and denounced him, whereupon God changed the man into a form similar to that of Jesus, and that he was seized and crucified.

For in depth analysis exposing the falsity of the Crucifixion myth I refer you to my book *"Contradicting Biblical Conjecture about the Crucifiction"*.

It was narrated that Ibn 'Abbas said:

*"There were kings after Jesus bin Mariam who altered the Tawrah and the Injil, but there were among them believers who read the Tawrah. It was said to their kings: 'We have never heard of any slander worse than that of those (believers) who slander us and recite: "And whosoever does not judge by what Allah has revealed, such are the disbelievers." In these Verses, they are criticizing us for our deeds when they recite them.' So he called them together and gave them the choice between being put to death, or giving up reading the Tawrah and Injil, except for what had been altered. They said: 'Why do you want us to change? Leave us alone.' Some of them said: 'Build us a tower and let us go up there, and give us something to lift up our food and drink so we do not have to mix with you.' Others said: 'Let us go and wander throughout the land, and we will drink as the wild animals drink, and if you capture us in your land, you may kill us.' Others said: 'Build houses for us in the wilderness, and we will dig wells and grow vegetables, and we will not mix with you or pass by you, for there is no one of the tribes among whom we do not have close

relatives.' So they did that, and Allah revealed the words: 'But the monasticism which they invented for themselves, We did not prescribe for them, but (they sought it) only to please Allah therewith, but that they did not observe it with the right observance.' Then others said: 'We will worship as so-and-so worshipped, and we will wander as so-and-so wandered, and we will adopt houses (in the wilderness) as so-and-so did.' But they were still following their Shirk with no knowledge of the faith of those whom they claimed to be following. When Allah sent the Prophet [Muhammad], and they were only a few of them left, a man came down from his cell, and a wanderer came from his travels, and a monk came from his monastery, and they believed in him. And Allah said: 'O you who believe! Fear Allah, and believe in His Messenger (Muhammad), He will give you a double portion of His mercy - meaning, two rewards, because of their having believed in 'Isa(Jesus) and in the Tawrah and Injil, and for having believing in Muhammad; and He will give you a light by which you shall walk (straight), - meaning, the Qur'an, and their following the Prophet; and He said: 'So that the people of the Scripture (Jews and Christians) may know that they have no power whatsoever over the Grace of Allah.'"

Source: Sunan an-Nasa'i 5400 Grade: Daif

Following is a inquisitive poem of advice by the Crusader era Muslim Scholar Ibn Qayyim al Jawziyyah entitled, "O Christ Worshippers":

أعباد المسيح لنا سؤال ... نريد جوابه ممن وعاه

Oh Worshippers of Christ! We'd like your most wise to answer our question.

إذا مات الإله بصنع قوم ... أماتوه فما هذا الإله

If our God was murdered by some people's actions, then what sort of God is this?

وهل أرضاه ما نالوه منه ... فبشراهم إذاً نالوا رضاه

And we wonder. Was he pleased by what they did to him? If so then blessed are they, for they must have achieved his pleasure.

وإن سخط الذي فعلوه فيه ... فقوّتهم إذاً أوهت قِواه

But if he wasn't pleased with them, then this must mean they overpowered him.

وهل بقي الوجود بلا إله ... سميع يستجيب لمن دعاه

So was the present entity left without a God, an All-Hearing being who can hear prayers?

وهل خلتِ الطباق السبع لما ... ثوى تحت التراب وقد علاه

And were the Heavens vacated, when he was placed under the earth and the dirt was above him?

وهل خلت العوالم من إلهٍ ... يدبرها وقد سُمرَت يداه

And was the Universe left without a God to manage it while his hands were being nailed down?

وكيف تخلت الأملاك عنه ... بنصرهم وقد سمعوا بكاه

And why didn't the Angels help him when they heard him cry out (in pain)?

وكيف أطاقت الخشبات حمل الإله ... الحق شد على قفاه

And how could any wooden beam holdup a True God, while He is being fastened to it?

وكيف دنا الحديد إليه حتى ... يخالطه ويلحقه أذاه

And could any iron ever be brought to Him so that it would be driven inside Him and cause Him pain?

وكيف تمكنت أيدي عداه ... وطالت حيث قد صفعوا قفاه

And how could ever His enemies' hands ever reach Him, so that they could whip him from behind?

وهل عاد المسيح إلى حياة ... أم المحيي له ربّ سواه

And did this Christ revive himself or was there another god that brought him to life?

ويا عجباً لقبر ضم رباً ... وأعْجَبَ منه بطن قد حواه

And how strange is it. That a grave could be enclosed on a god. And even stranger is the womb that enclosed him (before.)

أقام هناك تسعا من شهور ... لدى الظلمات من حيضٍ غِذَاه

Which he remained inside for nine whole months, in utter darkness being fed by blood.

وشق الفرج مولودا صغيرا ... ضعيفا فاتحا للثدى فاه

Then he emerged from the womb as a small child, completely helpless reaching out to be fed.

ويأكل ثم يشرب ثم يأتي ... بلازم ذاك هل هذا إله

Thus, he ate, drank, and after he answered the call which comes naturally. So is this really a god?

تعالى الله عن إفك النصارى ... سيسأل كلهم عما افتراه

High Exalted is Allah above the lies of the Christians. Each of whom will be asked about their fabrications.

أعباد الصليب لأي معنى ... يعظّم أو يقبّح من رماه

Oh Cross worshippers, for what reason is someone exalted (for accepting this) and blameworthy for rejecting it?

وهل تقضى العقول بغير كسر ... وإحراق له ولمن بغاه

And is it not logical that we should break and burn (what humiliated Christ) and the one that made it?

إذا ركّبَ الإله عليه كرها ... وقد شدت لتسمير يداه

Since (you claim) that God was forcefully crucified upon it, with his hands nailed to it.

فذاك المركب الملعون حقا ... فدسه لا تبسه إذا تراه

For truly what a cursed cross to carry? Which one should discard instead of kissing when glanced upon.

يهان عليه رب الخلق طرّا ... وتعبده فإنك من عداه

For (you claim) the Creator was abused upon it. Yet you appear to worship it, so are you one of His enemies?

فإن عظّمته من أجل أن قد ... حوى رب العباد وقد علاه

If you exalt it (i.e. the Cross) because it carried the Lord of all that exists,

وقد فقد الصليب فإن رأينا ... له شكلا تذكرنا سنا

then why don't you also prostrate and exalt the graves?

فهلا للقبور سجدت طُرّا ... لضم القبر ربَّك في حشاه

For it was the grave that held your (so-called) god in it.

فيا عبد المسيح أفق فهذا ... بدايته وهذا منتهاه

Oh worshippers of Christ, Wake up. For this is what the matter is all about.

Following are some excerpts from what the modern Muslim Scholar Rabi' Ibn Hadi 'Umayr Al-Madkhali wrote in his book "*An Advice to the Popes*":

"It has been reported on various media platforms — radio stations, newspapers, and satellite channels — that Pope Benedict XVI has insulted Islam and its Messenger Muhammad and described him and his message as evil and irrational. This is a strange and astonishing affair, and contradicts logic, reason, and the clear truth of Islam. By means of this religion, Allah brought humanity out of darkness into light, and from the injustice of religions to the justice of Islam. Even the just and intelligent enemies of Islam have testified to this truth. I shall not prolong in praising Islam and the Messenger, for the world has been filled with that already abundant with books in this regard. I shall briefly say: Muhammad is truly the Messenger of Allah who has been sent as a mercy for all of the worlds. Allah sent him as a witness, a bearer of glad tidings, a warner, as one who invites to Allah, and as an illuminating light. He came honoring the Prophets and their books, as well as, loving and believing in them and their books.

The Jews and Christians disbelieved in the Torah and the Injeel and did not act according to the beliefs and laws of these books. They belied Muhammad, who confirmed the messages the prophets preceding him came with, including the Torah and the Injeel. They disbelieved in Muhammad and his message, which substantiated all the previous prophets and gave confirmation of the beliefs and laws in the Torah and the Injeel, except for that which was abrogated by Islam. They (Jews and Christians) fought him (Muhammed) fiercely, especially their rabbis, monks, priests, and popes. Their fight was driven by arrogance, pride, envy, and tyranny — and after they distorted their books and tampered with the content - they turned their beliefs of monotheism into polytheism and blasphemy, and halted the application of those laws. So, if this was their behavior with their own scriptures which they claim to believe in, then it was no wonder that they disbelieved in Muhammad and the Quran that he brought, where no falsehood can come to it from before it, nor from behind it!

(I call to) The one who is called the Pope of the Vatican! Embrace Islam and find safety, and Allah will reward you twice. However, if you refuse, then you are responsible for the sins of your followers from both European and non-European Christians. So embrace Islam along with your fellow Christians, so that Allah may reward you with Paradise as wide as the heavens and the earth, prepared for the pious and the followers of the truthful messengers. Believe in this great Quran, which supersedes all the (previous) messages and scriptures, and advocates the correct beliefs and just

rulings that are supported by sound minds and innate nature! Believe (O Pope), you and your followers, in this Quran, which contains that which I have mentioned and its miracles have reached a level that no other affair, tangible or otherwise, can reach.

Allah challenged the jinn and humankind to produce something similar to the Quran, but they were unable to do so. Rather, they were unable to produce even ten chapters like it, in fact, not even a single chapter like it. They were unable, unable, unable, even if they helped and assisted one another. This alone is sufficient reasoning for the popes and their followers to believe in Islam, as long as they have a modicum of intelligence, prudence, understanding, and fairness. O Popes! Embrace Islam so that you may gain safety and enter a paradise as wide as the heavens and the earth. Otherwise, be assured of the severe and eternal punishment of a fire that Allah has prepared for the unbelievers — its heat is severe, and its pits are deep.

O you Popes! Do not let this present life deceive you, and do not let the chief deceiver (Satan) deceive you about Allah. O Popes! Know that your predecessors have distorted your Books, corrupted your religion, elevated humans to the status of gods, and claimed that Jesus is the son of God or the third of the three.

People of the Book! O Popes! All the Messengers, including Jesus, preached monotheism and fought polytheism.

Jesus commanded them to worship Allah alone, and declared that Allah is his Lord and the Lord of those addressed by His message. He also preached that anyone who sets up partners in worship with Allah will be denied Paradise, and the fire will be his abode.

O Christians and Popes! Cease from what Allah has warned you against regarding taking Jesus or other created beings as gods! Otherwise, you are upon disbelief and polytheism and the recompense of that is that you will reside in the Hellfire without any hope of entering Paradise. Do not be deceived by the traditions you inherited from your predecessors, your popes, your priests, and your monks, I swear by Allah, they adopted falsehood and disbelief and distorted the Torah and the Injeel, as mentioned earlier

Do not think that Jesus will intercede for you or enter Paradise and save you from Hell, for this is not in his hand. Remember that you have contradicted him and his creed – the creed of monotheism – and you have taken him as a deity. Jesus himself disavows you and your misguidance.

If you deny the facts and arguments contained in this address, then I invite you to invoke curses on the liars, just as Allah commanded His honest and truthful Messenger(Muhammad). Quran 3:61,

فَمَنْ حَآجَّكَ فِيهِ مِنۢ بَعْدِ مَا جَآءَكَ مِنَ ٱلْعِلْمِ فَقُلْ تَعَالَوْاْ نَدْعُ أَبْنَآءَنَا وَأَبْنَآءَكُمْ وَنِسَآءَنَا وَنِسَآءَكُمْ وَأَنفُسَنَا وَأَنفُسَكُمْ ثُمَّ نَبْتَهِلْ فَنَجْعَل لَّعْنَتَ ٱللَّهِ عَلَى ٱلْكَٰذِبِينَ

Then whoever argues with you about it after [this] knowledge has come to you - say, "Come, let us call our sons and your sons, our women and your women, ourselves and yourselves, then supplicate earnestly [together] and invoke the curse of Allah upon the liars [among us]."

I (Gregory Heary) end this book quoting two true prophetic hadith and sincerely hope for the reader blessed firm lifelong prophetic guidance and that we can all meet together with Jesus in paradise.

It is narrated on the authority of Abu Huraira that the Messenger of Allah (ﷺ) observed:

By Him in Whose hand is the life of Muhammad, he who amongst the community of Jews or Christians hears about me, but does not affirm his belief in that with which I have been sent and dies in this state (of disbelief), he shall be but one of the denizens of Hell-Fire.

Source: Sahih Muslim 153

Narrated Abu Sa'id Al Khudri:

Allah's Messenger (ﷺ) said, "If a person embraces Islam sincerely, then Allah shall forgive all his past sins, and after that starts the settlement of accounts, the reward of his good deeds will be ten times to seven hundred times for each good deed and one evil deed will be recorded as it is unless Allah forgives it."

Source: Sahih Bukhari hadith 41.